Date Due		
Jul 8 '63		
Apr 7 '64		
Feb 25 '65		
IN LIBRARY		
Jun 15 '67		
Jun 22 '67		
Dec 6 '67		
Jul 8 '68		
May 19 '71		
Mar 11 '75		
Apr 25 '80		
GB	PRINTED	IN U. S. A.

Jesuit Studies

Contributions to the arts and sciences

by members of the Society of Jesus

JESUIT STUDIES

Deception in
Elizabethan Comedy

John V. Curry, s.j.

LOYOLA UNIVERSITY PRESS

Chicago, 1955

TO MY MOTHER

AND IN MEMORY

OF MY FATHER

Although debts of gratitude are not paid with mere words, words may serve at least to place such debts on record. I wish, first of all, to thank my Superiors for the opportunity to write this book. The scholarly advice of Professor Oscar James Campbell of Columbia University and Professor Alfred Harbage of Harvard University has been extremely valuable. The late Doctor Richard H. Perkinson, one time of Fordham University, favored me with some helpful suggestions. The stimulating interest in the progress of the work shown by my friends and colleagues at Le Moyne College gave impetus to that progress, and the members of my family stood staunchly in the background as a reliable source of encouragement. Mr. John F. Judge, Miss Rose Marie Stanton, and Mr. Thomas J. Macpeak did valiant service in the tedious labors of proofreading. For courteous and absolutely essential cooperation I am grateful to the research librarians and loan-desk attendants at the libraries of Columbia, Fordham, and Syracuse universities and at the New York Public Library. Special thanks must go to Reverend Theodore J. Cunnion, S.J., director of the Le Moyne College Library, and his associate librarian, Miss Catherine Kenna.

I am glad to acknowledge my obligation to Cambridge University Press for permission to quote from *The Dramatic Works of Thomas Dekker*, edited by Fredson Bowers; to Ginn and Company for permission to quote from *The Complete Works of*

Shakespeare, edited by George Lyman Kittredge; to The Macmillan Company for permission to quote from *Representative English Comedies*, edited by Charles Mills Gayley and Alwin Thaler; to Methuen and Company, Ltd., for permission to quote from *The Jacobean Drama* by Una Ellis-Fermor; to Oliver and Boyd, Ltd., for permission to quote from *The Plays of John Marston*, edited by H. Harvey Wood; to Oxford University Press for permission to quote from *Shakespearean Comedy* by Thomas Marc Parrott, from *Ben Jonson*, edited by C. H. Herford, Percy Simpson, and Evelyn Simpson, and from *The Shakespeare Apocrypha*, edited by C. F. Tucker Brooke; to Routledge and Kegan Paul, Ltd., for permission to quote from *The Plays and Poems of George Chapman: The Comedies*, edited by Thomas Marc Parrott; and to the University of California Press for permission to quote from *Life and Literature in the Roman Republic* by Tenney Frank.

In all quotations I have followed the spelling and punctuation of the editions from which I took excerpts. Apart from a few necessary exceptions, the date of each play referred to is given only at the first mention of the play. The date is uniformly that of the first production of the play.

J. V. C.

Syracuse, New York
February 9, 1955

CONTENTS

Preface   vii

I.   Rare, Ingenious Knavery   1

II.   Deception and Its Agents   8

III.   More Deceivers   42

IV.   The Victims of Deception   71

V.   The Duper Duped   105

VI.   The Means of Deception   119

VII.   The Audience Appeal of Deception   141

VIII.   Conclusion   167

Bibliography   173

Index   181

CHAPTER I

Rare, Ingenious
Knavery

Toward the end of Dekker's *Old Fortunatus* (1599) Ampedo asks his more venturesome brother, Andelocia, what mysteries lie behind Andelocia's recent activities. He receives an answer ringing with overtones which an alert reader of Elizabethan comedy will not find too faint to detect or consider too fanciful to acknowledge. "Trickes, *Ampedo*, trickes, deuises, and mad Herogliphickes, mirth, mirth, and melody. O, there's more musicke in this, then all the Gammoth ares, and Sol fa Res, in the world."[1] Here Andelocia is striking a chord which must have vibrated with sympathetic amplification in the hearts of his Elizabethan audience, for if there was anything the Elizabethans loved to see on the stage, it was a play which gave them plenty of tricks, devices, and mad hieroglyphics.

What they were given, to be sure, was not confined, even in comedy, to merry shifts and stratagems devised by tricksters merely for the fun of it. Some traps had satiric or even sinister purposes behind them; some snapped with heartless finality on their victims. Occasionally within the one play villainous intrigue slipped in beside playful trickery, just as Andelocia, a

---

[1] *Old Fortunatus,* V, ii, 32-34. In Fredson Bowers, editor, *The Dramatic Works of Thomas Dekker,* Vol. I. Cambridge: Cambridge University Press, 1953.

few moments after he uttered the sprightly words just quoted, fell into the hands of victims of an earlier hoax of his and was strangled for his pleasantry. Sometimes little else seemed to appear in a play "but meere knauery, deceit, and coozenage."[2] Frequently simple woodcocks were all that were caught in the springes; and at other times, the odds being less unequal, the audience was regaled with "gull for gull, and wits at war with wits."[3]

In the fifth act of *Volpone* (*c.* 1606), after the sweaty perturbations of his perilous first appearance in court, Volpone suffers an emotional letdown. He begins to look about for a kind of merriment and intellectual stimulation which the wine he has been resorting to cannot seem to afford him.

> Any deuice, now, of rare, ingenious knauery,
> That would possesse me with a violent laughter,
> Would make me vp, againe! (V, i, 14-16).[4]

Somewhat similarly, one can readily imagine, whenever an Elizabethan playwright would feel that the comedy he was composing stood in need of another laugh, of some further spark or lift, he would probably cast his mind about for some device of rare, ingenious knavery (in one or another of its contemporary connotations: mischievousness, trickery, roguery, or rascality) to inject into his piece.

It will occur to readers of Elizabethan comedy, therefore, that the use of tricks, traps, stratagems, and devices must have infused a certain amount of deception into the action of the comedies of that period. The question arises whether deception was

---

[2] *The Puritan* (1606), V, iv, 38-39. In C. F. Tucker Brooke, editor, *The Shakespeare Apocrypha*. London: Oxford University Press, 1908.

[3] *All Fools* (*c.* 1604), IV, i, 377. In Thomas Marc Parrott, editor, *The Plays and Poems of George Chapman: The Comedies*. London: George Routledge and Sons; New York: E. P. Dutton and Company, 1914.

[4] In C. H. Herford, Percy Simpson, and Evelyn Simpson, editors, *Ben Jonson*, Vol. V. London: Oxford University Press, 1925-1952.

merely an incidental, fragmentary means of entertaining and maintaining interest or whether it was put to more structural and functional uses.[5] For instance, did the presence of deception contribute to any appreciable degree to that planned, incremental progression from situation to situation which may go by the name of dramatic action? Did plots get under way and were complications added by means of it? Was it made an instrument for the introduction, manipulation, and exhibition of characters? Did the presence of deception have any perceptible influence on the tone and atmosphere of a play? Were significant dramatic and comic effects produced with the help of deception? More briefly, to what structural and functional uses was deception put in Elizabethan comedy and in the infusing of what dramatic values was it instrumental? The desire for an answer to questions such as these prompted the analytic study of deception in Elizabethan comedy the results of which are presented in the following pages.

"Deception" here means simply what is ordinarily meant by the word: the deceiving of somebody by one means or another. The reason for calling this a study of deception and not using the word "intrigue" in the title is that the latter term may be applied to a number of quite different concepts, and hence might prove confusing. It may be used to refer to political or other forms of machination; it may mean a secret amour; or it may mean simply the plot of a story or play. Deception is of more univocal meaning. On the other hand, the scope of this investigation is not limited exclusively to the "comedy of intrigue"—that sort of comedy in which many ingenious complications are contrived and in which these complications are the main object

---

[5] "Structure" has taken on, in recent criticism, diverse and shifting meanings. In this study the term refers to the planned framework of a play. The word "functional" is perhaps best described negatively. It is here used to characterize that which is opposed to the merely ornamental, the incidental, the accidental, the unintegrated.

of interest. Deception, as will be seen in the course of this study, is found in many comedies which are not intrigue comedies in the strict sense.

In further limitation of the scope of this inquiry it must be noted that indeliberate deception, accidental misunderstandings, and mistakes which are the result of no conscious intention of a deceiver are excluded from consideration. Thus, for example, no attention is given to the instances of fortuitous mistaken identity in *The Comedy of Errors* (*c.* 1592).[6] Again, self-deception is not the direct object of scrutiny. There are, however, in Elizabethan comedy a number of characters whose self-deception is fostered and exploited by tricksters. Malvolio immediately comes to mind. When such cases occur, an oblique glance at the relationship of self-deception to the active ministrations of a duper will not be considered irrelevant.[7]

The first so-called "regular" comedies, *Roister Doister* (*c.* 1553) and *Gammer Gurton's Needle* (*c.* 1553), are the plays with which this study opens. The forward boundary of the investigation, therefore, lies somewhere around 1553. The terminal date is 1616. In that year both Shakespeare and Beaumont died, and Jonson published his *Works* and produced *The Devil Is an Ass,* the last of his comedies exclusive of the "dotages" which came a number of years later. Middleton began to collaborate with Rowley around 1616; and after this date, says Schelling, distinctly Middletonian comedy scarcely held the

---

[6] For the development of Shakespeare's use of the device of mistaken identity see John W. Draper, "Mistaken Identity in Shakespeare's Comedies," *Revue anglo-américaine* 11:289-97, avril 1934.

[7] See Viola Mitchell Evans, *Self-Deception in the Plays of Six Comic Dramatists* (unpublished dissertation, University of California, 1935). In this study an analysis of the comedies of Ben Jonson, Molière, Shakespeare, Etherege, Wycherly, and Congreve resulted in the conclusion that self-deception is the basis of the comedy of humors, character, and manners, and that it is the most frequently employed and most certain means of demonstrating incongruities in human nature and of arousing laughter.

stage.[8] The year 1616, therefore, marks, however faintly, a line of transition, and is accordingly a suitable terminal date.

The term "Elizabethan comedy" is here taken to embrace all the types commonly discussed in histories of Elizabethan drama under the designations realistic, satiric, romantic, fantastic, and humor comedy. Some of these terms, of course, are not mutually exclusive. Professor Harbage's *Annals of English Drama* has been a convenient guide in the selection of the plays to be studied.[9] Any extant, available play, written in English and published between 1553 and 1616, which has been designated as a comedy in Professor Harbage's book has been considered legitimate material for this investigation.

The organization of the work follows a natural sequence. Those first receive attention who are the agents of the deception. The planning and execution of the trickery in each play, it will be seen, is generally in the hands of a single character. We shall see, too, that the type undergoes many mutations and pursues a number of diverse objectives. One purpose, therefore, of the two chapters given to these characters is to classify them according to the objectives they seek. They all tend toward their objectives, of course, by indirection and deception, and in this some family resemblance should be displayed by all of them. Consequently another intention of this phase of the study is the tracing of the lineaments of this family resemblance in trait and behavior as well as in functional uses.

The victims of deception call next for consideration. *Plena stultorum sunt omnia,* sighed Cicero; and with an excess of fools the world is still surfeited. Man's susceptibility to deception is

8 Felix E. Schelling, *Elizabethan Drama—1558-1642*, Vol. I, p. 512. Boston: Houghton Mifflin Company, 1908.

9 Alfred Harbage, *Annals of English Drama—975-1700* (Philadelphia: University of Pennsylvania Press, 1940). Harbage's *Annals* is also, except where otherwise indicated, the authority followed in these pages in the dating of Elizabethan comedies. The date is uniformly that of first production.

ingrained in his nature. This weakness dramatists of all ages have hypostatized and have sent their embodiments of man's primeval and perennial folly strutting across the stages of the world to fall as a matter of course into the traps gleefully set up for them by their traditional enemies, the clever, the witty, and the deceitful. On the Elizabethan stage the race of dupes, both native and exotic, flourished in a prolific variety of breeds, and the hunting was both merry and determined.

The intended victim of a device, however, it is pleasant to note, does not always fall into the snare set for him. The trap may instead snap upon the one who rigs it. Indeed, upon occasion counterplots are set in motion, and the audience is favored with the delectable spectacle of the trickster tricked, the biter bit, the sapper blown at the moon by the successful snaking of an undershaft. Accordingly, frustrated deception presents itself as the next object of study. A deceiver would be ineffectual if he did not have an ample stock of tricks in his bag and devices to fit all varieties of prospective dupes and all manner of occasions for duping them. Therefore the very means themselves of deception open up another avenue of approach.[10] The investigation is finally rounded off by a study of the sources of audience appeal to be found in deception. What was it in the use of deception on the Elizabethan comic stage that appealed to the theatergoers of those days? Wherein lay its values as dramatic

---

[10] One of the most prevalent means of deception in Elizabethan comedy was disguise. See Victor Oscar Freeburg, *Disguise Plots in Elizabethan Drama: A Study in Stage Tradition* (Columbia University Studies in English and Comparative Literature, No. 51. New York: Columbia University Press, 1915). This study of Elizabethan plots in which disguise is a functional component treats of only one device or means of deception in Elizabethan plays of all kinds. The work is therefore both more limited in subject matter and broader in the field covered than is the present one. The same may be said of the chapter on multidisguise in William J. Lawrence's *Pre-Restoration Stage Studies*, pp. 227-98 (Cambridge: Harvard University Press, 1927), and of an article by John C. McCloskey on "The Plot Device of False Report," *Shakespeare Association Bulletin* 21:147-58, 1946.

and comic entertainment? The answers to these questions naturally lead to further observations upon the technique of Elizabethan dramatists in their exploitation of deception as an
element of dramatic construction.

As for the method employed, the investigation proceeds by
way of an analytical survey, from a succession of starting points,
of the uses of deception in Elizabethan comedy. Hence it is not
primarily a study of character types, of the intriguer and his
victims. Specimens of these types are examined mainly in their
relationship to deception. It is what they, by deceiving and being
deceived, contribute functionally to the plays that is the principal aspect under which they are scrutinized. As an analytical
study, furthermore, this inquiry does not concern itself with
sources, social or literary, ancient or contemporary, of plots,
situations, or characters. Resemblances are indeed occasionally
pointed out, but this is done by way of illustration rather than
as a disclosing of influences. Similar use only is made of such
brief glances as are given to the rogue, the fop, the usurer, the
Puritan, or other historical and social counterparts of characters
here commented on. Analysis of the plays themselves is the main
instrument of inquiry and the chief source of information. It
must be here emphasized that the plays discussed are not sum-
marized in any strict sense. What may look like résumés of the
plots are in reality analyses of the action from the one particular
avenue of approach being followed in each chapter.

CHAPTER II

Deception
and Its Agents

Several limitations of this first phase of the investigation must be carefully marked out. Only those characters are examined who employ deception and who in the use of it promote to a considerable extent the movement of the plot. Secondly, these characters are studied only insofar as they resort to deception in their activity. The first restriction excludes from consideration those who do indeed follow deceitful ways but whose trickery does not contribute more than incidental ornament or entertainment. The second limitation inhibits the author from attempting to limn a full-length portrait of all the characters discussed. Among those characters who indulge in an appreciable amount of deception in the course of a play, there are some whose nature and activities extend quite beyond this one aspect and function. Mention may be made, for example, of the wit-intriguers, like Macilente in *Everyman Out of His Humor* (1599), who exercise the double function of manipulating the action and of commenting on other characters. Insofar as they are satirical commentators or *raisonneurs* they are not the specific concern of this study. On the other hand, everything connected with the deceiver's use of deception—his objectives, his patterns of behavior, his relation to the movement of the plot and to other characters, and his characteristics to the extent

8

that they determine or take color from this particular activity of his—will be looked into.

In the following pages will be met such disparate characters as Diccon and Lemot, Cacurgus and Smallshanks, Duke Vincentio and Cocledemoy. Yet they are all legitimately included in a single discussion with a single point of view by the fact that they all use deception to gain their ends. Furthermore, in contributing to the action by means of deception, it is not unlikely that they will manifest beneath their divergencies certain common characteristics and will follow certain patterns of activities. These similarities will be noted in the course of the two chapters given to the agents of deception.

The unifying principle of this discussion of deceivers, therefore, will be our concern with those characters of Elizabethan comedy who by the use of deception contribute to the movement of the plot. The diversifying or classifying principle will be the primary objective sought by each agent of deception. His use of deception will entitle him to our scrutiny; the purpose to which he directs it will link him with deceivers following similar objectives and will distinguish him from those with different goals in mind.

Some characters in comedy seem to indulge in deception not so much for any ulterior purpose as for its own sake. In such cases the itch for trickery may originate in a love of fun or in an impulse toward mischief; or it may take its rise from a desire of the trickster to exercise and display his virtuosity in deception; or it may result from a combination of all three impulses. Such tricksters, if they have any practical purposes in mind behind their knavery, generally let it be understood that these are of subsidiary importance. These characters may be grouped under the name of the "mischief-makers," and each of them can well have said with Puck:

> And those things do best please me
> That befall prepost'rously.

In fact, Puck himself has some affiliation with these mischief-makers, and he has been spoken of by Ashley Thorndike as a "manipulator of mischief."[1] Most of the confusions in *A Midsummer Night's Dream* (*c.* 1595), however, are rather the result of accident and of Puck's mistakes than of the use of deception on his part. Accordingly, he will not come in for discussion here.

Probably the first so-called regular comedy in English was *Roister Doister*, written by Nicholas Udall.[2] Though the central figure is the braggart soldier, the most active character in the play is Merrygreek, who parades Roister and maneuvers him into one predicament after another. This he does mainly by means of deception. He slyly fosters the dupe's delusions of military prowess and irresistible appeal to women by flattering him and giving him false counsel; he covertly gives aid and comfort to his enemies in Dame Custance's household; and he conspires with them in belittling and mocking the one he is pretending to befriend. By these means he provides such rudimentary complications as there are in the play and brings things to a conclusion. Even the solution is engineered with the help of deceit, for the reconciliation between Roister and Dame Custance and Gawain, her betrothed, is built upon Roister's being persuaded by Merrygreek to take complacence in a completely nonexistent attitude of fear and trembling in the other parties.

Merrygreek is, therefore, a mischievous merrymaker, with a touch of cruelty in him, though "at the bottom of his heart, of good-nature."[3] Edward Flügel[4] rightly dissents from A. W.

---

[1] Ashley H. Thorndike, *English Comedy*, p. 104. New York: The Macmillan Company, 1929.

[2] In John Matthews Manly, editor, *Specimens of the Pre-Shakespearean Drama*, Vol. II. Boston: Ginn and Company, 1897.

[3] Introduction to *Roister Doister* in Charles Mills Gayley and Alwin Thaler, editors, *Representative English Comedies*, Vol. I, p. 100. New York: The Macmillan Company, 1903-1936.

[4] *Ibid.*, p. 101.

Ward, who seems to equate Merrygreek on all counts with the classical parasite of the Greek New Comedy and its Latin reproductions.[5] Merrygreek "prefers fun to food,"[6] and any character about whom that can be said is not just a parasite. The ancient parasite got his bread by providing entertaining talk and nonsense, but for him the fun was only a means to the food. A French scholar has done the type of classical parasite no injustice in thus characterizing it: "Quoi qu'il fasse, il a partout le même caractère: son âme est dans son ventre."[7]

In the very first scene of *Roister Doister* Merrygreek tells the audience that the reason he pays insincere adulation to Ralph is the sport he gets out of dancing attendance on the braggart and not principally the fact that he finds him his chief banker "both for meete and money."

> But such sporte haue I with him as I would not leese
> Though I should be bounde to lyve with bread and cheese
>   (I, i, 53-54).

Here, at the very beginning of the play, we see that Merrygreek's motives are not purely and simply those of a parasite. In a later scene he confirms what has already been said of him by Custance's friend, Trusty; namely, that the ambiguous assistance Merrygreek was giving Roister in the latter's wooing of the widow was all for a jest (IV, v, 58; IV, vi, 16-20). At first it is for his own enjoyment alone that Merrygreek abuses the braggart in this way, but later he does it also for the sport and mirth

---

[5] A. W. Ward, *A History of English Dramatic Literature to the Death of Queen Anne*, Vol. I, p. 257. London: Macmillan and Company, 1899.

[6] E. P. Vandiver, Jr., "The Elizabethan Dramatic Parasite," *Studies in Philology* 32:412, July 1935. For further material on the parasite see M. Evelyn Dilley, *The Parasite: A Study in Dramatic Development* (unpublished dissertation, University of Chicago, 1924) and Robert W. Withington, "'Vice' and 'Parasite': A Note on the Evolution of the Elizabethan Villain," *PMLA* 49:743-51, September 1934.

[7] Gustave Marie Michaut, *Histoire de la comédie romaine: Plaute*, Vol. I, p. 221. Paris: E. de Boccard, 1920.

of Custance and her friends.[8] This fun is provided by Merry-greek's acting in the capacity of a showman displaying, by means of rather elementary trickery, the folly of his dupe.[9]

The action of *Gammer Gurton's Needle*[10] moves along almost exclusively under the impulses given it by another mischief-maker, and these impulses are transmitted without exception through the medium of deception. It is true that Diccon, the Merry Bedlam, is not responsible for the loss of the needle, but he seizes upon this loss as the occasion for beginning his knavery. He plays two main tricks, and out of these arise the three confusions which make up the bulk of the play.

For his first trick he stirs up what must have been not very dormant animosities. He tells Dame Chat that her neighbor, Gammer Gurton, thinks that she (Dame Chat) has stolen a rooster of hers. He next tells Gammer that it is Dame Chat who has filched her needle. Especially to be noted are his efforts to cover up his tracks and preserve a necessary ignorance in his dupes by swearing each of them to secrecy as to the source of her information (II, ii, 51-52; II, iv, 42-43). Accordingly, when Dame Chat is accused by her irate neighbor of stealing, she

---

[8] It is not only his motives that differentiate Merrygreek from the classical parasite; he is also far more active than the other type of character usually is. In Roman comedy the parasite is generally not active in the movement of the plot; or if he is, he is merely an assistant of the master intriguer of the piece, as in the *Persa* of Plautus. In the *Curculio* of Plautus and the *Phormio* of Terence the parasite is the chief intriguer, it is true, but these are exceptional cases. In the *Captivi, Bacchides, Rudens,* and *Stichus* of Plautus his place is quite secondary, and he is used purely for comic effect or as one of the dupes. See Michaut, *Histoire de la comédie*, Vol. I, p. 220; Philippe E. Legrand, *The New Greek Comedy*, translated by James Loeb, pp. 73-78 (London: William Heinemann, 1917).

[9] ". . . he encourages him each time to his next exhibition, and at the same time sees to it that the exhibition shall prove him a greater fool. Thus one exhibition leads to another to the final one at the end of Act IV" (Thomas Whitfield Baldwin, *Shakespeare's Five-Act Structure: Shakespeare's Early Plays on the Background of Renaissance Theories of Five-Act Structure from 1470*, p. 399. Urbana: The University of Illinois Press, 1947).

[10] In Manly, *Specimens of the Pre-Shakespearean Drama*, Vol. II.

thinks it is the theft of the rooster she is being charged with, and there follows the burlesque battle between the two women.

The new trick begins with the coming of the curate, Doctor Rat, on the scene. As in the first case it was the loss of the needle, so here it is the unexpected summoning of the curate as a new element that gives Diccon an opening. This he pounces upon with alacrity. He tells Dame Chat the not-implausible lie that Gammer's farm hand, Hodge, is planning to creep through her window and that, as a revenge for the loss of the needle and for the beating sustained by him and his mistress in the fray, he intends to steal or kill her chickens. She and her maids prepare for an intruder, while Diccon tells Doctor Rat that, if he wishes to catch Chat with Gammer's needle, he will have to get into her house secretly. Doctor Rat takes the advice and falls into the trap set by the occupants for a marauder of lesser pretensions.

The third confusion, making up the last part of the play, is also the result of this second trick. Dame Chat denies all accusations about having done anything to Doctor Rat, since it is Hodge she believes she and her maids have set upon. In this scene Chat and Gammer Gurton first learn that they have both been getting their information from Diccon, and the "bailie" who is adjudicating their case feels that all the confusion rests "upon no other ground but only Diccons lyes" (V, ii, 167). Diccon is summoned and, after a moment of bluster and denial, admits he was the cause of the trouble; but far from evidencing any regrets for his knavery, he has this to say:

> I am sory for nothing else but that I see not the sport
> Which was betwene them when they met, as they them-selues
>   report (V, ii, 224-25).

By stirring up brawls with the help of deception for the fun he could get out of it all, Diccon shows himself a merry mischief-maker. We further perceive that Diccon's function is similar to that of the Latin tricky slave in that by his deception he initiates and manages the action. It is precisely by his agency

that what would have been ample matter for a Heywoodian interlude—namely, the simple loss and recovery of the needle
and the attendant horseplay—is expanded and complicated to a
degree which can be dignified by the name of plot. Furthermore,
though in Diccon's mischievous meddling we see vestiges of the
Vice of the moralities, there is an advance in realism in his characterization. In him the spectators could recognize a familiar
contemporary figure, the village beggar; he is no mere abstraction. In this element of realism, too, he is even further on than
Merrygreek, who is still something of a classical exotic, accli-
matized though he be.[11]

A quartette of tricksters who play tricks on their masters and
thwart their plans mainly out of a desire of stirring up mischief
are the diminutive pages of John Lyly's *Mother Bombie* (*c.*
1589).[12] No more description of their character need be given
than to apply to all four what was said of one of them: "though
bound vp in *decimo sexto* for carriage, yet a wit in *folio* for
coosnage" (II, i, 45-46).

How they deceive their masters and affect the movement of
the plot may be seen from the following simplified sketch of
their activities. Memphio, a householder, has a fool for his son,

---

[11] For discussions of the ancient tricky slave see Legrand, *The New Greek Comedy*,
pp. 104-15; Michaut, *Histoire de la comédie*, Vol. I, pp. 170-98, 270-306;
George E. Duckworth, *The Nature of Roman Comedy: A Study in Popular
Entertainment*, pp. 160-75, 249-51 (Princeton: Princeton University Press,
1952). The following monographs are also instructive: Erich Schild, *Die
dramaturgische Rolle der Sklaven bei Plautus und Terenz* (Basel: Hirzen,
1917) and Helen E. Wieand, *Deception in Plautus: A Study in the Technique
of Roman Comedy* (Boston: Richard G. Badger, 1920).

    The medieval Vice has been treated in the following: L. W. Cushman, *The
Devil and the Vice in the English Dramatic Literature before Shakespeare*
(Studien zur englischen Philologie, Hft. VI. Halle: Max Niemeyer, 1900)
and Robert Lee Ramsay, editor, *Magnyfycence, a Moral Play by John Skelton*,
pp. cxci-iv (Early English Text Society, Extra Series, No. 98. London: Kegan
Paul, Trench, Trubner and Company, 1906).

[12] R. Warwick Bond, editor, *The Complete Works of John Lyly*, Vol. III. London:
Oxford University Press, 1902.

and his neighbor, Stellio, has a half-wit for a daughter. Being ignorant of the condition of his neighbor's offspring, each determines to deceive the other as to the limitations of his own heir and to arrange a marriage. Both citizens enlist the aid of their pages in the project of cozening each other. As soon, however, as they hear their masters' intentions to marry off their foolish offspring, the pages, Dromio and Riscio, determine to trick their masters in some way, though neither of them knows exactly how he will do it, since it is only when the pages meet each other that they learn that there is a fool on either side of the proposed marriage. Their first plan, then, seems to be to aid and abet the marriage without letting their respective masters know they are being paid in the same coin they themselves are trying to deal with. When they hear from the other two pages about the objections of the fathers of another couple, Livia and Candius, to their love and how each of these fathers wishes to marry his child to one of the foolish ones, being ignorant of the mental condition of the latter, the pages plan to bring about the marriage of the lovers with the help of the other match. By disguising the two couples in each other's clothing they maneuver the fathers of Livia and her lover into giving their consent to the very betrothal they are trying to prevent. The pages are successful until almost the end of the play in keeping up their pretense of collaboration with their several masters while all the time contriving means and ways of embarrassing them. It can easily be perceived, therefore, that most of the dramatic action is directed and controlled by their trickery.

From Merrygreek, Diccon, and the pages of Lyly to Lemot, the king's minion in Chapman's *A Humorous Day's Mirth* (1597),[13] may seem a far cry, but the main motives animating all of these characters are really identical. They indulge in trickery for the sake of the fun and mischief they can thereby

---

13 In Parrott, *Plays of Chapman: Comedies.*

stir up. Since, however, Lemot has been marked out by scholars as exercising a new function in dramatic structure,[14] we shall classify him with Shakespeare's Maria and Jonson's Macilente as a separate type which is really a branching out and more sophisticated development, in certain respects at any rate, of the mischief-maker. The members of this group may be called exhibitors of folly.

Lemot is used by his author to play upon the gulls and humor types with which he is surrounded and to make their follies more ridiculous. He does this principally by tricking them into situations where their several "humors" will be given special occasion to vent themselves. It is he who starts the action going on all fronts. The means he employs in doing this is a merry sort of double-dealing. The hypocritical wife of a jealous husband, the henpecked husband of a jealous wife, the daughter of a dodderer who has a fatuous husband in mind for her, the king who has something of a roving eye, are all by one pretext or another lured or invited to a gathering at a tavern. When Lemot thinks he has them safely bottled up there in what will at least look like a compromising situation for all present, he summons or fetches the respective "humorous" husband, wife, father, and consort in the mischievous expectation of enjoying the sport of the ensuing spectacle. By reason of one accident or another, however, nobody is caught in a situation of even the slightest impropriety; but Lemot has had plenty of fun in badgering the jealous husband, the suspicious wife, and the doting queen, and in playing up their fears. He thus incites them to display their humors, and eventually to see the ridiculousness of their several idiosyncracies.

---

[14] See Charles Read Baskervill, *English Elements in Jonson's Early Comedy*, pp. 135, 167-68 (Bulletin of the University of Texas, No. 178; Humanistic Series, No. 12; Studies in English, No. 1. Austin: The University of Texas, 1911). See also Oscar James Campbell, *Shakespeare's Satire*, pp. 66-68 (London and New York: Oxford University Press, 1943).

Lemot, however, does not seem possessed of any intention to cure a single one of these "humorous companions." Not even with the Puritan lady does his mischievousness show any medicinal tendencies. After he has lured her to the tavern and tricked her into an open expression of love for him, he reveals just what he thinks of her in a rude enough fashion. But though she then fears that he will make her a "mocking stock to all the world," he does not expose her to the others. He does not even tell her to give up her pretense of peculiar virtue, but cynically bids her get back to her house, put on her Puritan weeds again, and assume once more her hypocritical role. None of his other victims show the slightest indication that any cure has taken effect. Each of them is finally given to understand that his or her suspicions on this particular occasion were unjustified or at least unproven, but no sign whatever of a permanent or deep-seated change displays itself in the disposition of any one of them.

Lemot's motive in all his double-dealing and manipulating is mainly love of sport and mischief. He sets out to provide entertainment for himself and for the king and his courtiers, though he has no scruples in making the king one of his victims. That these are his objectives is shown by several utterances during the play. In the very first scene he announces his intention to point out his humorous companions, and shortly thereafter he consecrates the day to mirth (Scene 2, line 67). This intention to enjoy the sport is repeated in Scene 8, lines 260-63. In the last scene, when the queen learns how she has been deluded by Lemot into thinking the king was in danger of bodily harm and indignity, the king, having himself barely escaped an awkward exposure, urges the queen to forgive the mischief-maker.

> Well, pardon my minion that hath fray'd you thus;
> 'Twas but to make you merry in the end (xiv, 88-89).

And later still, the king speaks of the happenings of that day "spent with unhurtful motives of delight" (*ibid.*, line 363). It

may be noted that Professor Parrott calls attention to the fact
that Chapman has kept Lemot free from all self-interest and
sensuality. He "loves mischief," says Parrott, "for its own sake,
and takes a purely intellectual pleasure in his intrigues."[15] This
is noticeable particularly in his affair with the hypocritical
Puritan wife, Florilla.

Another mischief-maker whose function is to play upon a
gull and to lead him into ridiculous situations in order to
exhibit his folly is Shakespeare's Maria in *Twelfth Night* (*c.*
1600).[16] She is the main deceiver in the plot against Malvolio.[17]
The steward's own nature, it is true, presents to his enemies the
means whereby he can be tossed into the fishpond of confusion,
but it takes a clear eye to diagnose his malady exactly and a
shrewd mind to devise the precise means of working effectively
upon that weakness.

> The devil a Puritan that he is, or anything constantly but a
> time-pleaser; . . . so cramm'd, as he thinks, with excellencies
> that it is his grounds of faith that all that look on him love
> him; and so on that vice in him will my revenge find notable
> cause to work (II, iii, 158-66).

Not only is the letter which she indites accurately aimed at the
chinks in Malvolio's armor, but in it she suggests to him the
precise behavior which is specifically calculated to irritate her

---

[15] Parrott, *Plays of Chapman: Comedies*, p. 689. For comment by Professor Parrott
on the intriguer in other comedies of Chapman see the same volume, pp.
708 and 804. The influence of Latin and Italian comedy upon the intriguer
in Chapman's comedies is traced in Paul V. Kreider, *Elizabethan Comic
Character Conventions as Revealed in the Comedies of George Chapman*,
pp. 70-73, 78 (University of Michigan Publications in Language and Literature, Vol. XVII. Ann Arbor: The University of Michigan Press, 1935).

[16] In George Lyman Kittredge, editor, *The Complete Works of Shakespeare*.
Boston: Ginn and Company, 1936.

[17] In his *Shakespeare: A Survey*, p. 176 (London: Sidgwick and Jackson, 1925)
E. K. Chambers calls Sir Toby the archplotter of the play, but reasons given
in the present discussion seem to warrant our accepting Maria as the main
deceiver, at least as far as the main victim is concerned.

mistress. Maria, therefore, can confidently predict the "fruits of the sport":

> He will come to her in yellow stockings, and 'tis a colour she abhors, and cross-garter'd, a fashion she detests; and he will smile upon her, which will now be so unsuitable to her disposition, being addicted to a melancholy as she is, that it cannot but turn him into a notable contempt (II, v, 218-24).

Maria further shows herself a skillful tactician in preparing her mistress, Olivia, to see some strange aberration in Malvolio (III, iv, 8-13).

In all this trickery she needs no assistance from Toby or anyone else; she asks but for an audience. "For Monsieur Malvolio, let me alone with him" (II, iii, 143-44). It is true that it is Sir Toby's idea to bind the victim and confine him to a dark room, but Maria caps this with the further refinement of having the holed-up Malvolio harassed by the clown disguised as the parson. The youngest wren of nine, therefore, is the instigator, deviser, and finisher of the plot against the archvictim of *Twelfth Night*. And in carrying it off she is so clever, witty, and impudent, and full of animal spirits that it is no wonder Sir Toby hails her as a "most excellent devil of wit."

It may be noted, in parting, that there is a touch of revenge seeking in the motives of Maria's tricking of Malvolio. She and Sir Toby are stirred to animosity by the steward's conceited presumption in aspiring to be Olivia's husband, his officious arrogance toward all in the household, and his congenital frigidity to cakes and ale. This seeking of revenge has not been observed in the mischief-makers thus far discussed. We see a bit of personal sting here that is not merely the light tapping of fun-loving mischievousness.

For the final example of the exposers of folly we may turn to Macilente in *Everyman Out of His Humor*.[18] During the first

---

[18] In Herford and Simpson, *Ben Jonson*, Vol. III.

part of Jonson's play Macilente is just an observer of and an envious commentator upon the follies and foibles of the various humorists who are paraded before him.[19] The preliminary exhibition of their humors is done without any active effort on his part except by way of bitter comment. "Most of them are related by blood or by marriage, and it is their natural encounters which excite them to self-revelation."[20] After the third act, however, Macilente begins to maneuver the other characters into situations in which their several humors will be mercilessly exposed and thus purged.

Macilente first informs Deliro, the doting husband, that Fastidious Brisk is of no importance at court. By this revelation Deliro, who has been supplying Fastidious with funds for his extravagances under the delusion that the fop has many intimates at court, determines to have him apprehended and to bring suit against him for the money owed him. Thus the pushing of Fastidious into a corner and the curing of Deliro's doting on his wife (who in her infatuation for the fop makes efforts to help Fastidious) are both set in motion (IV, ii). Next, Macilente plans and helps execute the trick whereby not only the conceited pretentiousness of Saviolina is laid bare, but the eyes of Fastidious, who had thought her the paragon of witty women, are opened, at least as far as she is concerned. Then by poisoning Puntarvolo's dog, he presumably does what he can to cure the knight of his humor for traveling. ("Well, by this time, I hope, sir Puntarvolo and his dog are both out of humour to travaile.") Immediately thereafter Macilente throws suspicion of the poisoning upon the parasitical braggart, Shift, and is therefore responsible for the shaming by Puntarvolo of that worthless

---

[19] This function as commentator is not relevant to the subject of the present study. See Oscar James Campbell, *Comicall Satyre and Shakespeare's Troilus and Cressida*, pp. 54-81 (San Marino: Henry E. Huntington Library and Art Gallery, 1938).

[20] *Ibid.*, p. 71.

fellow before the eyes of Sogliardo, on whom Shift had been sponging by telling him tall tales of his past days as a highwayman. Thus Shift is exposed and Sogliardo is disillusioned. Here again two humors are disposed of in a single moment.

At the meeting in the tavern, by egging on the scurrilous Buffone to jibe at Puntarvolo and by covertly prodding the knight into retaliation, Macilente successfully lures Buffone over the line of safety which the railer's own cunning sense of self-preservation would have prevented him from overstepping. If Buffone should ever again indulge his passion for railing, after the cruel punishment then and there administered to him, it certainly would not be in the presence of Puntarvolo.

Macilente's last moments in the play are spent dashing energetically from the tavern to Deliro's house and from there to the prison, first sending Deliro's wife and then fetching Deliro himself, by one false pretext and another, to Fastidious' cell. There he presides over the disillusioning of all three. The husband is shocked out of his doting by finding his wife in the arms of the fop; his wife accordingly will certainly no longer be able to indulge in her shrewish contrariness; and Fastidious, facing a prospect of years in the debtors' prison, will, whatever inclinations remain toward extravagant display, have no opportunity for yielding to them. Macilente's own special humor of envy could thereupon subside into quiescence.

Macilente is thus seen to be, at least in the latter and more active part of the play, the wit-intriguer of the piece. Buffone has no illusions about the nature of Macilente's activities: "Now is that leane, bald-rib MACILENTE, that salt villaine, plotting some mischieuous deuice" (V, iv, 24-26). The latter nudges the others into such positions *vis à vis* one another that their resultant interaction inevitably leads to mutual exposure and disillusionment and, in some cases at any rate, to self-improvement.

Macilente's part in the machinery of the plot is therefore different from Buffone's. Herford and Simpson refer to these two characters as the executants of Jonson's satirical purposes.[21] This assertion must be qualified. Both Macilente and Buffone, it is true, help to exhibit and expose the various humors by the kind of *comment* proper to each of them. But only Macilente is really an active agent in *maneuvering* the others into positions in which they give the supreme exhibition of their folly and have their eyes opened at the same time. He is the one responsible, directly or indirectly, for the cure in every case except that of Sordido. Buffone himself in his turn undergoes ignominious treatment through the double-dealing of Macilente.

Now, the means almost invariably used by Macilente in the exercise of this function is one form or another of deception. He plans the foistering of the country lout upon the lady, Saviolina, who is deceived into thinking and pronouncing him a gentleman; he casts suspicion of poisoning the dog upon a man he knows to be innocent of the deed; he makes a promise of help to Buffone which he has no intention of keeping. When he is actually telling the truth, he puts a completely false color on his motives for telling it, as when he lets Deliro's wife think it is friendship for her and for Fastidious that prompts his informing her of the latter's imprisonment.

What are the motives which actuate Macilente? Certainly he is not driven by any great urge for displaying his virtuosity in trickery, as is Cleanthes in Chapman's *The Blind Beggar of Alexandria* (1596).[22] He takes no delight in his cleverness, as Brainworm does in *Every Man in His Humor* (1598).[23] Neither is he like Lemot, who, though fulfilling a similar function in the construction of the plot, plays the puppetmaster more out of a mischievous spirit of mirth and laughter than for any other reason. Macilente's own humor gives us the clue. Envy in him

---

[21] Herford and Simpson, *Ben Jonson*, Vol. I, p. 387.
[22] *Infra*, pp. 155-56.
[23] *Infra*, pp. 36-37.

is a dynamic humor which not only issues forth in lip-curling censure of the other characters but drives him into corrective action against them. But back of his efforts to put the spotlight of revelation and rude awakening upon the others is no spirit of benevolence. In him, rather, is to be detected a certain maliciousness which makes him more akin to the medieval Vice than to the Plautine slave, who usually employs his wiles in the service of his young master and is not motivated by malevolence. The contrast between this sharp corrector and gay mischief-makers, like Brainworm and Lemot, "measures the distance traversed by Jonson in passing from comedy touched with satire to satire under comic forms."[24]

The pages of *Mother Bombie,* as has been seen, are principally bent on mischievous funmaking, but by their tricks they manage also to help a pair of lovers outwit their fathers. Attention may now be directed to those whose *main* objective is to help young lovers.[25] In this and in the succeeding section special consideration will be given to the relationship between the trickster and his young master or friend in the carrying out of the intrigues. This relationship, it will be seen, varies from one of almost abject dependence of the lover upon his helper to one of efficient employment and direction of the assistant by a more self-confident principal. The first plays to be discussed will be three rather free translations from the Italian.

The Bugbears (c. 1564)[26] is a fairly close adaptation, with additions, of Antonfrancesco Grazzini's *La Spiritata.* Formosus

---

[24] Herford and Simpson, *Ben Jonson,* Vol. I, p. 387.

[25] An unpublished Harvard dissertation (Maxwell I. Raphael, *The Lover's Helper: Studies in the Development of a Literary Type,* 1937) traces the literary uses of the male and female go-between from the *Iliad* to medieval romances. Neither the type studied by Raphael nor the ground he has covered is identical with the subject and scope of this section.

[26] This play is in R. Warwick Bond, editor, *Early Plays from the Italian* (London: Oxford University Press, 1911). The name of the author may be John Jeffrie (or Jeffere).

and Rosamunda, who have been clandestinely married, seek the sanction of a public ceremony.[27] The girl's father, ignorant of the existing connection, is willing that they be married but cannot raise the three thousand crowns demanded by the youth's father, Amedeus, as a dowry. The avaricious Amedeus, despite his son's protests, agrees to marry Formosus to the daughter of a dotard who can pay the dower. Formosus dares not tell his father he is already married for fear of being disinherited. Such is the opening predicament of the young man.

He enlists the aid of his servant, Biondello, who sets as their immediate objective the acquiring of three thousand crowns. The servant plans to steal this amount from the coffers of Formosus' father and to have an uncle of Rosamunda offer this money as though from his own pocket to endow the girl. But in order to furnish Amedeus with a satisfactory explanation of the disappearance of his money, the conspirators give him reason to believe his house is haunted. Next Trappola, an acquaintance of Formosus' servant, who has been brought into the conspiracy for his ability in impersonating a conjurer, brings his art to bear on the fathers of the boy and the girl and on the elderly rival. He confirms their belief that the house is haunted; and then after pretending to purge the place of the spirits by his magic, he intimates that the goblins have taken with them three thousand crowns from Amedeus' coffers. To the obliging uncle is secretly conveyed the money which provides the dowry and makes the match acceptable to the young man's father.

In this play, therefore, is to be seen a situation found in a number of Plautus' comedies of intrigue. We find the secret connection between a young man and a girl, the necessity of

---

[27] Bond's summary of the play intimates that this union is as yet an illegitimate one, though promise of marriage has been made. But several lines (for example, I, ii, 36-40) are evidence that those who speak of it consider it a marriage though there has yet been no public ceremony. See Bond, *Early Plays from the Italian*, p. 77.

securing a sum of money, which becomes the immediate objective of the deception, the duping of old men, and the predominance of servants in the manipulation of the action. There are some differences, the most obvious one being the social position of the girl and the nature of the match. In Roman comedy the girl is usually a foreigner, a courtesan, or a slave in the possession of a slave dealer, and therefore no likelihood exists, at the beginning of the play, of a marriage between the *adolescens* and his *amica*, though often enough she turns out, at the end, to be a long-lost daughter of a citizen and therefore eligible for a respectable marriage. As in the comedies of Plautus, the attention is focused in *The Bugbears* on the tricky servants and their dupes; and though here a second pair of lovers are introduced (in the manner of Terence rather than of Plautus), attention is directed at them but fitfully, and Rosamunda, the beloved of Formosus, is not seen on the stage at all.

It is Biondello, the servant of Formosus, then, who has planned the whole hoax.[28] But once he has summoned his accomplice, Trappola, and has sketched the part he is to play in the plot, to the latter is given the greater prominence in the deception. Biondello introduces Trappola to his old master, Amedeus, vouches for his skill in dealing with bugbears, and then leaves the old man and his fellow dupes in Trappola's competent hands. This trickster first secures their confidence and open-mouthed admiration by a disquisition, set forth with much parade of pseudoscientific lore, on the varieties of preternatural manifestations and their authors. He drenches them with such a cascading catalogue of "puckes, puckerels, hob howlard, bygorn & Robin Goodfelow," that one of them breaks out with "oh Godd what is it that thys man doth not know?" Another agrees that "neyther Baldus nor Bartolus hath thys skyll" (III, iii, 58, 59).

---

[28] "I can tell thee the matter, for I devised it" (I, ii, 25).

This skill, indeed, so works upon their superstition that they are like putty in his hands, and Amedeus swallows without question the explanation of the antics in his attic. Trappola's amazing gallimaufry of magical terms and astrological hocus-pocus is a real stock in trade that would serve many a trickster with shrewder victims in prospect. This weaving of a web of circumstantial and mesmerizing volubility around his dupes by a knowledgeable knave as artful preparation for a swindle or stratagem is a promise of such ampler things to come in Elizabethan comedy as Subtle's discourses on alchemy in *The Alchemist* (1610), Merecraft's nonchalant listing of his proliferating "projects" *(The Devil Is an Ass)*, the farcical Latin of the mock lawyer and clergyman in *Epicoene* (1609), and, in a different sort of situation, Volpone's mountebank eloquence before Celia's window.

In George Gascoigne's *Supposes* (1566),[29] another free translation of an Italian play, a young man from Sicily, Erostrato, has been living in secret intimacy with Polynesta at Ferrara. Erostrato has enabled himself to do this by exchanging identities with his servant, Dulippo, and working as a menial in the household of the girl's father. This situation is threatened with upset by the wooing of Cleanthes, an elderly lawyer whose suit is favored by the girl's father. In order to forestall an agreement between the father and the dotard, the servant of Erostrato comes in the guise and character of his master, pretends to seek the girl for himself, and wins the first skirmish by offering a more opulent dowry than Cleanthes can match. It now becomes imperative for him to back up his offer with something more authentic than his mere word. He provides this by intercepting an old Sienese on his way into the city, scaring him with a trumped-up story of an enraged duke and newly aroused animosities toward travelers from Siena, but offering him harbor-

---

[29] In Bond, *Early Plays from the Italian*.

age if he will agree to pose as his, the feigned Erostrato's, father in a projected deception. Having undertaken to play the part, the old man assures the girl's father of his intention to make good the offered dowry.

These shifts of the servant in behalf of his master are frustrated by two unexpected occurrences. The one is the discovery by Polynesta's father of the secret relationship between his daughter and the feigned Dulippo, who has been in his service. He has the culprit locked up. The other unlooked-for event is the arrival of the young man's real father in the city. This arrival really brings matters to a head. The feigned Erostrato sees that the only way to help his young master is to confess all to his old master and bring him to help his son. This confession provides the solution to the young Erostrato's difficulties, because his father agrees to accept the girl as his daughter-in-law and to supply the dowry.

It is not clear from the text which of the two, the young lover or his servant, is the planner of the main deception—the reciprocal disguise and the pretended wooing by the feigned Erostrato. The next trick, devised in order to give at least a momentary backing to the dowry proffered by the false suitor, is planned and executed by the servant. Yet it is to be noted that he seeks the advice of his master before bringing to him the old stranger whom he has induced, by trickery, to pose as Erostrato's father (II, i, 265-66). Furthermore, this same servant fails lamentably when presented with an unforeseen emergency in the arrival of his master's father. He shows a certain lack of resourcefulness here, though he is brazen enough when his old master's eye lights upon him. Therefore, though we have here another descendant of the tricky slave of Roman comedy, variations from the archetype can be seen in the feigned Erostrato's lack of resourcefulness in an emergency and in his looking for advice or at least permission from his master in playing the trick on the Sienese gentleman.

To a certain extent the plot of *Misogonus* (*c.* 1560),[30] which is probably a third adaptation from the Italian, depends on the deception practiced upon the father of a household by a servant. Cacurgus pretends to be a half-wit and uses his position as domestic fool to acquaint himself with the counsels of Philogonus, his employer. By communicating this knowledge to Misogonus, the young scapegrace of the family, Cacurgus enables the boy to evade the feeble, roundabout efforts of the father to curb him. In the course of the play Cacurgus makes an entertaining but ineffectual attempt to help Misogonus by impersonating an astrologer and magician and imposing on a pair of credulous country women.

Though this play does not center around a love affair to be helped along by a servant, Cacurgus is reasonably treated in this section of the study because the supposed fool does side with the wayward *adolescens* against the father. He has some characteristics of the medieval Vice in that he abets the young fellow in his pursuit of profligate ways, but the play itself is in the tradition of the "education drama" and is in form an imitation of Roman comedy.[31] Cacurgus also has the makings of an intriguing servant; but though his young master compliments him for being "as full of knaverie as an egge is full of meate" (I, iii, 26), his talents never really amount to much in the way of effective trickery. He deceives the father, it is true, as to his real character, but on the two occasions in which he tries to use definite pieces of information acquired by this deception, he is frustrated in his attempt to achieve his purpose. Among his characteristics are self-reliance and confidence in his ability to serve the young man by trickery. Though his motives for favoring Misogonus are not entirely clear, he seems to feel that by his

---

[30] In Bond, *Early Plays from the Italian.* The author of *Misogonus* is not known with certainty. See E. K. Chambers, *The Elizabethan Stage,* Vol. IV, pp. 31-32 (London: Oxford University Press, 1923).

[31] See Bond, *Early Plays from the Italian,* pp. xci-iii.

"pollicye" he prevents his young master from trying his father's patience beyond the breaking point.[32]

In discussing Shakespeare's *The Taming of the Shrew* (*c.* 1594) we need concern ourselves only with the subplot dealing with the wooing of the younger sister, Bianca. This plot goes back ultimately, and at least in some scenes directly, to George Gascoigne's *Supposes*.[33] Here too the main point of interest will be the relative positions of the young lover, Lucentio, and his servant, Tranio, in the conducting of the intrigue.

Upon falling in love with Bianca, Lucentio immediately turns to his servant:

> Tranio, I burn, I pine; I perish, Tranio,
> If I achieve not this young modest girl.
> Counsel me, Tranio, for I know thou canst;
> Assist me, Tranio, for I know thou wilt (I, i, 160-63).

This, to be sure, is much in the manner of the Plautine young man pleading for his slave's help in an *affaire de coeur*. But this convention of helpless dependence does not persist, for Lucentio immediately puts his own brains to work as well as his servant's, and they both seem to hit on an idea together. "Both our inventions meet and jump in one," says Tranio (I, i, 195); but when he sees difficulties in their initial plan of Lucentio's disguising himself as a tutor to gain entry to Bianca's house, Lucentio himself thinks of the ruse of having Tranio disguise himself as Lucentio to cover up his master's absence from his own house and duties. It is Lucentio, too, who directs Tranio to "make one among the suitors" in his character as the rich young Lucentio. Here we see the young lover taking command of the situation, making plans, and giving directions.

---

[32] In still another adaptation made from the Italian between 1576 and 1584 a young man is given muddled assistance by the pedant, a character of only mild interest. See Percy Simpson, editor, *Fidele and Fortunio—The Two Italian Gentlemen* (Malone Society Reprints. London: Malone Society, 1910).

[33] See Kittredge, *Complete Works of Shakespeare*, p. 326.

He does, however, make use of the servant in his intrigue, and Tranio does furnish considerable assistance. And in doing this the servant is left more or less to his own devices. Thus we see him outbidding the old Gremio in the matter of the dower, then supplying the need of a father to back up his extravagant offer by hoodwinking the pedant into assuming the role. Besides disposing of the old Gremio, he also lures the younger rival, Hortensio, out of the running by falsely intimating that Bianca is a bit too carefree in bestowing her affections and by entering with him into a pact to desist from wooing her (IV, ii, 11-47). Later he draws Bianca's father away from home for the signing of the feigned marriage preliminaries and makes it possible for his young master to run off with Bianca and be married. It is clear, therefore, that the young man himself plans the over-all strategy but that he is given essential aid by his clever servant, who is deputed to engage in diversionary tactics and who, indeed, must depend on his own devices while in the field.

Tranio fulfills his function in the plot with efficiency, but is not given the special highlighting which is often allotted the tricky servant. When confronted by the real father of his master, he is allowed even less opportunity than his counterpart in the *Supposes* to show the usual effrontery and insolence of the tricky servant when faced with exposure (V, i, 65-115). His motives in engaging in deception are simply obedience and devotion to his young master (I, i, 216-22).

The main intriguer, Anthony, in William Haughton's *Englishmen for My Money* (1598) is not a servant in the same sense as are the tricksters in the immediately preceding plays, but a tutor in the household of Pisaro the usurer. Anthony is discharged from his office at the beginning of the play for encouraging his charges, Pisaro's three daughters, in their attachment to three young Englishmen. While Pisaro bestirs himself to invite three foreign suitors to court his daughters, the English lovers urge the dismissed tutor to "deuise the means" to "ouer-reach the Churle." Assuming a disguise, Anthony enters the service of Pisaro as a French tutor. To bring things to a speedy and happy conclusion he employs three devices, one for each couple. He lets one of the girls go off disguised in his clothes, so that she can marry her lover. He instructs another lover to come to the house disguised as a neighbor's daughter seeking lodging for the night. Pisaro sends the "girl" to bed with one of his daughters, who, of course, is the one with whom this particular young fellow is in love. The third ruse is more elaborate. Anthony instructs Harvey, the last of the lovers to be provided for, to pretend to be dying and to draw up a deed of gift wherein all his property is made over to the daughter with whom he is in love. Pisaro is advised that this deed will be of no value when Harvey dies, for the young man's heirs will come into the property. The way to make the deed good would be to marry the girl to the dying man. Pisaro, therefore, not only agrees to allow the marriage, but he hypocritically forgives the young lover all the debts accumulated by Harvey in his heedless days of borrowing from the usurer. Thereupon Harvey leaps up and shows that he is very far from death's door. The frustrated father next discovers that his other two daughters and their English lovers have circumvented him. Knowing a *fait accompli* when he sees one, Pisaro accepts the situation with a good grace.

Thus the tutor, Anthony, plays the part of the lovers' helper by devising for them the means of outwitting the father. His devices amount to no more than a resort to hackneyed disguises and a feigned sickness unto death, but the working out of these devices constitutes much of the action of the play.

Another lovers' helper is the magician, Peter Fabel, in the anonymous *The Merry Devil of Edmonton* (c. 1602),[34] who

---

[34] William Amos Abrams, editor, *The Merry Devil of Edmonton—1608, And a Reprint of The Life and Death of the Merry Devil of Edmonton, by T. B., 1631.* Durham: The Duke University Press, 1942.

undertakes to cross the plots of Sir Arthur Clare and help his young friend, Raymond Maunchensey, elope with Clare's daughter. For all his talk about setting "wit and Art" to work against "age and craft," Fabel employs only the pedestrian mummery of disguises, and the threadbare disguise of friars' weeds at that. The corrupt state of the text in the last scenes indicates, however, that we may have lost some of his "art."

One of Chapman's most captivating characters is Rinaldo, who initiates most of the action in *All Fools* in his efforts to assist two pairs of lovers. But since that play contains an even more entertaining dupe, it will more fitly be discussed in a different chapter.[35] Chapman has another lively figure who plays a similar role in *May Day* (*c.* 1602).[36] As it stands, this play can hardly be considered original, since Chapman took over practically the whole plot and most of the characters from the *Alessandro* (*c.* 1545) of the Italian author Alessandro Piccolomini.[37] The English playwright, however, recast the entire play, leaving out and adding features freely with an eye toward making his offering more suitable for the English stage. One of his most important changes was the substitution of the jaunty intriguer, Lodovico, for the passive and colorless Italian gentleman, Alessandro, of the original.[38]

Lodovico is not only the most active member of the cast (although the servant, Angelo, runs him a close second), but he serves as a structural link binding all the elements of the play together. Having overcome, by urbane mocking and avuncular joshing, the feigned indifference of his kinswoman, Aemilia, for her lover, Aurelio, and the timidity of Aurelio himself, he undertakes to outwit parental opposition and to help them see each other. In order to do this he enlists the aid of Aurelio's witty

---

[35] *Infra*, pp. 76-78.
[36] Parrott, *Plays of Chapman: Comedies.*
[37] *Ibid.*, p. 734.
[38] *Ibid.*

servant, Angelo, who has told him of the senile passion of Lorenzo, Aemilia's father, for Franceschina. He instructs Angelo
to lure Lorenzo away from his house with the promise of an
assignation to be arranged with Franceschina. But in order to
let Lorenzo have an unmolested afternoon with the lady, Lodovico himself assumes the task of drawing off her husband, the
sharking captain, Quintiliano, by introducing him to a rich gull
and inviting both to a tavern for a carouse. Thus he knits
the Aurelio-Aemilia, the Lorenzo-Angelo-Franceschina, and the
Quintiliano-Innocentio-Giovanello elements together, while getting, to boot, a burnt finger in an incidental and spontaneous
attempt at delving into still another pie, the disguised-boy and
disguised-girl situation.

In Lodovico's utilization of one strand of deception for the
strengthening of another thread of intrigue, we see that Chapman has achieved a more sophisticated exploitation of deception as an element of plot construction than is perceptible in
Haughton's *Englishmen for My Money*. The energetic and good-
humored activities of this fellow serve as a bond of unity.

Organically, therefore, Lodovico is the most important figure in the play. It is he who initiates much of the movement,
though not all of it. In furthering his designs, however, he takes
advantage of movements which have been set going independ-
ently of him, making use on the one hand of Lorenzo's amorous
angling, through Angelo, for the favors of Franceschina, and on
the other of Quintiliano's sponging upon simpletons. It is to
render his adroit management less than justice, therefore, to say,
as Paul Kreider does, that "he definitely accepts and follows
the suggestions of the lady who actually manages the intrigue."[39]
After he has jogged the lover out of his excessive fear of looking
upon his beloved and bullied the lady out of what he calls her

---

[39] Kreider, *Elizabethan Comic Character Conventions*, p. 74. Kreider refers to
May Day, I, i, 197-278; II, i, 110-224.

"superfluous nicety," Lodovico is entreated by them, it is true, to help them, but there is never any doubt as to who will do the planning and the arranging. Chapman himself evidently thought much of this character, and Professor Parrott is right in calling attention to the interesting light cast upon Chapman's technique of comic structure by his introduction of Lodovico into his play.[40] It shows that the playwright considered an intriguer of Lodovico's ubiquitous activity of importance enough to encourage him to depart from his Italian original in introducing him, a departure more drastic than any other of the changes he made in the plot of the Italian play.

There is in *May Day* a dexterous and witty servant, Angelo, who in some ways is very much like the Plautine clever slave and the Italian Arlequino. He plays his tricks, however, under the direction of Lodovico, and is not the main intriguer in the play. The intriguing servant is much better studied in Savorwit, in the play next to be discussed, who is more independent in action and has more directional control of the intrigue than Angelo has in *May Day*.

Two plots run side by side in Middleton's *No Wit, No Help Like a Woman's* (*c.* 1613; revised version by Shirley, 1638).[41] In one of them we find a clear imitation of the clever slave of Roman comedy. It was the servant, Savorwit, who before the action of the play had suggested to Philip, his young master, the plan of bringing home Grace, the young man's secretly acquired wife, and presenting her to Sir Oliver, Philip's father, as the long-lost sister whom Philip had been sent abroad to ransom from pirates. When this makeshift is threatened by the proposal of Sir Oliver to marry his "daughter" to a rich simpleton, it is Savorwit who persuades the father to marry her to Sandfield,

---

[40] Parrott, *Plays of Chapman: Comedies*, p. 734.
[41] A. H. Bullen, editor, *The Works of Thomas Middleton*, Vol. IV. London: J. C. Nimmo, 1885-1886.

Philip's friend, and to allow Philip to marry a girl named Jane
to whom Sandfield really intends to be married. The servant
then urges the young couples to pretend to comply with this
invalid matchmaking so that each can secretly enjoy his real
wife's company—a deception rendered the easier by Sir Oliver's
willingness to have both couples live in his house.[42] Savorwit
also plays the typical clever servant's game by attempting to
discredit a Dutch stranger whose unexpected advent bids fair to
uncover the whole hoax.[43] His quick thinking and witty nonsense, in the scene in which he pretends to interpret the little
Dutch boy's remarks to the effect that the boy's father is at certain times of the moon troubled with mental disturbances, are
calculated only to gain time (I, iii). Later the untoward appearance on the scene of Philip's mother, who had been represented
to the father as having died, and her subsequent conclusion that
the girl Philip had married is really her lost daughter and therefore his sister, presents the servant with two awkward problems.
The first one he manages with skillful address, but in the second
one he recognizes something no adroitness of his can manipulate.

> . . . there wit must stay,
> It cannot pass where fate stops up the way (IV, i, 273-74).

All is set to rights, however, by the discovery that Jane, and not
Grace, is the daughter of Sir Oliver and his wife, and that therefore Philip has not married his sister.

Most of the action, therefore, in that half of the double plot
in which Savorwit has part is initiated and controlled by this
tricky servant. Out of loyalty to his young master, who depends
abjectly on his servant's help, Savorwit meets emergencies with
at least temporary expedients. These emergencies constitute
crises in the action and inject suspense; the dodges by which he

---

[42] A similar situation is contrived with Rinaldo's help in Chapman's *All Fools*.
[43] Compare Tyndarus' efforts in Plautus' *Captivi*, vv. 547 ff.

extricates himself provide much amusement. None of his shifts and devices can really be of any permanent help, but they at least delay the day of reckoning. (In comedy, from the time of Menander down, nobody seems inclined to worry about the distant future.) The final solution of Philip's difficulties is not due to any of Savorwit's deceptions.

For an interesting variation from the type of which Savorwit is an adequate illustration we may look at Brainworm in Jonson's *Every Man in His Humor*.[44] At the first glance Brainworm might seem to be a faithful copy of the Plautine tricky slave in the latter's capacity as contriver of intrigue and lovers' helper. It is indeed true that Brainworm superficially conforms to the type. He aids Edward Knowell in what the young man's father fears to be profligate ways. He is called artificer and architect. He is granted monologues in which he indulges in triumphant chortling over his own cleverness and in confident predictions of further knaveries (II, iv, 1 ff.; II, v, 133-48). These knaveries are the object of applause and commendation by Justice Clement at the end of the play, as well as of appreciative comment by young Knowell and his friend, Wellbred, in the course of it. In all this Brainworm is following the conventional pattern, and Jonson evidently meant him to be recognized as being in the tradition of the tricky slave.

Despite these resemblances a closer reading of the play reveals that Brainworm breaks quite definitely through the envelope of conventional typing both in characterization and in structural uses. Jonson would not suffer his character to remain an exotic or a mere abstraction; and Brainworm, though fashioned after an ancient and foreign pattern, is cut out of native English cloth and garnished with contemporary, realistic detail. Furthermore, he does not have as much of a guiding hand in the forward movement of the plot as the Plautine slave or as the

---

[44] In Herford and Simpson, *Ben Jonson*, Vol. III.

more rigorous English imitations of the type such as Savorwit. For the greater part of the play his deceptions and disguises do not seem to lead to anything practical or helpful. What, for instance, is the point of his passing himself off on young Knowell and Stephen as a soldier when he first meets them? His professed object in assuming the disguise was to help the young fellow. He could have informed Knowell at that first meeting in Moorfields of his father's sallying forth to spy on him.

Since, however, he uses his devices to provoke displays of eccentricity and fatuity on the part of the humor characters and gulls in the play, and since the exhibition of the humors seems to be the main function of the plot in this particular play, it must be said that Brainworm's trickery is functional enough in the structure of the work.[45] Then, too, in the second half of the play he does help Edward Knowell in his vaguely motivated resort to stratagem in getting Bridget out of Kitely's house to marry her. This assistance is given, however, under the direction of Edward's friend, Wellbred, who does the planning, gives the directions, and employs Brainworm to put the ruses into execution.[46] When all is said and done, Wellbred remains the chief lovers' helper in this tepid affair. It is he who finally enables Bridget to run off and marry Knowell by his two-faced ruse of telling each of the Kitelys that the other of them is at Cob's house for no good reason. He thereby gets both husband and wife out of the house at the same time.[47]

Not always is the young lover in comedy in need of a helper. In the comedies of Terence and especially of Plautus, it is true, the *adolescens* is usually a colorless sort of fellow who is reduced to hysteria and intellectual impotence when obstacles are

---

[45] See Herford and Simpson, *Ben Jonson*, Vol. I, pp. 343, 350.

[46] See, for example, IV, v, 1-11; IV, viii, 61-70.

[47] See the analysis of this play in Elizabeth Woodbridge Morris' *Studies in Jonson's Comedy*, pp. 51-53 (Yale Studies in English, No. 5. Boston: Lamson, Wolffe, and Company, 1898).

put between him and his beloved; and he must necessarily have recourse to his tricky slave, who thereupon takes over the management of the whole affair. In fact, in some of Plautus' comedies the love affair is but the occasion for bringing on the *fallax servus*, who becomes not only the chief engineer of the intrigue but the most dominating personality in the play and the center of attention. This is the case in *Pseudolus, Epidicus, Bacchides, Asinaria,* and *Mostellaria.* In *Miles Gloriosus,* it is true, Palaestrio shares the spotlight with the braggart, but the slave is on the stage for a longer time, and he is the one who is pulling the strings which make all the other characters move. In most of the English comedies thus far analyzed in this study, the relationship between the young lovers and their helpers is much the same as it was in the Plautine comedy. But in the plays now to be discussed the relationship is shown in the process of being modified and reversed.

The intrigue of Gascoigne's *Supposes* supplied the author of *The Taming of a Shrew* (c. 1589)[48] with material for one of the plots, the wooing of the two sisters of the shrew. This plot is rather watery, and the only thing that interests us in it is the fact that whatever is done to thicken it is contributed by Aurelius, the young lover, entirely by himself and without the guidance of any intriguing servant or friend. There is a servant, to be sure; and Aurelius makes use of him in his wooing, by disguising himself, for instance, in his servant's clothes and disguising the servant on one occasion as a music master to take the shrew's eye off her younger sister, and on another occasion by sending the servant to impersonate himself, Aurelius. But it is the young man who makes the decisions, devises the tricks, and engineers the intrigue, such as it is. The servant merely obeys orders and does no devising on his own part.

---

[48] In Thomas Amyot and others, editors, *A Supplement to Dodsley's Old Plays,* Vol. IV. London: Shakespeare Society, 1853.

Another young lover who can plan and execute deception to further his own love affair without the help of a servant is Sebastian Wengrave in *The Roaring Girl* (*c.* 1610), by Middleton and Dekker.[49] Sebastian's father forbids him to marry Mary Fitzallard, the girl he loves. In order to bring his father around, young Wengrave pretends he is in love with Moll Cutpurse, a notorious girl who is commonly seen in male attire. Both Mary and Moll cooperate with him in this deception. The father, distraught at the idea of his son's throwing himself away on a girl about whom he has heard unpleasant rumors, sets afoot counter-intrigues in order to dislodge his son from the supposed infatuation. He is tricked, however, into giving his blessing to the marriage between Sebastian and Mary when his son maneuvers him into making a promise to consent to Sebastian's marriage with any girl provided it be not the infamous Moll.

Gerardine, a similarly self-reliant young gallant in the main plot of Middleton's *The Family of Love* (*c.* 1602),[50] loves Maria, the niece of Glister, a "doctor of Physic," but he is not permitted to marry or even to visit the girl. After trying an unsatisfactory trick which involves a pretended departure on a journey and a secret conveyance of himself inside a trunk into Maria's house, Gerardine inaugurates another scheme. He rumors it abroad that Glister, her uncle and guardian, is responsible for Maria's pregnancy. He also contrives to make Glister's wife believe this false report, and thus she is prompted to have her husband haled before a court for infidelity. The "court" is provided by the ingenious Gerardine, who dresses himself up as the judge and has his cronies appear as lawyer and other officials. After forged evidence has been presented the "judge" informs Glister that the case looks very strong against him, but he suggests that it might be possible to free him from all suspi-

---

[49] Bullen, *Works of Thomas Middleton*, Vol. IV.
[50] *Ibid.*, Vol. III.

cion if the physician would be willing to give Maria a dowry and allow her to marry Gerardine. The distressed physician agrees, articles are properly signed and sealed, and then the intriguing lover uncovers himself and the whole deception, but the marriage and the settlement stand.

It can be seen that Gerardine is willing to go to any lengths to encompass his end, even to besmirching the reputation of the girl he wishes to marry. The atmosphere surrounding this love affair, therefore, is hardly a romantic one. The interest here seems to be directed more toward the intrigue than to the love between the young people. This intrigue is initiated, planned, and executed by the young man without the guidance or the assistance of a tricky servant and without more than incidental assistance from any friend.

In a later chapter another of Middleton's self-confident young lovers will receive extended notice in the discussion of *A Mad World, My Masters* (*c.* 1606).[51] Occasion will also be taken later to speak of the determined young lady in Marston's *Parasitaster, or The Fawn* (*c.* 1605) who unassisted plays the role of the intriguer in her own love affair.[52]

In the aforementioned plays which are built upon a love intrigue three varieties are distinguishable in the relationships between the lover and his associates. In some comedies we find the young love in complete, and sometimes abject, dependence upon his servant, who makes the plans, gives the orders, and exercises general control over the whole intrigue. This is also the relationship usually obtaining in the comedies of Plautus. In other plays the lover is ruled and directed by one not in the inferior position of a servant but rather in the status of an equal—a friend or a relative such as Lodovico in *May Day*, Wellbred in *Every Man in His Humor*, and Rinaldo in *All*

---

[51] *Infra*, pp. 107-10.
[52] *Infra*, pp. 78-81.

Fools.[53] A third variation is to be seen in the competent assuming of the reins of control in their own love intrigues by the self-reliant Gerardine, Follywit *(A Mad World, My Masters)*, Sebastian *(The Roaring Girl)*, and Dulcimel, "the quick, deviceful, strong-brain'd" young woman in *Parasitaster*. Something of the same sort of departure from the ancient, conventional relationship between a young master in love and his servant is reported to have taken place in the Spanish theater of the sixteenth and seventeenth centuries. In the plays of Lope de Vega and his predecessors the *gracioso*, although often mixed up in the conducting of the love intrigue, usually was merely the instrument who worked under the orders, and carried out the plans, of his master. One explanation offered is that it would have gone against the grain of the *caballero* to take directions from his own servant.[54]

[53] Another character who helps an equal in a love affair is Nevill in Nathan Field's *Amends for Ladies* (c. 1610-1611), in William Peery, editor, *The Plays of Nathan Field* (Austin: The University of Texas Press, 1950).

[54] Maria Heseler, *Studien zur Figur des Gratioso bei Lope de Vega und Vorgängern*, p. 48. Hildesheim: Franz Borgemeyer, 1933.

More
Deceivers

The classes of deceivers remaining to be studied are rogues, testers, exposers, protectors, enviers, and revengers. The most numerous of these, as well as the best known, are the rogue intriguers. The rogue's place in the life of Elizabethan England, in popular literature, and in the drama of the period has been well investigated, as also have the interacting influences of all these spheres.[1] The present study does not concern itself with the vestiges of contemporary social or literary sources to be found in the comedies to be discussed. Nor is there any intention to assess the degree of realism with which the rogue has been presented in these plays. We are interested in the dramatic re-

---

[1] Several monographs may be mentioned: Frank Aydelotte, *Elizabethan Rogues and Vagabonds* (Oxford Historical and Literary Studies, Vol. I. London: Oxford University Press, 1913); Frank Wadleigh Chandler, *The Literature of Roguery* (Boston: Houghton Mifflin Company, 1907); Mildred Gayler Christian, *Non-Dramatic Sources for the Rogues in Middleton's Plays* (Chicago: University of Chicago Libraries, 1936); James Howell, *The Rogue in English Comedy to 1642* (unpublished dissertation, University of North Carolina, 1941); Burton Alviere Milligan, *Rogue Types and Roguery in Tudor and Stuart Literature* (unpublished dissertation, Northwestern University, 1939). The theme of roguish intrigue is also touched upon in Wilbur Dwight Dunkel, *The Dramatic Technique of Thomas Middleton in His Comedies of London Life,* pp. 9, 59 (Chicago: University of Chicago Libraries, 1925).

productions of this type of character only insofar as they are put to organic uses in the comedies in which they are found.

Rogues might be subdivided and classified in several ways, but for our present purposes it will be sufficient to follow a very simple division. Some of the rogues here collected for contemplation are petty cozeners, sharpers; some of them are swindlers on a larger scale who show both an ampler imagination and a more clever approach in their "projects"; still others are distinguished from their unwashed congeners by the superior level of their education and breeding. The dominant characteristic of all rogues seems to be that they are intent on getting their hands, by wit, dexterity, and sharp practices, on somebody else's money or property.[2]

No mere journeyman in the "crafty company of Couzoners and Shifters"[3] but a master of some adroitness and experience is Canby, the rogue who exerts much influence on the movement of the comic subplot in *The Blind Beggar of Bednal Green* (1600).[4] The victim of most of his tricks is Tom Strowd, a simple country fellow who has yearnings for finer feathers than his solid yeoman stock would seem to warrant him. Tom is all fire and threats over a minor cozening at the hands of Canby which occurs early in the play, but he is so suavely handled by his duper that he shortly finds himself introducing Canby and a confederate to his father as "honest proper Gentlemen." Thereafter the young fellow is so hoodwinked by Canby that, when his father is in danger of hanging, the only one he can think of appealing to for help is this petty cheat, whom he naively

---

[2] Chandler, *Literature of Roguery*, Vol. I, p. 4; Howell, *Rogue in English Comedy*, p. ix.

[3] The phrase is found in Awdeley's *Fraternitye of Vacabondes* (1561), and is quoted in Aydelotte, *Elizabethan Rogues and Vagabonds*, p. 117.

[4] W. Bang, editor, *The Blind Beggar of Bednall Green* (Materialien zur Kunde des älteren englischen Dramas, Vol. I. Louvain: Uystpruyst, 1902). This play was written by Henry Chettle and John Day, and perhaps William Haughton.

believes to have influence at court. Canby steals from young
Strowd the hundred pounds with which he was to pay for a
reprieve for his father and then gives his grateful gull a counterfeit reprieve which he says he has got from the Duke of
Gloucester. After Tom is told to his dismay that the reprieve is
a forgery, he is sent to hunt down the rogue and his fellows.
Upon coming to them, however, Tom is again beguiled by
Canby's ready wit and is induced to join their band of cozeners.[5]
But his plain-speaking, honest kersey nature does not allow him
to maintain membership long in this fraternity, and he helps
frustrate the rogues as well as their employers in their plot
against the "blind beggar" and his daughter. In the end Tom
gives Canby a beating in a trial by combat. The latter is pun-
ished by banishment, though he does not seem to look upon this
as an unbearable sentence. "We'll do you more good," he tells
the duke, "by cheating your enemies abroad, than ever we did
hurt by cozening honest subjects at home" (lines 2626-28). His
alternate cheating and mollifying of young Strowd comprise the
entire comic element of the play.

The fun in Marston's *The Dutch Courtesan* (*c.* 1604)[6] is
supplied by the trickery of Cocledemoy, a merry and clever
rogue, who has no trouble at all in cozening on several occasions
the victim to whom he gives his undivided and persistent attention. The tricks he uses are distinct ones and are not stages in
a single preplanned intrigue. He takes each opportunity as it
comes along to administer a new dose of his wit to Mulligrub,
the Puritan innkeeper. Yet there is this connection between his

---

[5] In joining up, though only temporarily, with his victimizers, Tom is following
the pattern set by at least some real-life Elizabethan gulls. After finding
themselves ruined, these would sometimes become assistants to conycatchers
to hunt for gulls among their own friends from the country and would thus
make a living cozening others as they themselves had been cozened. See
Aydelotte, *Elizabethan Rogues and Vagabonds*, p. 79.

[6] In H. Harvey Wood, editor, *The Plays of John Marston*, Vol. II. Edinburgh and
London: Oliver and Boyd, 1934-1939.

devices, that each of them gives him some help in working the next one. After he has "dry-shaved" and fleeced Mulligrub in his disguise as barber, he uses his knowledge of this incident to satisfy Mistress Mulligrub's demand for a token from her husband to vouch for the authenticity of Cocledemoy's alleged commission to fetch a silver plate. Then, after Mulligrub has discovered the loss of the plate and has railed at his wife for letting herself be deceived, Cocledemoy has the effrontery to dash into the house again during a momentary absence of Mulligrub. He glibly tells the bewildered woman that her husband has only been playing a joke on her in denying he had sent anyone for the plate. He further persuades her to give back to him the "jole of salmon" he had offered her as corroborative detail to lend color to the previous lie whereby he has cozened her out of the plate.

Later, when he is almost caught by his lurking victim and loses a cloak in escaping, he shows mental as well as physical agility by using this very cloak, which Mulligrub naturally picks up, as a means of bringing the unfortunate fellow very near to hanging. Next, while the dupe is moaning in the stocks under suspicion of stealing the cloak, he is allowed by his victimizer, now disguised as a bellman, to give him his purse that he may bear witness to the constable as to his probity. Cocledemoy takes it with the ironical leer: "Tis more than I deserve sir," and he does just the opposite to what Mulligrub expects him to do.

Mulligrub has no chance with this clever rogue, and it is only when the latter hears the victim of so many of his dodges forgiving him as he mounts the scaffold and saying that if he (Mulligrub) were to live longer, he would not attempt to prosecute the knave who had tormented him, that Cocledemoy throws off his current disguise and declares that all his tricks were played just to display his wit.

> No knave worsh. [worshipful] friend no knave, for observe
> honest *Cocledemoy* restores whatsoever he has got, to make you

know, that whatsoere he has done, has bin only *Euphoniae
gratia*, for Wits sake: I acquit this Vintner as he has acquitted
me, all has bin done for *Emphises* of wit my fine boie, my
worshipfull friends (V, i; p. 136).

This is a bit of a surprise for us as well as for the vintner, and
it may be remarked that Cocledemoy first made sure that Mulligrub was willing to forgive and forget. If the vintner had per-
sisted in cursing his victimizer as he mounted the scaffold, one
fears that Cocledemoy would have seen him turned off without
a qualm.

Cocledemoy is mentioned by Freeburg in his chapter on
rogues in multidisguise,[7] but it must also be noted that this
rogue has more than a change of beard and costume in his bag
of tricks. He is naturally clever and quick-thinking. Attention
has already been directed to his use of a previous escapade to
help along another one. Then, too, disguise alone would not
have served him when he presented himself the second time to
Mulligrub's wife and talked her out of the salmon even though
her husband had just told her she had been bamboozled by this
very knave. This called for brazen derring-do and the ability to
tell a convincing lie in quick enough time to prevent an outcry
upon his reappearance. His characteristics, therefore, are bold
cleverness, dexterity, and a talent for making the best of the
slightest opening. His series of pranks upon Mulligrub comprise
the whole action of the comic subplot of *The Dutch Courtesan*.

Pursuing our investigation into an upper order in the hierarchy of roguery, we may observe deception being used in the
illegal quest of grander profits in Middleton's *Michaelmas Term*
(*c.* 1606).[8] The main plot has to do with the swindling of a
country gentleman, newly come to town and ignorant of its
ways, out of his property. This swindling is done by a London

---

[7] Freeburg, *Disguise Plots*, p. 135.
[8] In Bullen, *Works of Thomas Middleton*, Vol. I.

linen draper, Quomodo, with the assistance of a pair of artful
dodgers, Shortyard and Falselight.

In the defrauding of Easy five cleverly integrated stages
may be discerned. First of all, the trap is prepared by Quomodo
in his careful and exact briefing of Shortyard on how he is to
approach the selected victim (I, i). Secondly, these instructions
are carried out by Shortyard in outfitting himself as a gallant,
striking up an acquaintance with Easy under false pretenses,
and enticing him into gambling and extravagant entertaining.
He professes himself willing to supply Easy with more funds
even if he has to put himself in debt to do so (II, i, 79 ff.). When
this eventually becomes necessary, Shortyard, accompanied by
Easy, approaches Quomodo in his shop for a loan. Thirdly,
when the need for further funds inevitably arises, Easy is
tricked into cosigning a series of bonds with which Shortyard
is apparently burdening himself in order to supply Easy with
money (II, iii; III, i, 140-44). These bonds are all, to be sure,
primarily binding on Shortyard; but in every case Easy has
been maneuvered, merely "for custom sake," as he is given to
think, into adding his signature for surety. For the fourth move
Shortyard disappears when the bonds fall due, and Quomodo
has Easy arrested by a pair of counterfeit minions of the law as
the only signer and debtor attachable. By threatening his victim
with imprisonment for not paying the seven hundred pounds due
him, Quomodo frightens Easy into making a final agreement
binding all his property as security to "two citizens of good
account" who agree to stand bail for him until Shortyard returns to make good the debt. Shortyard, of course, does not
return; and the fifth step is reached and the trap finally sprung
when the "two gentlemen," who are none other than Shortyard
himself and an accomplice in another set of disguises, lay claim
to Easy's lands and goods, which they then make over to Quomodo (III, iii and iv; IV, i). By such devious but closely inter-
linked processes is the victim's inheritance taken from him.

The scene in Quomodo's shop is a most interesting and instructive one. Because it illustrates Middleton's exploitation of contemporary swindling devices as machinery for an intrigue plot, it will be worth detailed analysis. It is to be noted that it is Shortyard who is to borrow the money so that out of pure friendship, as he protests, he may supply Easy's immediate needs. This immediate need for money on the part of Easy is necessary for the plan of the confidence men, and this need Shortyard has created by inveigling Easy into inviting some gentlemen to a party that evening. Upon being approached, Quomodo according to plan regretfully says he cannot at the moment lend Master Blastfield (Shortyard's alias in his dealings with Easy) the two hundred pounds he requires, though he insists he will be able to do so in three days. This, of course, will not do, for Easy feels it would be to his everlasting shame if the banquet invitations were to be revoked for lack of funds (II, iii, 143-44). But then Easy remembers the names of the two other moneylenders whom Shortyard (to impress the dupe) had mentioned earlier as being able to supply him with cash any time he asked for it. Shortyard perceives that "the trout will be a little troublesome ere he be catched"; but he is prepared for this minor emergency, and he pretends to send his boy to Master Gum and Master Profit to tell them of his needs. The boy, of course, makes his contribution to the swindle by coming back shortly with the news that these two "uncles" are out of the city for the day. Only then does Quomodo propose that Shortyard accept, in lieu of ready money, a quantity of cloth which he assures Shortyard and Easy they can easily sell to any one of a number of merchants for the sum they need. Quomodo manages this difficult phase very cleverly. Taking Easy aside, he suggests that he persuade Shortyard to accept this proposal, and when Shortyard then pretends to be indignant at the very idea ("Would he ha' me turn pedlar now?"), we find Easy persuading him to take the cloth and to sign the bond for its value.

Shortyard yields with some show of reluctance. "Well, master Easy, none but you could have persuaded me." Here we have the ironical situation of the dupe's persuading the duper to join in cheating him.[9] Quomodo, on his side, allows a slight huff to show toward Shortyard because he has demurred at the idea of taking a loan in commodity.

The next step is to get the dupe to sign the bond, too, as security. Though it is only Shortyard who is taking the loan, it is customary, they tell him, to have two citizens sign the bond. "The second man enters but for custom sake." But when Shortyard suggests that Easy be allowed to be this second signer, it is Quomodo's turn to make a show of reluctance. "Alas, sir!" he objects to Shortyard, "you know he's a mere stranger to me: . . . although I grant the chief burden lies upon you, yet we are bound to make choice of those we know, sir." Easy's self-esteem is so jarred at this that he is by way of walking off in high dudgeon and proves difficult to placate. "Cuds me," exclaims Quomodo under his breath, "I'm undone! he's gone again." Shortyard, too, feels that the "net's broke." But here again Shortyard is equal to the occasion; and by reminding Easy of the eternal loss his prestige would suffer if he had to cancel the supper that night, he brings him around. The bond, finally, is signed by both of them. Quomodo immediately exults to himself, thinking of Essex logs and Christmas on his soon-to-be-acquired estate.

The next move is to send out the cloth by a porter to be sold. The porter, an accomplice in disguise, returns to report that, owing to circumstances, no merchants are willing at the moment to buy the commodity. Shortyard is downcast, Easy desperate, and Quomodo sympathetic. Professing his anxiety to help, Quomodo tells them of a tradesman newly set up who will perhaps

---

[9] Dapper finds himself in an identical situation with his two leeches, Subtle and Face (*The Alchemist*, I, ii, 28-90).

buy the goods, but he warns that the price paid will probably be very low. The porter accomplice is again sent out to fetch this tradesman, and he immediately returns disguised as master Idem, the tradesman who is willing to buy but who will pay only sixty pounds for the cloth for which Shortyard and Easy have bonded themselves to pay two hundred. Easy accepts perforce what is offered and he finally has some ready cash for his entertaining; but, as Quomodo in high feather sums up the day's work, "First have I caught him in a bond for two hundred pound, and my two hundred pounds' worth a' cloth again for threescore pound. Admire me, all you students at inns of cozenage" (II, iii, 484-87).[10]

This scene in Quomodo's shop, at the sign of The Three Knaves, is one that would be hard to surpass in comic interest and suspense. This spectacle of the two spiders winding their filaments of simulated friendship and chicanery around their fluttering victim, flattering him, cajoling him when he shows fitful signs of bolting, even subtly bullying him with the "loss of credit" his reputation would sustain if he failed to feast the gentlemen whom Shortyard has coolly invited in his name; the busy shuttling in and out of the other accomplices on their feigned errands to other moneylenders; the nudging of the fly into deeper and deeper depths of the web by subtle gradations, nothing being done too hastily, nothing (or almost nothing) out of prearranged order; the ironic overtones of Easy's urging the seemingly reluctant Shortyard to take the loan in commodity, with these overtones becoming audible in such lines as the scrivener's, "Nay, 'tis done now, past mending" and Easy's own exclamation, "O horrible! are there such fools in town?"; the sympathetic and solicitous but impotent hovering "above" of

---

[10] Readers of Elizabethan rogue literature will recognize as the background of this scene the common commodity swindle. See Aydelotte, *Elizabethan Rogues and Vagabonds*, pp. 78-79; Milligan, *Rogue Types and Roguery*, pp. 138-39; Bullen, *Works of Thomas Middleton*, Vol. I, pp. 253-54 (Bullen's note).

Thomasine, Quomodo's wife—this spectacle of bustling, conniving activity focusing and closing in upon one pliant and unsuspecting figure adds up to a *tour de force* of fluid movement and immediacy which hides the consummate artistry and skill that went into making this scene the little masterpiece of dramatic art that it is.

It should not be inferred from what has just been said that Middleton's art is confined to the fabrication of effective but disconnected scenes. In this comedy a series of scenes presents the successive and interrelated phases of a carefully preplanned swindle which is masterminded through to its consummation. Each of these scenes in the Quomodo-Easy plot is interesting in itself, but they are all interwoven by the strands of the intrigue whose purpose is the transfer of Easy's property to the possession of Quomodo. The use of deception as an element of plot construction has come a long way since the employment of the rather disjunct tricks of Merrygreek as the framework of the plot in *Roister Doister*.

Although working under the instructions of his chief in the defrauding of Easy, Shortyard is a suave practitioner in his own right. He slides himself without difficulty into Easy's confidence, and by some impressive talk and the offhand mentioning of a few names he instills in his dupe a totally unfounded respect for his reputation for sufficiency among the moneylenders of the city. He puffs the gull's aspirations to be a man about town and edges him along the ways of extravagance by blandly issuing invitations in his name. Once or twice, when he or Quomodo overplays the line and the "trout" almost slips the net, Shortyard handles the emergency with adroitness. Modern confidence men could take lessons from this fellow. Still, it is Quomodo who selects the victim, plans the whole swindle, gives directions, controls all phases of the operation, and pockets the lion's share of the "take." He is the main intriguer of the play and its dominant personality. At the moment at which we leave him, his fortunes are at flood tide. How and why they ebb at the end of the play will be considered in a later chapter.[11]

Other rogues, the scope of whose imagination and the cleverness of whose technique can compare favorably with Quomodo's, are Jonson's Subtle and Face in *The Alchemist* and Merecraft in his *The Devil Is an Ass*. Since, however, *The Alchemist* will be the object of scrutiny in another chapter,[12] only Merecraft will be discussed here, and that briefly.

Merecraft, the most active individual in *The Devil Is an Ass*, is a "projector" who is "an adept in a variety of current methods of rascality."[13] He is the deviser and manager of most of the swindling schemes which are tried out successively on Fitzdottrel, the dupe of the play. Three of these schemes, in particular, may be characterized as bogus speculation, bogus settlement of quarrels by the laws of dueling, and sham demoniac possession.[14] Though Merecraft is not witty as other intriguers often are, and though he gives no indication of taking pleasure in his trickery as trickery, he is intelligent and is gifted with an eloquence all his own. His brain just spawns "projects," and he fluently invests them with a colorful speciousness that would be the envy of a modern wildcat promoter. He amazes and impresses the wide-eyed Fitzdottrel by "talking in millions" and by making airy references to noble and powerful clients. He is quick to surmount obstacles thrown in his path and to pick himself up after having one of his schemes blown up by a counter-intrigue. For instance, he silences a blackmailer threatening to reveal his true purposes by thinking up a new project on the spot, getting his dupe to finance it, and letting the blackmailer sluice off some of the golden stream. Similarly, when creditors press upon him at a most uncomfortable moment with threats of

---

11 *Infra*, pp. 106-07.
12 *Infra*, pp. 142-43.
13 Herford and Simpson, *Ben Jonson*, Vol. II, pp. 152-53.
14 *Ibid.*

arrest, he diverts them from their intentions by pretending he is on the point of letting them share in a lucrative project. Again, when he beholds his main scheme foiled by the counterplotting of Wittipol, who is helping Fitzdottrel's wife save the latter's estate, he immediately starts thinking how he can trump Wittipol's ace, and he improvises his last trick of having Fitzdottrel pretend to be possessed by a devil. In the end he is frustrated, but not before he has paraded a full display of swindling devices. The planning and the working out of these devices upon the gullible dupe, the counterintrigue they occasion, and the momentary embarrassments and ultimate frustration they meet with constitute much of the substance of the play, provide the complication and denouement of the plot, and are a primary source of interest and entertainment.

In our third class of intriguing rogues we may group some examples of those fast young men of good family or at least of superior education who, by dissipation or recklessness, have lost their property and patrimony and are either reduced to living by their wits or are pictured as being in the process of attempting to regain some of their property by underhanded means. In Middleton's comedies are to be found several instances of this type. Witgood in *A Trick To Catch the Old One* (*c.* 1605) and Follywit in *A Mad World, My Masters* are perhaps the most interesting of these, but they will be treated in other places in this study.[15] A gentleman rogue who will be worth examining is George Pieboard in *The Puritan*[16] (probably by Middleton).[17] Instead, however, of tracing the thread of deception through the plot of this comedy and seeing how it contributes to the move-

---

15 *Infra*, pp. 87-89, 107-10, 160-62.

16 In Brooke, *Shakespeare Apocrypha.*

17 Bullen, *Works of Thomas Middleton*, Vol. I, p. lxxxix, and Wilbur Dwight Dunkel, "The Authorship of *The Puritan*," *PMLA* 45:804-08, September 1930. Marston has also been mentioned as a possible author. See Chambers, *The Elizabethan Stage*, Vol. IV, p. 42.

ment of the play, it will be sufficient to indicate some of the typical characteristics of the chief trickster of the piece which qualify him for a place among his peers, the "shifty gentlemen" of Elizabethan comedy who live by their wits.

Whatever may have been the cause of his present penury, George Pieboard is portrayed as a man of education. At the beginning of the play he tells a confederate that, since his wits are his only patrimony, he intends by shifts, wiles, and forgeries to continue to make his belly beholden to his brain (I, ii, 48-119). His main device is to represent himself as a conjurer and to impose on the ignorance and credulity of a Puritan widow, her brother, and her daughters. But he does not depend on one device alone. He is fertile in stratagems, and thinks up and tentatively considers a few which he really does not need (I, iv). When presented with a problem, he strikes the traditional plotter's attitude of calling upon his brain for some excellent device: "Well, I must cast about some happy slight./ Worke braine, that euer didst thy Maister right!" (I, iv, 41-42).[18] He is absolutely self-reliant and cocksure, bids his assistants not to ask questions about just how he intends to carry out his plans. "Leaue that to me and my directions" (I, iv, 255). They are to do what he tells them. Especially to be noticed are his elaborate efforts at arousing in his prospective dupes, the widow and her family, the necessary confidence in his ability to do the marvelous things he claims he can. He gives them reason to think he has knowledge of the future by foretelling events he is making sure actually will happen (II, i, 262). He proves to their satisfaction that he knows their secrets by casually mentioning matters which he has got from eavesdropping (II, i, 328-34). By drugging a confederate and resuscitating him from "death," he

---

[18] Is not Hamlet himself also in this tradition, at any rate the tragic branch of it, with his "About, my brain! Hum, I have heard/ That guilty creatures, sitting at a play . . ."?

implants in them the belief that he has supernatural powers. Having thus worked upon their credulity, there is nothing he cannot get out of them. By means of all this he intends to deliver his friend, the captain, from prison, and with his help "to beguil as I see occasion." But he also indicates a by-product of all this trickery, which casts an interesting light on his type: that his wits will be "applauded among schollers and souldiers for euer" (II, i, 356-57).

Later, however, in the very moment of exaltation, when he feels that he has brought matters to such a head that his "deuise can no way now be crost," he is arrested for debt. He sees all his schemes tumbling about his ears; for he knows that, once in prison, he will be kept there indefinitely with the suits of other creditors who will press upon him. But in this extremity he is not long at a loss.

> All my meanes is confounded: what shall I doe? has my wits serued me so long, and now giue me the slippe (like a Traynd seruant) when I haue most need of 'em? no deuise to keepe my poore carcase fro these Puttocks?—yes, happines! haue I a paper about me now? yes, too! Ile trie it, it may hit: *Extremity is Touch-stone vnto wit* (III, iii, 105-13).[19]

The brazen trick by which he extricates himself from his predicament need not be recounted, nor is it necessary in this place to show how in the end, for all his cleverness, he is frustrated of his aims upon the widow and her family.

This play is not of any exceptional merit and its hero is not endowed with any outstanding individuality, but these very defects make it easy to analyze and present the features which are typical of the class of gentlemen rogues he represents. He has just the characteristics one would expect him to have and does just the sort of thing his type would do.

---

[19] See Volpone's commendation of Mosca: "Good wits are greatest in extremities" (*Volpone*, V, ii, 6).

In *Ram-Alley*,[20] by Lording Barry, a more highly individualized young man seeks to recuperate his losses by guile. The main plot of this play is quickly outlined. A profligate younger son, William Smallshanks, sets out to achieve two objectives. The one is to win back his property forfeited through unpaid debts to Throat, a lawyer and usurer; the other is to make "an honest woman" out of his mistress by marrying her to "a man of worship." By using one objective as a means toward effecting the other, he succeeds in attaining both. The way he does this is by making it known that he is about to marry a rich heiress. Bringing the girl (who is, of course, no heiress, but his penniless mistress) to the lawyer's house, he asks the latter's assistance in keeping her ignorant of the fact that he is not a rich man's son as he says he has told her, but a spendthrift who has lost all his property. Being allowed to speak to the "heiress" for this purpose, the lawyer does just what has been expected of him, and betrays Smallshanks by telling the girl the truth about her intended husband and putting in a strong bid for her hand himself. She professes to be shocked and disillusioned, encourages Throat, and later runs off with him when he ambushes the wedding party on its way to the priest. Smallshanks, putting up a show of frustrated fury, agrees to give up all claims to the "heiress," provided the lawyer will pay off his present debts and give him back the mortgage he had squeezed out of him by usury. Throat, who has the papers already drawn up, agrees

---

[20] Claude E. Jones, editor, *Ram-Alley or Merrie-Trickes—A Comedy by Lording Barry* (Materials for the Study of the Old English Drama, Vol. XXIII. Louvain: Uystpruyst, 1952). There have been various conjectures as to Barry's first name. See Chambers, *The Elizabethan Stage*, Vol. III, p. 215. In this latest edition of the play Jones (p. viii) favors "Lording" as a Christian name, not merely as a courtesy title of "Lord." He gives as his authority C. L'Estrange Ewen, *Lording Barry, Poet and Pirate* ([London:] The Author, 1938). With regard to the date of the play Jones (p. x) says ". . . it appears that *Ram-Alley* was probably first produced between March 10 and July 28, 1608."

with alacrity and, complacently thinking he has been too clever
for the young fellow, sets his hand and seal to the documents
which mark him down as a dupe.

We have here no sad tale of a simple country cousin or a
credulous dodderer being deluded, but the spectacle of a pettifogger and a sharper in his own right falling ignominiously at
the very moment when he was priding himself it was most fit
that "hee should haue state that riseth by his wit" (III, i; 1515).
It is not, however, by a shot in the dark or by a lucky accident
that he was brought down. Smallshanks, his adversary, succeeded because he knew his man and proceeded on that knowledge. His technique was to draw before the lawyer's nose a bait
which, from what he knew of the avaricious and double-dealing
character of the lawyer, he foresaw would be a most potent lure.
The author had carefully brought out these traits of Throat, by
showing him in one scene slavering over his moneybags and
relishing the "indirect and cunning meanes" by which he had
gained them, and by showing him in another scene chuckling
over fees accepted from both parties to a dispute (I, i; 428-79
and II, i; 723-40). And Smallshanks is assured that he was
right in his choice of the bait, when his whispered question
to the "heiress," "Has the gudgeon bit?" gets the bait's delighted answer that he has been nibbling. Smallshanks had also
carefully prepared the ground by instructing an accomplice,
Boutcher, not only to tell the lawyer of his debtor's prospective marriage to an heiress, but to deceive Smallshanks' older
brother with the same lie. This was done precisely with the intention that the elder brother might accompany the "heiress"
and her *soi-disant* betrothed to the lawyer's house and unwittingly add to the credibility of the hoax (I, i; 161-77). But
most important of all, the active cooperation of the prospective
victim was looked for and was necessary, and Throat could
blame nobody more than himself for his gulling. He garroted
himself with the very noose he thought he was rigging up for

another. And the rope of course had been deliberately put into his hands by that other.

Smallshanks is built on the lines of Middleton's young intriguing rogues. He is shrewd and determined in pursuing his ends and not at all scrupulous in choosing his means. He picks his victim's weakness, prepares his approach with thoroughness, and deftly presses home his attack, while all the time letting his adversary think that it is he who is keeping the initiative. He is decidedly not a colorless imitation of his predecessors. A deliberate attempt to insure the spectators' sympathy for Smallshanks in his intrigue against the lawyer can be seen in the treatment he is made by the author to give to his mistress. Despite the broad and breezy freedom of his way of speaking to her, he shows a certain loyalty to her in his determination to get her properly married (albeit to someone else), or, if he cannot, to continue to support her. Barry has endowed him with a racy and voluble vocabulary and a vigorous temperament. His bumptious vitality is most startlingly brought out in his whirlwind wooing of the widow Taffeta in one of the subplots, into which we need not pursue him further than to quote the final words of his amazing marriage proposal:

> . . . ift be a match,
> Clap hands, contract, and straite to bed,
> If not, pray, forgiue, and straight goes off your head (V, i;
>   2240-42).

It will be convenient to bring together for more or less simultaneous treatment the next three classes of deceivers; namely, testers, protectors, and exposers. The members of these groups are diversified, it is true, by their different objectives, and distinguishable objectives constitute the main principle of classification in this chapter and the preceding one; but these three groups are related to one another in that the individuals of all three assume disguise as their primary means of deception. Furthermore, though their ultimate objectives are different—namely, to test, or to expose, or to protect—yet in most of these characters the *immediate* purpose of assuming their common means of deception, disguise, is to spy on someone. In a number of them, finally, we find interesting combinations of ultimate objectives; some are both testers and exposers, some are protectors and exposers, while others are a combination of all three types of deceivers who resort to disguise as their chief form of deception. There seems to be ample justification, therefore, for discussing them all in one section.

One objective of characters who pretend to go away or pretend to die and then return in disguise is to test and observe the fidelity of those who are apparently left behind or bereaved. The type of character doing this most often in Elizabethan comedy is the suspicious husband. Most of those plays listed in Freeburg's *Disguise Plots in Elizabethan Drama*[21] as employing this situation can be dismissed very briefly. Lyly's *The Woman in the Moon* (c. 1593) uses it but momentarily. In Chapman's *The Widow's Tears* (c. 1605), not the disguised husband, but his brother, Tharsalio, is the chief deviser of stratagems. In *The Coxcomb* (c. 1609),[22] by Beaumont and Fletcher, the spying-husband role is exploited rather as an excuse for farcical beatings and frustrations for the husband in order to show how well he deserves the name of coxcomb than as an opportunity given him to control the action of the play. Quomodo, the chief swindler in *Michaelmas Term,* dons disguise himself only toward the end of the play in order to observe how his wife and son cherish his memory. This device is the final, characteristic recourse to trickery which recoils upon him and proves the undoing of the knave.

---

[21] Pp. 141-50.

[22] In Arnold Glover and A. R. Waller, editors, *The Works of Francis Beaumont and John Fletcher*, Vol. VIII (Cambridge: Cambridge University Press, 1905-1912). *The Coxcomb* may have been revised later by Massinger or W. Rowley. See Chambers, *The Elizabethan Stage*, Vol. III, p. 224.

One who has somewhat more to do with the plot than the characters just mentioned and who is by way of being a tester of his wife's fidelity and the exposer of the infidelity of other men's wives, though unsuccessful in either capacity, is Justiniano in *Westward Ho!* (1604), by Dekker and Webster.[23] Having reason to suspect his wife, Justiniano pretends to go on a journey, but stays close at hand in disguise. His wife's tentative straying from the paths of conjugal fidelity, however, is cut short by disgust at the overtures of her elderly suitor rather than by any stirrings of remorse on her part or by any contriving by her husband. Moving into the other plot of the play, Justiniano makes use of his disguise somewhat in the fashion of an exposer of enormities by abetting the wives of certain citizens in their dallying with gallants and in trying to move them into a situation in which they will be caught by their husbands. In this last activity he is unsuccessful, and there is some talk about the ladies' being found chaste after all, but not much can be said for the wholesomeness of this play. Nor can much be said for its dramatic movement, which is badly articulated.

Another object a character may have in indulging in trickery is to keep watch upon a loved one and eventually to help him by indirect ways. Thus, the father in the anonymous *The London Prodigal* (*c.* 1604)[24] disguises himself, brings a false report to the wayward son that his father is dead and has disinherited him, takes service with the son, and suggests a device of drawing up a feigned will to trick the father of a girl into marrying her to him. Then, to bring his son up short, the disguised father conspires with the young man's uncle to have the prodigal arrested on his wedding day for not having paid a fictitious debt. After the prodigal shamefully mistreats his newly wedded wife,

---

23 In William Hazlitt, editor, *The Dramatic Works of John Webster*, Vol. I. London: John Russell Smith, 1857.
24 In Brooke, *Shakespeare Apocrypha*.

the father helps her in turn to follow the wastrel as a disguised servant. She is thus eventually enabled to prove her loyalty to him and to bring him around to repentance and a resolution to live a better life.

The reasoning behind the father's alternately abetting and scheming against the prodigal seems to be that, by giving him enough rope to let him come perilously close to hanging, he will eventually bring his son to his senses and induce him to reform his ways. Though the prodigal is the most important character in the play, it is his father who with the help of his disguise and other means of deception initiates much of the action and directs the movements of the others.

An even more active intriguer with benevolent intentions is the whimsical old gentleman, Friscobaldo of *The Honest Whore, Part II* (*c.* 1605),[25] who aroused the enthusiasm of William Hazlitt. This play, written by Dekker with the help of Middleton, is remarkably similar to *The London Prodigal* in many aspects, and these similarities have been pointed out by Freeburg.[26] It will be sufficient here to remark that in Dekker's play Friscobaldo also is a father who disguises himself as a servant in order first of all to observe whether his daughter, Bellafront, is really leading a reformed life as has been reported of her; and then, when he has been satisfied on this account, to help her in her troubles with her wayward husband. In doing so he resorts to all kinds of tricks and devices, including shifting out of his disguise to confront his daughter and her husband in his own person and back into disguise to accentuate the irony of vicious remarks made in his disguised presence about Bellafront's father by her husband. In the end he throws off his disguise in time to testify to the chastity of his daughter and save her from

25 In Hazelton Spencer, editor, *Elizabethan Plays*. Boston: D. C. Heath and Company, 1933.
26 Freeburg, *Disguise Plots*, pp. 152-53.

condemnation as a loose woman. Evidence for this testimony he was enabled to acquire by disguised omnipresence and efficacious finesse.

The Captain (*c.* 1612),[27] by Fletcher with the help perhaps of others, is another comedy in which a father disguises himself and resorts to other means of deception with the purpose of helping and protecting a daughter.

We may look, finally, at those characters who don disguise to spy out and expose wickedness. Freeburg mentions several plays in which disguised dukes or kings observe rogueries, eventually expose them, and in some cases punish them.[28] This is done in *Measure for Measure* (*c.* 1604), Marston's *The Malcontent* (1604) and his *Parasitaster* (*c.* 1605), and in Middleton's *The Phoenix* (*c.* 1604), all of which seem to have been produced within the same two or three years. The same use of disguise to hunt down roguery is seen in Middleton's *Your Five Gallants* (*c.* 1607), though it is a private individual and not a duke who here so disguises himself. *The Malcontent* will be discussed in the chapter on frustrated deception.[29] In *Parasitaster* the most active intriguer is not the disguised duke, whose activities are mostly confined to flattering the knaves and fools at the court he is visiting, though he does serve in the end as the author's mechanism for revealing these creatures for what they are and thus exposing them to scorn and ridicule. It is Dulcimel, the daughter of the Duke of Urbino, who does the most effective and entertaining hoaxing in the play. In *The Phoenix* a duke's son pretends to go forth on his travels but remains behind in his realm in disguise to see what he can see. He is brought face to face with an assortment of sins and knaveries, but it is more by accident that he meets with one incident after another than

---

[27] In Glover and Waller, *Works of Beaumont and Fletcher*, Vol. V.
[28] Freeburg, *Disguise Plots*, pp. 160-75.
[29] *Infra*, pp. 115-18.

by any active manipulation on his part. He has a catalogue of observed crimes drawn up, and in the end one after another of the culprits is drawn to the scene of exposure and there denounced. The prince uncovers himself and corroborates *viva voce* what had been set down against them. Therefore, in this play, there is really no over-all intrigue; there are merely episodes, succeeding one another, though with some sort of continuity and coherence being given by the connection of the various personages among themselves and by the presence of the disguised prince.

In Shakespeare's *Measure for Measure* is achieved a more functional use of the disguised duke than in any of the other comedies employing this device. As is to be expected, Duke Vincentio is also a more highly complex character than his literary progenitors or descendants. His objectives, for one thing, in employing trickery cannot be reduced to a single category. That he seeks to test and prove the character of his deputy, Angelo, and observe how the possession of power will affect a precisionist can be seen in his remarks at the beginning of his feigned departure:

> Moe reasons for this action
> At our more leisure shall I render you;
> Only, this one: Lord Angelo is precise,
> Stands at a guard with envy, scarce confesses
> That his blood flows or that his appetite
> Is more to bread than stone; hence shall we see,
> If power change purpose, what our seemers be (I, iii, 48-54).

Then, too, he exploits his disguise for observing what enormities are rankling in his dukedom and eventually for exposing them. He resorts, finally, to much turning and double-dealing and not letting his left hand know what his right hand is doing in order to protect Isabella's chastity and her brother's life and to provide for the happiness of the melancholy maid of the moated grange. In this disguised duke, therefore, we have a combination of tester, exposer, and benevolent protector. In pursuing these objectives he not only initiates much of the action of the play, but controls its progress and in the end unties all tangles deliberately knotted by himself. In all this his means of locomotion, as it were, is one form of deception or another.

What seems to be a parody of the type of exposer and protector in disguise as seen in the plays just discussed is Justice Overdo's assumption of disguise "to spy out enormities" at Bartholomew Fair. While under disguise he is subjected to various humiliations, persists in his mistaken protection of the worst criminal at the Fair, and though in the end he does ape his spying predecessors in presiding over a closing scene of revelation and reckoning, he is somewhat chastened by the discovery that what he thought would prove the "chiefest enormity" turns out to be the indiscretion of his own wife, who had been indulging in the vanities of the Fair in a disguise of her own. Jonson's parody of the disguised and busy exposer and protector of other plays consists in this, that instead of protecting the innocent and setting evil to rights, Overdo unwittingly protects true evildoers, makes redress, it is true, for wrong done by himself in the past, but reimburses the wrong person (Quarles disguised as the wronged madman), and exposes his wife in a compromising situation—the last thing he would care to do (*Bartholomew Fair*, V, vi).[30]

The above examples will suffice as illustrations of testers, protectors, and exposers. To bring to an end our classifying of deceivers in Elizabethan comedy, we will give very brief notice to those who are prompted by envy or a desire for revenge to plot real harm against their intended victims. These may be designated as enviers and revengers. There is Don John of Shakespeare's *Much Ado about Nothing* (*c.* 1598), who pro-

---

[30] In Herford and Simpson, *Ben Jonson*, Vol. VI. *Bartholomew Fair* was first produced in 1614.

tests his villainy too much to be convincing. Envy arouses in him a vengeful desire to hurt Claudio because the latter has conducted himself with honor in the recent campaign and is now a favorite with Don Pedro, the duke. Don John, accordingly, with the help and contriving of the tool villain, Borachio, plots the disgrace of Hero, Claudio's betrothed, and thus sets up the complications of the main plot.

Another character who is impelled by a desire for revenge to resort to villainous intrigue is Franceschina in Marston's *The Dutch Courtesan.*[31] Because her former lover, Freevill, has cut himself off from her in anticipation of an honorable marriage, she demands that his friend, Malheureux, who has in his turn fallen in love with her, kill Freevill. Unless he does so, she swears, she will not allow him to have anything to do with her. She suggests that a quarrel be forced upon Freevill and that he be murdered in the ensuing duel. Her real purpose is not only to have Freevill killed by his friend but to betray to the authorities the murderous intention of the survivor in forcing the duel. Franceschina is frustrated in the end by Freevill, who allows her villainy to have some play in order that the eventual revelation of it may shatter Malheureux's infatuation for the woman.[32]

The planning and execution of the trickery in each play, we have seen, is generally in the hands of a single character. The Elizabethan comic trickster, duper, deceiver, guller, to call him by his various designations, belongs to an archetype which has an ancient, if not entirely honorable, lineage. In some of his characteristics he harks back to the tricky slave of Roman comedy. The Elizabethan deceiver also owes some of his features and some of his modes of operation to the native Vice of the medieval moralities. The agent of deception in Elizabethan

---

[31] In Wood, *Plays of John Marston*, Vol. II.

[32] Mendoza, the villainous intriguer in Marston's *The Malcontent*, will be discussed at length in another chapter (*infra*, pp. 115-18).

comedy, however, is not stereotyped and conventionalized to the extent to which the Roman tricky slave is, or the medieval Vice. The Elizabethan deceiver shows many mutations and pursues a number of diverse objectives, and the characters discussed in the second and third chapters were classified according to those different objectives. A final check of the objectives sought by means of deception and the types of characters pursuing them will be helpful.

The most common end a deceiver may have in view in Elizabethan comedy is the furthering of a love affair. The chief intriguer in such an affair may be the servant of the lover, or a friend, or a resourceful, self-reliant young gallant managing his own intrigue. Another frequent objective is the getting of money or property. The rogues seeking this objective are shown to be of varying reach and grasp. There are the petty sharper, the swindlers of greater intelligence and wider range, and finally the young gentlemen of superior education and breeding but of decayed circumstances. By others, trickery is used primarily for the sake of the mischief and fun arising out of it, though even among some of these relatively harmless tricksters a sharper spirit of revenge may be seen lurking behind their jollity. Still other purposes directing the use of deception are the exhibiting of the victim to scorn and ridicule, the uncovering of knavery, and the testing of fidelity. Leaning toward the viciousness of villains in tragedy is the malice of those intriguers who, out of a desire for revenge for real or fancied injury or out of envy, practice their wiles in order to bring real harm on the ones they deceive. Opposed to such purposes is the objective of the friendly deceivers whose goal is to do good to the very persons they deceive.

The justification for including in one study characters seeking such diversified objectives and exhibiting quite diversified characteristics is the fact that these characters all resort to deception in their pursuit of their objectives and in so doing affect to a considerable extent the flow of the plot. Now, with this much in common, it is not surprising that these characters manifest many similarities in trait, in behavior, and in dramatic function. It will be useful, accordingly, to sketch the outlines of a portrait of what might be called the archetypal deceiver of Elizabethan comedy. This will serve as a further summary of what has been written thus far and as a more explicit unfolding of the implications in the given data.

As for traits, the Elizabethan comic intriguer is nothing if not clever. This cleverness shows itself first of all in his ability to diagnose the precise weaknesses of his prospective victims, in the deftness of his touch in playing upon those weaknesses, and in the artfulness of his approach in winning the confidence of his dupes. He is resourceful and fertile in trickery and often thinks up more devices than are really called for by the situation. He is completely self-reliant and self-assured; and though he may employ assistants, he keeps absolute control of the stratagem, often refusing to give reasons to his henchmen for his commands and directives. Sometimes, it is true, he has uncomfortable moments when he wishes he were well out of the coil his busy ingenuity has begun to wind, but he almost invariably rises to emergencies by calling upon his wits for some shift or device. He adapts himself speedily to new and unforeseen circumstances, taking advantage of fresh openings or of new victims appearing on the scene. Very often, even while being quite businesslike and self-seeking in his activities, he extracts huge enjoyment out of the trickery by which he achieves his objectives.

A certain pattern also emerges in the tactical behavior of the intriguer. There is usually a preliminary scene of planning the intrigue or the trick to be played. Then this plan may be repeated to someone else. Next comes the preparation of the victim by the winning of his confidence. This may be done by flattering him, or by making protestation of friendship, or by presenting him with spurious evidences of the competency or the credibility of the deceiver. Often a scene shows the deceiver in triumphant self-congratulation over his own cleverness and glee over the gullibility of his dupe, or there may be an interlude in which he comments on his success so far and anticipates the early consummation of the intrigue. Sometimes it is in this very moment of gloating that he is sent on the way to frustration or at least to momentary embarrassment. More often, however, these emergencies present the intriguer with a further opportunity of proving his ingenuity and slipperiness or of manifesting his brazen effrontery in the face of detection. A favorite device of tricksters in such scenes of confrontation is to attempt to belittle the credibility of the confronter by casting doubts on his sanity.

The ways in which deceivers move toward their objectives show a certain recurrent variety. Sometimes the deceiver has but one objective and plans in advance the whole trickery by which he intends to achieve his objective. Such is the case in *The Bugbears;* this is true also, as will be seen later,[33] of the way in which Dulcimel in *Parasitaster* achieves her objective of marrying the young ambassador to her father's court. Again, a deceiver with one definite objective but with no ostensible plan will employ a series of devices as need arises. It is in this way that the young lovers in *The Taming of the Shrew, The Family of Love, The Scornful Lady* (c. 1613), and the lovers' helpers in *Englishmen for My Money* and *All Fools* further their own or their friends' intrigues. Thirdly, the deceiver may start out with only a general or indefinite objective but will play tricks as opportunities present themselves. This is the kind of objective and manner of procedure followed by Merrygreek *(Roister Doister)*, Diccon *(Gammer Gurton's Needle)*, Lemot *(A Humorous Day's Mirth)*, Cocledemoy *(The Dutch Courtesan)*, and

---

[33] *Infra,* pp. 78-81.

Canby *(The Blind Beggar of Bednal Green)*. A fourth group is made up of those deceivers who begin with one objective but pick up another in the course of the intrigue and use one objective to achieve the other. Such are the tricky pages in *Mother Bombie*, Lodovico in *May Day*, and Witgood in *A Trick To Catch the Old One*,[34] Mistress Low-water in the Lady Golden-fleece-Mistress Low-water plot in *No Wit, No Help Like a Woman's*, and Duke Vincentio in *Measure for Measure*. A fifth relationship between objective and movement toward it by the deceiver is to be seen in *Ram-Alley*, in which Smallshanks junior has two objectives to start out with: to make an "honest woman" of his past mistress by marrying her off to someone and to regain his property. He makes use of one objective to gain the other.

Functionally, the deceiver is often the key figure in the construction of the plot. As such, he initiates the action, serves as a device for the grouping and shifting of characters, and may be involved in the providing of a denouement. Crises in the action and consequent intensification of suspense often have their origin in the momentary checks and embarrassments he meets with. In some plays, by parading humor characters and other objects of ridicule and contriving the tricks whereby they are exposed and "dishumored," he implements the author's satirical intentions. In most cases he amounts to something of a master of ceremonies. The interesting thing is that the author himself sometimes becomes so intrigued with the intriguer that he suffers him to become the main attraction. In such instances the resplendent and scintillating ringmaster draws and holds the eyes of the audiences to himself rather than to the performers he is putting through their paces. Thus it sometimes happens that a character who was introduced into a play primarily as a *machine à fraude* or as a device for manipulating and spotlight-

---

[34] *Infra*, pp. 87-89.

ing other characters is himself crystallized into a full-bodied creation, though some of the other characters fail to take on a third dimension.

In all these uses of the deceiver, deception is shown in the process of becoming, as the period under study progresses, increasingly and more artistically involved as an organic and pervasive element of the structure of Elizabethan comedies.

CHAPTER IV

The Victims
of Deception

Whenever we come upon active deception, we shall find a victim as well as an agent of the deception. Furthermore, if any dramatic value is to result from the carrying out of the deception in a comedy, something should be contributed by the dupe other than his mere presence as a beating stock or, as one of the Elizabethans put it, as a virginals in a barbershop which any man may play on. This by no means negligible contribution by the dupe will usually be one form or another of cooperation in his own duping.

Tricksters are often in need of accomplices to help them carry out their schemes. Sometimes, however, the willing assistance of another cannot be procured or counted upon, and the deceiver finds himself under the necessity of tricking someone into unwitting cooperation in the duping of others. This puts the one giving the assistance in the category of dupe, for he is being used as an instrument rather than an accomplice. To mention a single example from tragedy, this is the relationship between Roderigo and Iago in *Othello*. Such a situation in a comedy offers more interesting and dramatic possibilities than the mere use of an accomplice because the chief intriguer must keep his assistant from discovering that he is merely a pawn in a game. There can be variations in this situation.

The pedant in the *The Taming of the Shrew* is used as an instrument by Tranio in deceiving the father of Bianca, the girl his master is plotting to marry. In his disguise as one of the wooers Tranio has outbid the old rival, Gremio, in the matter of the dower offered, and his next move is to get someone to act as his father and go surety for the bond. Accordingly we see him pouncing on the traveler from Mantua, filling him with false fears for his life if he should enter the city in his own character as a Mantuan, and suggesting that he assume another identity and take asylum with him. Incidentally, as it were, he lets the credulous pedant understand that he can be of service to him by passing "assurance of a dow'r." The pedant seems to enter into his new role with complete acquiescence, for we next see him pompously giving his "approval" to the proposed marriage (IV, iv), and in a later appearance he joins vigorously in facing up to the real father upon the latter's unexpected arrival (V, i). Throughout all this the pedant knows he is assisting in an imposture, but he believes that his disguise is primarily helpful in saving his own life and, at least in the beginning, he does not realize he himself is being imposed upon.

The distinction between an accomplice and a mere instrument will be readily seen in examining the way in which William Smallshanks in *Ram-Alley* makes use of his friend, Boutcher, and of his father and elder brother. Boutcher is told of Smallshanks' intention to outwit the lawyer, Throat. As a friend, Boutcher is asked to help, his main task being to arouse Throat's cupidity by mentioning Smallshanks' seeming prospects of a fortunate marriage. He is also instructed to create this same false impression in the minds of Smallshanks' doddering father and stupid elder brother. The purpose of this is that the two kinsmen may be brought around to look upon the young scapegrace more favorably than had been their wont. This new respectful attention from his family and the added fact that the elder brother is induced to accompany William Smallshanks and his "rich heiress" to the lawyer's office is intended by the rogue to impress Throat and contribute an air of authenticity to the whole imposture. This effect is achieved; and thus, with the help of an accomplice, two lesser dupes are maneuvered into an unwitting cooperation in the ensnaring of the main victim.

In *The London Prodigal*[1] Flowerdale, the young wastrel, draws up a spurious will in which all the nonexistent goods of the young man are bequeathed to the girl he desires to marry. This document he gives the foolish Weathercock with the stipulation that he divulge its contents to no one until after the death of the prodigal. The inane busybody does exactly what was expected of him and brings the document immediately to the girl's father, thereby making the father more favorable to young Flowerdale and losing the girl he himself had been courting. In this way Weathercock serves as an instrument in his own as well as the father's duping.

In *The Puritan*[2] are several instances of very active and effective assistance being exacted from minor dupes. The general intention of the gentleman rogue, George Pieboard, it will be remembered, is to live by his wits.[3] This intention is canalized, for a good part of the play, into efforts to rescue from prison a friend who will help him later in his cozening schemes. Visiting his friend, Captain Idle, in the prison, George sets himself to excogitate a plan. And pat comes in Nicholas, a foolish cousin of the captain's, who happens to be a servant in the household of the Puritans who are to be the principal victims of George's schemes, and who is himself one of the "brethern." George immediately sees in him a fit subject "to work a 'scape upon," and proposes that the captain should suggest to Nicholas that he steal a gold chain from his master so it can be pawned

---

[1] In Brooke, *Shakespeare Apocrypha.*
[2] *Ibid.*
[3] *Supra*, p. 54.

and provide a purchase for the captain's liberty. Nicholas is horrified at the very idea. "Any thing else that I can do, had it beene to rob, I would ha don't; but I must not steale: that's the word, the literall, *thou shalt not steale;* and would you wish me to steale, then?" (I, iv, 162-65). George admits that would be demanding too much, but asks him if he would be willing to "nim" the chain. Knowing of no commandment which explicitly mentions nimming, Nicholas gladly assents. Instead, however, of having this foolish tool bring him the chain to be pawned, George modifies his original plan and instructs Nicholas, once he has taken the chain from his master's house, to hang it in the rosemary bank in the garden. When his master discovers the loss of his chain, Nicholas is to tell him that he has a kinsman "of such exquisit Art, that the diuill himselfe is french Lackey to him"—one who would find the chain for him—"tho twere hid vnder a mine of sea-cole." Sir Godfrey, being even more gullible than his servant, determines he must have the services of this conjurer; and when told that he is in prison, he promptly procures a pardon for him. The captain, following George's instructions, lives up to advance notices, restores the chain "by his art," makes a great impression on the Puritan household, and, along with George, almost succeeds in getting himself a wealthy wife.

Two other tools are employed by George to further his designs. He has been posing as one with more than natural knowledge; and to impress the members of the Puritan household with his ability to foretell the future, he has told them that blood would be shed within a few hours in front of their house. He has arranged for two accomplices, Peter Skirmish and the corporal, to fight a sham duel at a stipulated moment at that place. But the corporal does not know that George has instructed Skirmish really to wound the corporal in the leg (II, i, 339-40; III, i, 56-57), nor does he know that George intends to give him a sleeping potion to make the wound seem a fatal one.

Skirmish, on the other hand, does not know he will be clapped into prison and brought within an ace of hanging (III, i, 68). All this George has arranged so that, when he rescues Skirmish from the gallows by dramatically raising the corporal "from the dead" at the precise moment when the effects of the sleeping draught wear off, his stock will soar with the Puritans and he will accordingly be able to induce them to do anything he wishes. The corporal and the soldier think they are George's henchmen, but in all this they are merely his dupes and are used by him as mere means to an end.

> These emptie creatures,
> Souldier and Corporall, were but ordaind
> As instruments for me to worke vpon (III, i, 77-79).

In Middleton's *A Trick To Catch the Old One*[4] Witgood, the archdeceiver, makes use of two accomplices, his mistress and the tavern host, in his victimizing of the two usurers, Hoard and Lucre. The host, however, though giving valuable assistance, is not vouchsafed quite complete knowledge of Witgood's intentions. In fact, he himself is deceived on certain essential matters all through the play, and by means of this deception his contribution to the intrigue is drawn out of him. Once Witgood has determined to try the rich-widow trick on his uncle, he sees the necessity of outfitting his penniless mistress, who is to pose as the "widow," with an equipage and a manservant. He selects a tavern host, who has not known the courtesan, and tells him that a widow, all for his (Witgood's) love, has "regardless of vainglorious ceremony" run off unfurnished and unattended to marry him. But if she discovers that he is without property, he confides to the host, that love may cool, and he may lose out on the match. Therefore his rich uncle must be maneuvered into supplying him with enough credit to enable him to make quite

---

[4] In Bullen, *Works of Thomas Middleton*, Vol. II.

sure of the "widow." On the other hand, lest the uncle should see the lady without servants or horses and think she is not all she is claimed to be, Witgood suggests to the host that he supply her with horses out of friendship to Witgood and go along with her himself in the role of servant (I, ii). The host assents and proves of real help to Witgood and the courtesan throughout the intrigue. But his horses and his services are obtained by deceiving him. All through the play, until, presumably, the recognition by others of the courtesan for what she is, the host believes she is really a rich widow; and though he is helpful in playing off the main victims against each other and drawing them into Witgood's net, he is all along under the impression that Witgood himself intends to marry the "widow," and that he is only using the usurers as a means of keeping his credit high enough to make sure of her. This false impression gives rise to certain interesting situations where the effect of a double-edged irony is achieved. For instance, the host-servant receives bribes from Hoard to speak favorably of him to his mistress, but he says in an aside that he knows the "widow's" mind and that her real intention is to marry only Witgood (III, i, 146-47). He is undoubtedly helping deceive the usurer, but he does it only because he himself is deceived.

Besides making use of the unwitting assistance of a dupe in the victimizing of another, a deceiver may sometimes count upon the cooperation of a gull in the ensnaring of himself. This can be especially interesting when, to use the words of Plautus, who had a flair for contriving such situations, "the dolts feel that they are foxing others at the very moment they are gulling themselves."[5] We have already seen how Throat, the lawyer in *Ram-Alley*, suffers exactly this fate. Another play in which this situation is elaborated calls for more detailed analysis. Rinaldo, who is the chief agent of deception in Chapman's *All Fools*, is

---

[5] ". . . i se quom frustrant, frustrari alios stolidi existumant" (*Bacchides*, v. 548).

the friend of one young lover and the brother of another.[6] His friend, Valerio, is afraid that his stern father, Gostanzo, will discover that he is secretly married. Rinaldo's brother, Fortunio, complains that he cannot even get near his beloved because of parental restrictions. By an initial lie to Gostanzo that the lady seen in Valerio's company is the wife of Rinaldo's brother, Fortunio, Rinaldo finds himself involved in an attempt to help the two young couples. Bidding the lovers be ruled by him and giving directions as to how they are to play their parts, he turns his attention to Gostanzo. An intuitive reading of the old man's character enables Rinaldo to gain his complete confidence by stroking him just where he is most susceptible to flattery.

Among Gostanzo's weak points is his conceited conviction that, because of his stern methods of bringing up Valerio, the latter is an industrious and obedient son. He also considers himself a man of "policy" and an efficient manager of other people's affairs, especially those of Marc Antonio, his neighbor whom he disparages as an overindulgent father and as

> An honest knight, but simple, not acquainted
> With the fine sleights and policies of the world
> As I myself am (III, 1, 96-98).

He *talks* "by the book" of Machiavelli fluently enough; but instead of being an active deviser of stratagems, as he thinks, he is all the time being led by the nose, and the initiative is in the hands of Rinaldo and Valerio much more than he is ever allowed to understand.

Once Rinaldo has gained the confidence of his dupe ("I like his learning well," says Gostanzo to Marc Antonio later, "make him your heir"), he is able to make suggestions to Gostanzo which the latter carries through unquestioningly. Thus it is that Gostanzo joins Rinaldo in a series of stratagems whose succes-

---

[6] Parrott, *Plays of Chapman: Comedies.*

sive objectives, he is given to understand, are, first, to show Marc Antonio how to bring up his son, and later, to play some tricks on his neighbor. As is counted on by Rinaldo, Gostanzo characteristically adds a few flourishes and coils of his own to the deception and thus winds the subterfuge around to its real objective, the hoodwinking of Gostanzo himself.

Rinaldo has but to recognize the nature of the material he has to work upon and mold it accordingly. This he does by keeping his dupe under the impression that he is the most active conspirator of them all, deftly stimulating his appetite for meddling, and flattering his conviction that he alone is a man of policy. In a word, Rinaldo merely lets Gostanzo entangle his feet with a lime of his own mixing. If an epigram were called for here, one might aptly use the last verses of "To Candidus" by Chapman's contemporary, Guilpin:

> And to conclude, who selfe conceitedly,
> Thinkes al men guls, ther's none more gull than he.[7]

A character who in some ways resembles Gostanzo, and to whom most attention is given in Marston's *Parasitaster, or The Fawn*, is Gonzago, the father of the girl Dulcimel.[8] In his youth, Gonzago admits, he had wit, but age has deepened that to wisdom. Now he knows "Dimensions and termini/ Of all existens." The "Being and the *quid* of things" are no secrets to him. He keeps constantly by him a companion, Granuffo, whose complete silence he interprets as awed admiration of his sapience. But his daughter knows just how deep this wisdom lies. Having fallen in love with Tiberio, who had come as ambassador to arrange a wedding between his father and Gonzago's daughter, "the quick, deviceful, strongbrain'd Dulcimel" makes her father her instrument in communicating with the man he has warned her not to

---

[7] Everard Guilpin, *Skialetheia, 1598*, Epigrams, No. 20. (Shakespeare Association Facsimiles, No. 2.) London: Shakespeare Association, 1931.

[8] Wood, *Plays of John Marston*, Vol. II.

encourage. Thus, Gonzago is told by his daughter that the young envoy has spoken in his own behalf to her. For the alleged effrontery the young man is straightway chided by Gonzago, who thereby opens Tiberio's eyes to the fact that the lady is making advances to him; and the love which he never felt before is aroused. The next lie Dulcimel tells her father is that, instead of being deterred from his suit, Tiberio has sent her a scarf and love letters which she dutifully hands over to Gonzago. He, of course, confronts the astonished young man with these proofs of his impudence and assures him his dissembling has been smelled out. Tiberio cannot but be convinced now that Dulcimel is angling for his love. And when finally Gonzago in a great heat breaks it to Tiberio that his daughter, who has wit "to gull a thousand easie things like you," has obediently informed him that Tiberio was planning to climb a tree to get access to her chamber that night and that he had asked her to have a priest on hand to marry them, what can the young prince do but follow directions thus blatantly conveyed to him by the one who is convinced he is wisely preventing any such thing from happening? By means of her father, therefore, Dulcimel first stirs to life in Tiberio a love which he had not before been aware of; then by remote control she directs him through the various stages of the intrigue until she draws him up the tree to her chamber and marriage, without having spoken a word to him after the first harmless interview when he presented his credentials at her father's court.

Gonzago is an excellent example of a dupe being used as an instrument in his own duping. In Gonzago is also to be seen one of those interesting cases of self-deception being played on and manipulated by a clever deceiver. He thinks himself wise and politic, and these illusions are puffed by the obsequious obeisances of his wordless shadow, Granuffo, by the provocative flattery of the disguised Faunus, but most especially by the mock adulation of his daughter. She plies him with such hyperbolic

phrases as "my Nestor-like father," "my oraculous father," and
"royally wise and wisely royal father" that he says upon one
occasion, "I thinke that eloquence is hereditary." Gonzago himself gives voice smugly and persistently to appreciation of his
own wisdom, and these utterances are usually made in circumstances which render their ironical thrust as palpable as an
elbow in the ribs.

> I will deale wisely, and be provident,
> Your father shall not say I pandarizde,
> Or fondly winkt at your affection,
> No weele be wise . . . (III, p. 188).

This is spoken to the young prince to whom he has just shown
the scarf and the letters given him by his daughter and to whom
he is about to mention the very tree whereby he can climb to
her window. He cannot get over "what overweening fooles these
young men be, that thinke us olde men sottes!" And at the moment when the prince is secretly being married to Gonzago's
daughter, this wise old sot is singing a paean to his own triumphant generalship:

> . . . this night we will exult, O let this night
> Be ever memorizd with prouder triumphes,
> Let it be writ in lasting Character,
> That this night our great wisdome did discover
> So close a practice, that this night I say,
> Our policy found out, nay dasht the driftes
> Of the young Prince . . . (V, i; pp. 214-15).

And so the great moment arrives toward which the audience
has seen this self-deceived and practiced-upon dupe precipi-
tously hastening. The disguised duke, Hercules, masquerading
as Faunus, who by his flattery had been inducing other foolish
individuals as well as Gonzago to display their several fatuities,
announces that he is about to expose for the delectation of all
the court a really special treat in the line of fools, an opponent
of two lovers who "Was by their cunning made the goe be-

tweene./ The onely messenger, the token carrier . . ." Gonzago does not believe that "such an egregious Asse" lives and demands whether one may have the sight of such a fellow for nothing. He is granted his request; and the light tappings of irony, which unperceived by himself have been tagging him all through the play, solidify now into an unmoving finger of scorn which he realizes with a shock is pointing at himself and himself alone.

Gostanzo and Gonzago are duped fathers; we may now turn our attention to some instances of husbands who cooperate in their own duping. Sir Petronel Flash, the shifty knight of *Eastward Ho!* (1605) by Chapman, Jonson, and Marston,[9] not content with cheating his newly wedded wife out of her property and sending her off on a journey to his imaginary castle, plans to seduce and take away with him on his voyage to Virginia the wife of the usurer, Security. In order both to lure Security away from his house so that Winifred, his wife, can flee and also to add a dash of ironic pungency to the cuckolding, Sir Petronel tells Security he is about to run off with the wife of Bramble, Security's lawyer, and asks him if he will draw the lawyer out of his house and bring him to the Blue Anchor Tavern by Billingsgate. He further informs Security that the lady will be brought in disguise to this same tavern, and hints at the opportunity for sport at Bramble's expense which this situation will afford them all. Security enters into the spirit of the thing with such gusto that he hops back into the room several times to suggest some new refinement to this "prettie, pithie, and most pleasant project," as he calls it.[10] His "best device" and most helpful suggestion comes when Petronel and his fellow conspirator,

---

[9] In Gayley and Thaler, *Representative English Comedies*, Vol. II.

[10] Professor Parrott, who argues that the whole Petronel-Winifred intrigue is Chapman's work, calls attention to the similarity between Security's delight in the proposed gulling of his neighbor and Gostanzo's attitude in *All Fools*, III, i, 76-112. See Parrott, *Plays of Chapman: Comedies*, p. 845.

Quicksilver, are racking their brains for a convincing disguise for the lady. Security comes running in to them with his wife's gown and proposes that they dress the lawyer's wife in it "for two great reasons":

> One is, that Maister Bramble may take hold
> Of some suspition that it is my wife,
> And gird me so perhaps with his law wit;
> The other (which is pollicie indeede)
> Is that my wife may now be tyed at home,
> Having no more but her old gowne abroad,
> And not showe me a quirck, while I fyrke [cheat] others.
> Is not this rare? (III, ii, 294-301).

That evening at the tavern Security takes malicious enjoyment in making covert jibes at the lawyer and in mocking him when he voices a suspicion that the masked lady who has been brought in is really the wife of the usurer. Hilariously, Security proposes a toast "to all that are going eastward to night towardes Cuckolds Haven; and so to the health of Maister Bramble" (III, iii, 101-03). This is comic irony in the vein of Middleton, this spectacle of a husband enthusiastically helping in deceiving himself and toasting all that will be cuckolded that night. That the whole project was frustrated by the storm and that his wife returned to the house in time to convince Security that she was still his ever-faithful wife is not to his credit. He did all he could to help her and the flashy knight in their project of making a dupe out of him.

Something very similar to the use made of her father by Dulcimel is seen in *The Widow* (c. 1616), by Middleton and perhaps Fletcher and Jonson.[11] The wife of Brandino forges a soliciting letter and signs it with the name of a man she secretly loves. This she shows to her husband, who immediately hies him to the alleged would-be seducer and by showing him the letter

---

[11] In Bullen, *Works of Thomas Middleton*, Vol. V.

and berating him for an attempt he has not dared to make, un-wittingly acquaints him of the lady's willingness to receive any attentions that might in the future be paid. The young man takes the hint and does not find it hard to convince the husband that his intentions in penning the letter were entirely honorable. Indeed, he so works on Brandino that the foolish fellow soon finds himself inviting his wife's lover to make free of his home. And later, when the young man is delayed from the proposed visit by being arrested at another's suit, Brandino himself stands bail for him and has him released (II, ii). The entire intrigue therefore is based upon a suggestible and gullible husband who can be hoodwinked into acting as a go-between and door opener for his own wife. That he is known to be gullible is shown by the wife's remarks that she knows her husband for a fool, and that it would have been as impossible for him to keep the letter from the lover as it would be for him to be young again (III, ii, 15-16). His credulity is also emphasized by his quick changes of opinion which follow the utterances of the one who speaks to him last (I, i, 172-226; II, ii, 139-63). It is to be noticed that this intrigue fails to run its full course because of the repentance of the lover, which is aroused by what he mistakenly appre-hends as a supernatural vision.

Harebrain, the principal dupe of the minor plot in *A Mad World, My Masters*,[12] is another husband who is shown supply-ing his wife with one means after another for playing him false, while all the time he thinks he is taking wise and provident steps to keep his wife's thoughts and actions chaste and devout. His introducing his wife to a bawd under the inexplicable impres-sion that he is providing her with a pious companion, and his fatuous insistence on his wife's visiting the lodging of this "vir-tuous virgin," when the bawd pretends to be ill, give rise to situations whose ironic potentialities are exploited to the utmost

---

[12] *Ibid.*, Vol. III.

by Middleton. Here again the fact that the wife's lover is given a scene of such repentance and repugnance for his sin that he converts the lady to better ways is not due to any prudence of the husband, nor does it serve to save Middleton from the charge of cynicism in his attitude toward moral questions, "particularly towards those involving sex relations."[13]

Briefer mention may be made of Bellemont's hoax by which Greenshield in *Northward Ho!* (1605), by Dekker and Webster,[14] is induced to volunteer to fetch the supposed "Yorkshire lady" to brighten the evening of the melancholy Mayberry. Greenshield does not know the lady under her mask nor does she know that her disguised conductor is her own husband. In the one moment of revelation he discovers that his wife has been roaming with a longer tether than he had been aware of and that he has been tricked into helping to make himself a laughingstock before his fellows.

Tricking a dupe into being a cooperator in his own hoodwinking adds a touch of complexity to a simple duping. A further twist is thrown into the coil when one victim is played off against another, and both are used as reciprocal instruments of each other's confusion. Among plots and situations of this kind especially worthy of study are those in which the prospective victims are themselves cunning and tricky.

One need not do more than refer to the fact that the barnyard imbroglio in *Gammer Gurton's Needle* was primarily a matter of setting two truculent neighbors by the ears by means of a sly dropping of lies and a judicious covering up of tracks. The credulous and choleric dispositions and the underlying antagonisms could be counted on to come to quick heat and flame once the tinder was touched. The merry mischief-maker, Diccon,

---

[13] Thomas Marc Parrott and Robert Hamilton Ball, *A Short View of Elizabethan Drama*, p. 170. New York: Charles Scribner's Sons, 1943.
[14] In Hazlitt, *Works of John Webster*, Vol. I.

was favored with more cooperation than he had any right to
expect from his dupes in making them reciprocal instruments
of each other's confusion.

In the subplot of *The Merry Wives of Windsor* (*c.* 1600)
Anne Page's father wishes her to marry Master Slender, while
her mother is bent on her marrying the French Doctor Caius.
Anne herself is for young Fenton. Matters come to a head on
that evening in Windsor Forest when Falstaff goes down to final
and ignominious disaster. Each of the interested parties plans
to put the masking and pageantry at Herne's Oak to his or her
own purposes and to outwit the others. Accordingly Master
Page bids his daughter to slip away with Slender during the
activities and marry him before her mother discovers her absence. To effect this he desires her to dress all in white so that
her eloping partner may know her in the dark. Her mother, on
her part, secretly enjoins Anne to dress in green and run off to
a parson with Caius, who is given the countersign. Anne knows
her own mind. Simulating assent to both her mother's and her
father's commands, she uses their mutual efforts at deceiving
each other as a means of outwitting both of them and the un-
worthy suitors. She dresses one boy in white, another in green,
gives them their instructions, and lets each of them run off with
the designated dupe, while she and Fenton steal away to be
married by a parson provided by the host of the tavern.

Glister, the physician in Middleton's *The Family of Love*,[15]
is enamored of Mistress Purge, the wife of the " 'pothecary."
Two gallants, however, Lipsalve and Gudgeon, are also in love
with her. They both come to him separately, asking him to use
the magic powers he is reputed to have in their behalf and win
for them the favors of the lady. The physician does not tell
either of them that the other is making advances to the same
lady, nor does he indicate that he is interested in her himself;

---

[15] In Bullen, *Works of Thomas Middleton*, Vol. III.

but to discourage them from pursuing Mistress Purge further, he plays a trick on them. He tells Gudgeon that he will have a spirit transport the lady of his desires to the rooms of his friend, Lipsalve. But since the apparition of a spirit would be too terri- fying a spectacle to look upon, it will come, he says, in the form and appearance of Lipsalve. When it comes, Gudgeon is in- structed, he is to take a whip and apply it vigorously to the apparition, which will thereupon disappear, leaving the lady with Gudgeon. These same instructions, with appropriate varia- tions, are given to Lipsalve, who is likewise given a whip to use on the spirit which will look like Gudgeon. It is only after simul- taneously belaboring each other that the two perceive that they are thoroughly gulled gallants.

In *Jack Drum's Entertainment* (1600), by Marston and others, occurs a farcical episode in which the heroine's maid makes two of her lovers serve as mutual instruments in each other's gulling. And of course in *Twelfth Night* Shakespeare has given us Sir Toby's befooling of Sir Andrew Aguecheek and Viola-Cesario in the matter of their duel.

At contriving situations in which one dupe is played off against another for the profit or the delectation of a trickster Jonson is an acknowledged master. In *Epicoene*[16] two gulls, Jack Daw, the pretender of learning, and Sir Amorous La Foole, de- scendant of a long line of La Fooles, are each deceived into thinking that the other is seeking mortal satisfaction for an insult not intended by either of them. The main trickster here is the lively Truewit, who plays upon the cowardice of each of his dupes and brings each to the point of offering to make humiliating satisfaction to the other. Upon being blindfolded, one victim permits himself to be kicked, and the other suffers his nose to be tweaked, while each of them thinks he is thus saving himself from far greater punishment. The resemblance

---

16 In Herford and Simpson, *Ben Jonson*, Vol. V.

between this situation and the burlesque affair of honor in *Twelfth Night* is obvious.

Not merely a single episode, but the whole intrigue in *Volpone,* is built up around the playing off, not only of two dupes against each other, but of a whole series of dupes against one another.[17] Mosca, and not his master, is usually the one directly in contact with the victims; and upon his cleverness and agility in keeping several balls in the air at one time without letting them fall foul of one another depends the success of Volpone's villainies. But instead of trying to prevent each of his dupes from discovering that others are playing at the same game of *captatio,* Mosca allows each of them to see the gifts that have been brought by the others, and thus he arouses their competitive and avaricious spirit and induces them to bring even greater gifts. This is a more difficult and dangerous game to play than trying to keep them all ignorant of one another's interest in Volpone's will. But he manages until the very end to maintain each of them in the conviction that he is the one most in the good graces of the "dying" Volpone.

Special interest attaches itself to those situations in which the victims who are played off against each other are themselves expected to be cunning. Such a situation is to be found in Middleton's *A Trick To Catch the Old One,*[18] which is one of the best of the realistic comedies turning on the outsmarting of greedy usurers by attractive young scapegraces. Young Witgood, ruined by his extravagance and the usury of his uncle, Lucre, plans to trick his uncle into giving back the property he had forfeited to him through unpaid debts. He lets it come, as though inadvertently, to his uncle's ears that he has fair hopes of marrying a rich widow. The one he induces to pose as the widow is his own mistress, who has no more possessions than the clothes

---

[17] *Ibid.*
[18] In Bullen, *Works of Thomas Middleton,* Vol. II.

on her back. The uncle determines to help him sew up the match, not out of any altruistic motive, but in the hope of eventually getting his hands on the "widow's" property through the improvidence of his nephew (II, i, 180-84). An even stronger reason is the opportunity he sees in this marriage for turning the laugh on Hoard, a swindling competitor, who has mocked and taunted him publicly because of the decayed state of his spendthrift nephew (II, i, 206-14). This determination is whipped almost to a passion when Lucre hears that Hoard is also putting himself forward as a suitor of the "widow." Hoard, in his turn, is motivated by a desire to annoy and spite his enemy in frustrating the nephew's hopes for a wealthy marriage as well as by greed for her reputed fortune (II, ii, 44-54). Now, when Witgood learns that Hoard is after the woman, he urges her to let the old fellow catch her. He feels that he is thus helping her to some security in life and making amends for having seduced her.

The young blood then plays off the two greedy old enemies against each other. By letting his uncle, Lucre, see that Hoard is making progress with the "widow," Witgood, with the artful assistance of his mistress, works Lucre into giving back to him the mortgage on his property so as to make him more acceptable to the lady. By allowing Hoard, on the other hand, to appear to outmaneuver him by secretly informing the "widow" that Witgood is really an impecunious scapegrace and thus persuading her to marry him instead, Witgood first of all sets her up in marriage. Then, when by an unexpected setback his various creditors have him arrested, he gets Hoard to pay all his debts in return for his releasing the "widow" from an alleged precontract to marry—a precontract which Witgood and she claim they had entered into.

Despite the fact that much of the action has its origin in Witgood's determination to win back by some trick his forfeited property, he is not endowed with any striking individuality.

William Smallshanks, the young fellow who fulfills an identical function in *Ram-Alley*, is much more highly individualized. Witgood is just another of the "million of men in the world that only sojourn upon their brain, and make their wits their mercers" (I, i, 24-26). He is a character whose presence and typical gifts are necessary if the author is to write this sort of play at all. The interest in *A Trick To Catch the Old One* is directed more to the story than to characters, and it is a plot which never lags. The playwright, however, has given a certain amount of attention to the characterization of the two covetous old curmudgeons whose mutual antagonism provides Witgood with a weapon he is quick to direct toward his own ends. He is therefore another duper who maneuvers each of two dupes into helping him outwit the other.

A sufficient number of situations and plots have been analyzed in the foregoing section to illustrate the several ways in which dupes make contributions to their own duping. In so doing they emphasize in their own way the usefulness of deception as both material and machinery of dramatic action in Elizabethan comedy. A grouping of the victims of deceptions according to conventional types will now be offered, and query will be made *pari passu* as to the special qualifications presented by the members of each type to warrant the type's being imposed upon so persistently.

Through which of the conventional character types of Elizabethan comedy are victims of deception distributed? This question may be answered in brief fashion.

Fathers are the type most frequently abused and duped in Elizabethan comedy. This, of course, is not a privilege peculiar to the father on the Elizabethan stage. The eternal conflict in life between the young and the old has had its long-lived counterpart in the history of comic drama. Young people and their henchmen or abettors were the instigators and agents of deception in the ancient and in the Italian forms as well as in the

Elizabethan. Now, young people are privileged characters in comedy, the more so if they are in love. Those who oppose them, therefore, arouse the spontaneous antagonism of the audience, just as those who abet them are drawn into the warm stream of sympathy that flows out to the young and the lovely. But among those who stand always and imposingly in the forefront of the opposition are the fathers, the conscious symbols of domestic authority. Hence in the comedy of Rome, in the *commedia dell' arte*, and in Elizabethan comedy fathers were generally the victims of dupery, and Tranio's delighted observation could stand as a pertinent comment on both life and comedy: "Here's no knavery! See, to beguile the old folks, how the young folks lay their heads together."[19] Samples of duped fathers in Elizabethan comedy are the following: the fathers in *Mother Bombie*, Amedeus *(The Bugbears)*, Sir Arthur Clare *(The Merry Devil of Edmonton)*, Master Page *(The Merry Wives of Windsor)*, Gostanzo *(All Fools)*, Gonzago *(Parasitaster)*, Sir Oliver Twilight *(No Wit, No Help Like a Woman's)*, and Knowell *(Every Man in His Humor)*.

Husbands form another class of characters very frequently duped. Some of these are of so suspicious a nature ("jealous," as the Elizabethans would say) that they are forever imagining themselves being cuckolded or are shown as taking fearful and ridiculous precautions against the possibility. This opens them up to suggestion and makes them easy prey for busy and insinuating rogues.[20] Such are Cornelio *(All Fools)* and Kitely *(Every Man in His Humor)*. Others are actually deceived by

---

[19] *The Taming of the Shrew*, I, ii, 138-40. Tranio's remark is a sufficiently accurate epitome of what happens in the anonymous *The Wit of a Woman* (W. W. Greg, editor, *The Wit of a Woman—1604*. [Malone Society Reprints.] London: Malone Society, 1913).

[20] See Robert Stanley Forsythe, *The Relations of Shirley's Plays to the Elizabethan Drama*, pp. 86-87 (Columbia University Studies in English and Comparative Literature, No. 48. New York: Columbia University Press, 1914), for a listing of Elizabethan plays in which "imaginary cuckolds" are featured.

their wives, who, however, are generally prevented from going the full length of infidelity.[21] Such husbands are Brandino *(The Widow)*, Harebrain *(A Mad World, My Masters)*, and Security *(Eastward Ho!)*. Unique in the class of husband dupes is Antonio in *The Coxcomb*, by Beaumont and Fletcher, who professes himself willing to put up with a wife's infidelity rather than give pain to one he overoptimistically considers a friend. Yet he persists throughout the play in testing his wife's fidelity in one foolish disguise after another. She does indeed play him false but manages to preserve in him the delusion that he has both a true wife and a true friend. A pleasant variation from the atmosphere of some of the situations here alluded to is to be found in the ring episode of *The Merchant of Venice* (*c.* 1596) where Portia and Nerissa merrily play ducks and drakes with their husbands' peace of mind with the help of the rings cajoled from Bassanio and Gratiano under cover of disguise.[22]

Another type of victim is the ridiculous lover. A comic character may be considered to be ridiculous as a lover and hence a fit object of trickery because he is elderly or because he is fatuous or because he is a foreigner. Examples of the amorous *senex* are the following: the elder Smallshanks in the minor plot of *Ram-Alley*, Lorenzo in *May Day*, the lawyer in the *Supposes*, Sir Bounteous Progress in *A Mad World, My Masters*, and the Falstaff of *The Merry Wives of Windsor*. Among the stupid lovers are Sir Andrew Aguecheek *(Twelfth Night)*, La Besha *(A Humorous Day's Mirth)*, Weathercock *(The London*

---

[21] Allowing for exceptions, we call attention to Professor Thomas M. Parrott's generalization: "Italian stories made a jest of adultery; the Elizabethan dramatic code, while allowing married women to skate over very thin ice, brought them in the end safe to shore and left their suitors struggling in the water" (Thomas Marc Parrott, *Shakespearean Comedy*, p. 255. New York: Oxford University Press, 1949).

[22] There is a monograph which the author was not able to see: Antoinette S. Jenkins, *The Jealous Husband in the Plays of Chapman, B. Jonson, Heywood, and Shakespeare* (unpublished thesis, University of North Carolina, 1928).

Prodigal), and Sir Giles Goosecap in Chapman's (?) play of
that name (*c.* 1603). Lovers who are made sport of mainly, it
seems, because they are from across the seas, are Doctor Caius
(The Merry Wives of Windsor) and the three foreign suitors
in *Englishmen for My Money.* An anomalous group of duped
lovers, who are not shown to be inept for any of the reasons
above mentioned but who are nevertheless for one reason or
another made displeasing to the audience and are accordingly
represented as gulled and frustrated gallants, is made up of
such hot-livered fellows as Lipsalve, Gudgeon, and Laxton in
Middleton's *The Family of Love* and the outwitted rivals in
the same author's *Your Five Gallants* and *No Wit, No Help
Like a Woman's.*

In the comedies of Plautus, though not in Terence's, the
type most persistently made the victim of trickery, next after
the fathers, was the *leno.* The slave-dealing procurer was usually a most unpleasant character, and the tricky slave would take
much glee in enabling the *adolescens* to enjoy the affections of
the slave girl by outwitting, to the great satisfaction of the audience, the procurer who had legal possession of her. In Elizabethan comedy the usurer took the place of the ancient *leno* as an
object of special antipathy on the part of the audience and as
the legitimate butt of tricksters and deceivers. In Elizabethan
drama there are seventy-one plays (of all kinds) in which
usurers are to be found, and in forty-five of these plays usurers
are important characters.[23] Among these plays are a number of
comedies whose plot or subplot evolves the story of a gallant
cozened by a usurer and succeeding in recovering his wealth by
some ruse or series of stratagems, one of which might be marrying the usurer's daughter or other relative and taking along with
him some valuables belonging to the usurer. Mention need be

---

[23] See Arthur Bivens Stonex, "The Usurer in Elizabethan Drama." *PMLA*
31:190-210, 1916.

made here of only a few of such comedies: *Englishmen for My Money, The Fair Maid of the Exchange*,[24] *A Trick To Catch the Old One*, and *Greene's Tu Quoque*.[25] In *Ram-Alley* and in *Wily Beguiled*,[26] furthermore, the chief victims are sharking lawyers, Throat and Churms respectively, who may well be classified with the usurers.

A character type whose origin and characteristics have been amply discussed by scholars is the gull.[27] As a literary type it was the creation of the 1590's. English epigram writers and authors of rogue literature furnished the principal elements which culminated in the type of gull as seen in the plays of Chapman and Jonson.[28] Within the one decade of the '90's there was a development in the meaning of the term. In its earlier use it connoted a credulous simpleton who was easily imposed upon. During the latter part of the decade the word assumed a specific application to a definite type of simpleton: the would-be gallant and affected fool, the witless pretender to accomplishments and valor.[29] We are interested in this type only insofar as it furnishes victims of deception. Specimens of the would-be

---

24 In *The Dramatic Works of Thomas Heywood*, Vol. II (London: John Pearson, 1874). The date of *The Fair Maid of the Exchange* is c. 1602. The authorship is in dispute. See Chambers, *The Elizabethan Stage*, Vol. IV, p. 13.

25 In W. Carew Hazlitt, editor, *A Select Collection of Old English Plays Originally Published by Robert Dodsley in the Year 1744*, fourth edition, Vol. XI (London: Reeves and Turner, 1874-1876). The author is Jo. Cooke; the date, 1611.

26 W. W. Greg, editor, *Wily Beguiled—1606* (Malone Society Reprints. London: Malone Society, 1913). *Wily Beguiled* was first produced within the years 1596-1606.

27 See, among others, Baskervill, *English Elements in Jonson's Early Comedy*, pp. 108-20; Herford and Simpson, *Ben Jonson*, Vol. I, pp. 345-46; Jack Steward Schell, *The Gull as a Type Character in the Plays of G. Chapman, B. Jonson, and Shakespeare*, pp. 9 ff. (unpublished thesis, University of Southern California, 1933).

28 Baskervill, *English Elements in Jonson's Early Comedy*, pp. 109-11; Herford and Simpson, *Ben Jonson*, Vol. I, pp. 345-46.

29 Herford and Simpson, *Ben Jonson*, Vol. I, pp. 345-46; Schell, *The Gull as a Type*, p. 12. See also Oxford English Dictionary, *s.v. gull*.

gallant and affected fool are La Besha *(A Humorous Day's Mirth)*, Stephen *(Every Man in His Humor)*, Fastidious Brisk *(Everyman Out of His Humor)*, Innocentio *(May Day)*, and Sir Andrew Aguecheek *(Twelfth Night)*. In the rogue literature of the period gulls are shown as being frequently imposed upon by conycatchers and swindlers.[30] This species of gull is reflected in Elizabethan comedy in such cases as Tom Strowd *(The Blind Beggar of Bednal Green)*, Easy *(Michaelmas Term)*, and Dapper *(The Alchemist)*.

A figure which came in for its share of obloquy and ridicule on the Elizabethan stage was the Puritan.[31] This type was also frequently the victim of trickery. The sanctimonious Florilla *(A Humorous Day's Mirth)*, the Mulligrubs, husband and wife *(The Dutch Courtesan)*, the family of Puritans as well as their servant, Nicholas *(The Puritan)*, and the saints Tribulation, Wholesome, and Ananias *(The Alchemist)* were among those who were merrily tweaked and tormented for the delectation of the audience. Shakespeare's Malvolio might be thought of in this connection, but he really is too complex a character to be contained under so simple a designation.

Finally, it is clear that several of the above characters are prime material for duping on two or more counts. Lorenzo *(May Day)* is both father and elderly philanderer; Security *(Eastward Ho!)* is jealous husband and usurer; Gripe *(Englishmen for My Money)* is father and usurer and foreigner to boot; and the gulls are sometimes ridiculous lovers (Sir Andrew Aguecheek and La Besha).

Running through the names of the victims of deception one meets in reading Elizabethan comedies, one is impressed by the fact that, just as there is a great variety both of types and of

---

[30] Aydelotte, *Elizabethan Rogues and Vagabonds*, pp. 78-79.

[31] Wilhelm Creizenach, *English Drama in the Age of Shakespeare*, translated by Cécile Hugon, pp. 104-09. London: Sidgwick and Jackson, 1916.

characterization of individuals within types, so too a certain amount of variety is to be perceived in the levels of intelligence among dupes. Some are unmistakably fatuous. Others are just as clearly endowed with a considerable degree of cunning and ability to take care of themselves. Others still there are whose mental capacity seems to fall somewhere between fatuity and cunning. It will be interesting, therefore, to attempt a grouping of victims of deception according to the levels of intelligence manifested by them.

On the lowest ledge we find the louts such as Hodge *(Gammer Gurton's Needle)*, Peter Plod-all *(Wily Beguiled)*, and Nicholas, the servant in *The Puritan*. Right alongside these we can, without any uncharitableness to either group, lodge such simpletons as Thurio *(The Two Gentlemen of Verona)*,[32] Sir Andrew *(Twelfth Night)*, Slender[33] *(The Merry Wives of Windsor)*, La Besha *(A Humorous Day's Mirth)*, Innocentio *(May Day)*, Sim *(Michaelmas Term)*, Dapper *(The Alchemist)*, and Stephen *(Every Man in His Humor)*. All of these, both the louts and the ninnies of loftier pretentions, are represented as utterly fatuous and afflicted with some ingrained and deep-seated inanity which, however, betrays itself in a variety of manifestations.

In a second class of characters are those who are neither doltish nor fatuous, nor yet completely without experience. They are, nevertheless, numbered among the notoriously abused. We immediately think of Malvolio, whom nobody will bid lie beside Sir Andrew Aguecheek on the level of utter fatuity. There is Falstaff, whose wit was made a Jack-a-Lent by the merry wives. No matter how gross a falling off one sees here from the admirable dexterity of the *Henry IV* Falstaff, one will hardly bracket him with the Slenders and the Plod-alls. Gostanzo of *All Fools*

---

[32] The date is *c.* 1593.

[33] "A very potent piece of imbecility" (Hazlitt).

fancies himself a politician and a shrewd manager, an opinion by no means founded on fact; but though his self-deception is played upon and turned toward his own duping, he is not shown to be an absolute nincompoop. Bassiolo, the character playing the title role in Chapman's *The Gentleman Usher* (*c.* 1602), is not represented as a simpleton with no brains whatever, as Poggio is in the same play. Bassiolo has a certain vigor and cogency of speech at times and can paint as satirical a portrait as the best of scoffers, as when he jeers at the idea of the duke's being a suitor for Margaret's hand (III, ii, 340-44). Further-more, though he is tricked into writing with his own hand a couple of letters from Margaret to her lover, he has sense enough to see later that these letters, having been preserved, put him into a compromising position, and also to perceive that the young couple hold a trump card which forces him to help them further. Conceit, ridiculous presumption, or some other form of self-deception is what makes characters of this class susceptible to, and fair game for, stratagems.

The members of a third class of characters who fall victim to deception are neither stupid nor self-deceived but are pos-sessed of some shrewdness and cunning, and may even have been successful practitioners in deception in their own right. In the forefront of this group are the usurers, Gripe *(Englishmen for My Money)*, Security *(Eastward Ho!)*, Lucre and Hoard *(A Trick To Catch the Old One)*, and the pettifoggers, Churms *(Wily Beguiled)* and Throat *(Ram-Alley)*. These are not only to be presumed to be shrewd from the fact that they are mem-bers of dramatic types conventionally represented as having craftiness as one of their traits, but each of these characters is shown as actually indulging in some double-dealing or knavery and manifesting a degree of wily cunning. Then there is Glister the physician *(The Family of Love)*, who is shown quite com-petently looking after his own interests and gulling certain gallants on more than one occasion. In *The Roaring Girl* Sir

Alexander Wengrave, who is tricked by his son, Sebastian, is not represented as an old fool but as an intriguing sort of fellow not at all averse to using underhanded means to discredit the girl he believes his son is infatuated with. Most of these characters are overreached, it seems, because they have been so successful in deceiving others that they have become overconfident. They are too crafty for their own good. It is their own resorting to deception that exposes them to trickery.

One can hardly be accused of oversubtlety in pointing out that the members of the above three groups lie along appreciably distinct levels of intelligence. It may even be possible, without slicing hairs too finely, to introduce two further categories on either side of the central group. Some characters are not represented as sottish or doltish, yet are shown as ignorant, uneducated, and superstitious. Beneath their rusticity or uncouthness a native spark of intelligence gleams fitfully enough to raise them a cut above their witless companions and to present to a duper a less inert material to work on. Such are Gammer Gurton and her neighbor, Dame Chat, who are by no means as lumpish as Hodge, yet they accept Diccon's glib lies at their face value and swing into immediate action. Here too we may place Mulligrub, the repeated victim of Cocledemoy's tricks. Both the old Sienese in the *Supposes* and the pedant, the corresponding character in *The Taming of the Shrew,* are spoken of by those who use them as their instruments as "none of the wisest" (*Supposes*, II, i, 105), "of small experience" (*Supposes*, II, i, 205), and "credulous" (*The Taming of the Shrew*, IV, ii, 67); and yet they are not fools absolute, for each of them carries out his assigned part in the imposture of his respective vehicle quite according to instructions and with some degree of vigor. So too, though young Tom Strowd is gulled time and again by the rogue, Canby, in *The Blind Beggar of Bednal Green,* he does not impress one as a nitwit. He certainly does not talk like a fool, even when he is telling of his own misfortunes. His is the most refreshing idiom of the play, as the following lines will illustrate:

> I was set ore for a reckoning of 40 shillings, and as fair a Sattin suite t'other night, as a man shall lightly see in a Summers day; but if ere it be my fortune to meet with that ill fac'd Gypsie that stole it, I'll teach him his teripoop for steal-ing, whilst he hath a day to live again, so woll I: Nay nothing griev'd me *Swash*, but that the slave perswaded me to lye naked for fear of the Fleas; which when I had done he stole me away as fair a shirt of my Mothers own spinning, as a man shall need to pull o'er his ears; and Sirrah in the morning when mine Hostis came up to call me, I was as naked as your *Norfolk*-Dumplin, as I am a christen man I blush'd out of all—
>
> *Swash.* Nay Master I told you at first you should find a sower fellow of that Gypsie (II; 729-41).

He has unlimited vitality and plenty of physical courage as well as the strength to implement it. In the end he helps to frustrate the conycatchers and their gentlemen employers. But he is woefully ignorant of human nature and of the dodges of the underworld. He comes back to Canby time and again and presents the rogue with new opportunities to cozen him.

Thus, in between the Hodges and Sir Andrews, the Sims and the Slenders, on the one hand, and Malvolio, Bassiolo, Gostanzo, and Falstaff on the other, we may slip such victims as Gammer, the pedant, and Tom Strowd. In still another class of characters who are shown as succumbing to trickery are to be found such as Claudio and Benedick of *Much Ado about Nothing*, Valentine *(The Two Gentlemen of Verona)*, and Easy *(Michaelmas Term)*. The first two are romantic characters who are certainly not represented as stupid nor ignorant, though they may legiti-mately be suspected of not being very cautious. At any rate, they are not in the class of the usurers and pettifoggers as far as well-practiced cunning goes. And Easy is clearly distinguished as being a gull of a different feather from Sim by the rogue who bilks them both. Sim, according to Shortyard, "From his conception was entail'd an ass," whereas for Easy, "Only good confidence did make him foolish,/ And not the lack of sense." Though a country gentleman and a scholar, Easy is new to the city and unwary, and "worldly craft beats down a scholar's wit" (IV, iii, 15-20). We may well assign these a place, therefore, between Malvolio and his compeers and the shrewd men of the world, like Throat, Glister, and Hoard.

It is undeniable, then, that the victims of deception in Elizabethan comedy do not all manifest the same degree of intelligence. At the lowest level lie the fatuous and the lumpish; then come those who are not stupid but who, because of lack of education and culture, are ignorant and superstitious; above these are victims who, while not entirely stupid nor ignorant, are egoistic or self-deceived with respect to some particular phase of their own character or powers; we find next some who are not justly classified with any of the above groups, but are shown as unwary and overtrusting; and finally there are those who are rather cunning and deceitful and quite experienced.

The line between one level and another may be a thin and wavering one, and it would not always be easy to decide on just which shelf each of the victims of deception should be deposited. The examples given above are merely illustrative, and it is quite possible that the placing of the characters mentioned may not be acceptable to all on all counts. It would be difficult, nevertheless, to deny that the different strata do exist.

Now, this fact gives rise to some interesting questions. The more intelligent a character is shown to be, the less susceptible should he habitually be to deception. In other words, along with the variation in levels of intelligence discernible in the victims of deception there is a variation in what one might call their antecedent susceptibility to deception. Whence the following two related but not identical questions may be asked: (1) Is there any correspondence in Elizabethan comedy between the degree of antecedent susceptibility to deception on the part of the one deceived and the facility with which he is actually deluded? (2) Is there, generally speaking, less ingenuity displayed by a deceiver in bamboozling a lout than in overreaching a much more cunning and canny opponent?

A priori, it would seem that the greater the antecedent susceptibility to deception, the easier the fall should be. But Malvolio, who is not fatuous, falls just as readily into the gin set for him as does Sir Andrew. For that matter, Viola-Cesario, who is as bright as a new penny, is deceived and befooled by the same trick as is Sir Andrew, and with no more show of suspicion that she is being gulled. And the usurious, conniving Gripe in *Englishmen for My Money* succumbs to the trickery of the tutor and of the young Englishmen as easily as his doltish fellow dupes, the foreign suitors. Rinaldo *(All Fools)*, who can fool Gostanzo to the top of his bent, is thrown by a countertrick played by one he has no reason to trust. Follywit *(A Mad World, My Masters)*, who presumably is to be credited with more brains than the gullible Harebrain in that play, is taken in by pretty nearly the same pretenses on the part of the "demure and maidenly" courtesan as is Harebrain, and with much more permanent results. In *The Scornful Lady* (by Fletcher and Beaumont, with the help perhaps of Massinger), the hard-to-get lady outwits her lover in his first two attempts to trick her into a declaration of love and into marriage, but she is trapped by his third trick. She has not lost her cleverness in the last act nor is the successful trick conceived or executed more brilliantly to any appreciable extent. The first two tricks did not succeed because that would have ended the play or at any rate the main plot. The third was carried off because it was time to end the play. Stupid dupes therefore do not necessarily fall more easily than the more intelligent ones do.

Again, in answer to our second question, it would seem *a priori*, that a trickster would display less ingenuity in leading by the nose a leash of simpletons than in outfoxing a wily adversary. But this is not borne out by the facts. In *The Puritan* George Pieboard and his accomplice, the captain, expend as much energy and make as careful preparations to deceive the family of Puritans, whom George knows to be foolish and excessively credulous,[34] as does Witgood in *A Trick To Catch the Old One* in outmaneuvering the cunning old usurers, Hoard and Lucre. In *Volpone* Mosca displays at least as much ingenuity in playing off the avaricious dupes against each other as in setting up and springing the "fox trap" on his crafty employer. And though among the dupes Voltore, the lawyer, is described as one who can give forked counsel, and take gold from both parties of a dispute as a retainer, and is presumably more cunning than the others, nevertheless Mosca is not shown as summoning up more guile in handling him than in working upon the other dupes. Trappola, in *The Bugbears*, speaks of the simplicity of the three old men, and accounts it "no great mastery to blynde & bleare their eye"; but that does not prevent him from overwhelming them with his flowing and learned volubility in impressing them with his knowledge of bugbears, pucks, and puckerels. Likewise, Merecraft in Jonson's *The Devil Is an Ass* gradually and carefully prepares the ground for the swindling of Fitzdottrell, whose name tickets him accurately, by impressing him with his grandiloquent talk of "projects."

In general it may be said that, no matter how simple and credulous the prospective dupe is known to be, his duper does not on that account stint in making elaborate preparations to build up the dupe's confidence in him and otherwise ready him for a fall. Hence the degree of antecedent susceptibility in a dupe would seem to have no real bearing on the degree of ingenuity displayed in the deceiving of him.

---

[34] ". . . I may now perceiue in 'em a naturall simplicitie which will easily swallow an abuse, if any couering be ouer it" (II, i, 334-37).

There is a quotation in *Michaelmas Term* which would seem to militate against this position. "I'll ha' the lands," says Shortyard, speaking of the property which Sim has apparently inherited from his father, Quomodo, who has allowed himself to be thought dead,

> . . . I'll ha' the lands,
> Let him study law after; 'tis no labour
> To undo him for ever: but for Easy,
> Only good confidence did make him foolish,
> And not the lack of sense; that was not it:
> 'Tis worldly craft beats down a scholar's wit.
> For this our son and heir now [Sim], he
> From his conception was entail'd an ass,
> And he has kept it well, twenty-five years now:
> Then the slightest art will do't; . . . (IV, iii, 13-22).

Shortyard here, as has already been pointed out, makes a distinction between his two dupes. Such a difference in levels of intelligence is basic to this discussion of dupes; but Shortyard also concludes from this difference between the two that it will be no labor to undo Sim, though there was considerable ingenuity exerted in deceiving Easy. This would seem to contradict the conclusions reached in the present section that a lesser degree of intelligence in a prospective victim need not call for a lesser exercise of a deceiver's specialized talents. This contradiction, however, is only a seeming one. The cheating of Sim out of the property he has inherited is not presented on the stage; Shortyard is merely shown later leafing through the deeds he has just cozened out of the simpleton. It was "no labour" for him to do it, just as in real life it would have required but "the slightest art" to cheat a booby like Sim. But if that cozening had been acted out on the stage as the fleecing of Easy had been, it would most likely have been a matter calling for more effort, or at least favored with more effort. If Middleton was only to mention a swindle as being perpetrated off stage, he could well have a swindler speak about it as an easier matter than the one seen done on the stage; but that was not because the victim was an easier mark in the one case than in the other, but simply because he was not shot at before the spectators. It was the exhibition of skill the spectators were interested in, and they were granted that in the swindling of Easy.

This is not equivalent to saying, of course, that all dupes are favored with an equal amount of ingenious attention by their deceivers. The point is simply this, that the different degrees of ingenuity displayed by the intriguer and of difficulty experienced in bringing down the chosen victim are not proportionate to the different degrees of stupidity or credulity with which they are afflicted. If the plot requires it, the more intelligent victim will fall as readily as a fatuous one. And if the author feels his audience is delighted with "plots, projects, correspondences, and stratagems," he will have his deceiver oblige withal, even though the focal point of all this artifice be the veriest woodcock who could be caught by the most palpable and patent of springes.

The significance of this answer to the questions proposed in this section lies, it would seem, in this, that Elizabethan comic dramatists did not strive for complete realistic fidelity to the conditions of actual life in this matter of the degree of ingenuity shown in duping and cheating, but rather were guided by the requirements of their plots and by the Elizabethan taste for the display of trickery on the stage.

In this chapter attention centered on one of the essentials of plays in which the action runs on the wheels of deception—the victims of trickery. Not merely the presence of a victim is required in such plays, but his dramatic cooperation is necessary if he is to provide anything more than inert material to be worked on by the intriguer and if there is to be any effective dramatic action and reaction. We have seen that a dupe could enter into the process of his own duping with different degrees of cooperation. First, he could be used as unwitting instrument in the victimizing of others and in so doing would himself be victimized. Next, he could enter actively into his own gulling. Of special interest here were those dupes who provided the lime and thread to entangle themselves. One is reminded of the art of jujitsu, in which the expert presses gently and allows his unskilled opponent to tie himself into knots. Then there were plays in which an intriguer played off two or more dupes against one another so that they became reciprocal instruments of discomfiture and thus helped promote the plans of the archtrickster. Here again of special interest were those who, in being thus maneuvered, were kept in the illusion that they were controlling matters by pulling strings in their own insidious ways. It is evident that in all these different kinds of situation deception is a very useful element in the dramatic structure of the plays discussed. Out of the interwoven strands of trickery, gullibility, and self-deception was constructed the web of incidents, episodes, and whole plots.

A breakdown of the dupes into the conventional types of Elizabethan comedy led to suggestions as to why such types were considered apt subjects for duping. A different kind of grouping (according to levels of intelligence) involved the asking of two questions. The negative answer given these questions opened the way to a further brief insight into the aims and norms of Elizabethan comic dramatists in their use of deception.

CHAPTER V

The
Duper Duped

Not always is the intended victim of deception practiced upon with complete success. For all his cunning, the would-be victimizer may find himself thwarted in the end. Stratagems are sometimes frustrated in Elizabethan comedy by mere chance or by the intrusion of a *deus ex machina*. Inasmuch, however, as the subject of this study is the functional uses of deception, it is permissible to limit the discussion of frustrated deception to those plots in which the resort to trickery is the direct source of the frustration of it. This frustration may happen in two main ways: the intriguer may find himself caught in the very web of deception he himself wove for the ensnaring of others, or the initial intrigue may be foiled by a counterintrigue.

Scholars have called attention to the fact that the one who spends most of his sober hours in abusing others in *Twelfth Night* is himself given a toss with his own device.[1] Sir Toby's mistaking the twin brother, Sebastian, for Cesario and his resultant broken crown can be checked off as the direct outcome of the knight's plotting to play off Viola-Cesario and the gull, Sir Andrew, against each other and back them into a mock duel for which neither of them felt any desire.

---

[1] See Chambers, *Shakespeare: A Survey*, p. 176.

105

Similarly, in Middleton's *Michaelmas Term*[2] we see a clever swindler being upset not so much by any counteraction taken by an adversary as by his own mistakes. In the moment of Quomodo's luxurious anticipation of the ride into the country to the estate which he has taken from Easy by fraud, the temptation comes to the knave to indulge in some further trickery. This time the purpose of the deception is to get a preview of what would most probably happen to his property after his death. He has hopes of "preventing that by policy, which without it must needs be destiny" (IV, i, 95-96). He pretends to die so that in disguise he may have opportunity of observing how his widow and his son, the foolish Sim, whom he has made his heir, will carry on. All sorts of reactions take place at once, though he is not immediately to become aware of some of them. His wife marries his erstwhile victim, Easy, who thus recuperates some of his losses; his henchman, Shortyard, fleeces his heir out of the property left him, which is, to be sure, mainly the estate bilked from Easy; the part taken by this confederate in the swindling of Easy is exposed by the wife, and Shortyard is forced to give up to Easy what he had just taken from Sim. Unaware of these developments, Quomodo at the funeral is made confident of his wife's devotion to his memory by the sight of her momentary and quite counterfeit grief. In his disguised capacity as a beadle he has apparently done some services in connection with his own funeral, and he is now paid by the "widow," who in businesslike fashion, admired by Quomodo, demands a receipt in which he is to acknowledge that he has received all that he can claim in that house. Instead of ripping off his disguise in a forthright fashion, he characteristically determines to reveal himself by indirection. Without bothering to read it through, he deliberately signs the receipt with his own name, so that the lady, on reading "Ephastian Quomodo," may be given a shock which he

---

[2] In Bullen, *Works of Thomas Middleton*, Vol. I.

trusts will be a pleasant one. She is surprised, indeed, by the revelation, but the shock is much greater for himself when he realizes that he has put his hand to what amounts, because of its wording, to a disclaimer of all rights and property.

Ward calls this a cleverly contrived trick,[3] but it seems a mistake to see here a deception deliberately played by Easy and Quomodo's wife on the swindler. Similarly, Dunkel speaks of the alertness and cleverness of Easy in regaining the property with the help of the "widow,"[4] but the alertness is shown rather in the grasping of an opportunity put into his hands than in any active and planned contriving. The text gives no indication that Easy and Quomodo's wife planned the receipt as a countertrick. Neither of them had any suspicion that the "beadle" was Quomodo in disguise. This is proved by their unfeigned surprise when he reveals himself (V, i, 118-32).

It is all at bottom Quomodo's own doing. It is by playing dead, disguising himself, and then taking a roundabout way of revealing himself that he presents his henchmen with the opportunity of cheating his son, gives his wife the freedom of action required to expose the earlier swindling of Easy and to compensate the victim, and puts himself in the position of signing away his rights. "My deeds have cleft me, cleft me," he wails, not in any spirit of sorrow for his evil-doing but in chagrin over his being the cause of his own ruin (V, iii, 96). "Deceit is her own foe" is the comment of the judge in the final scene.

Another play in which a deceiver indulges in just too much trickery for his own good is Middleton's *A Mad World, My Masters*,[5] the main plot of which has to do with the successive ruses whereby young Follywit tricks his grandfather, Sir Bounteous Progress, out of sufficient sums of money to enable him to

---

[3] Ward, *English Dramatic Literature*, Vol. II, p. 515.
[4] Dunkel, *The Dramatic Technique of Thomas Middleton*, p. 13.
[5] In Bullen, *Works of Thomas Middleton*, Vol. III.

live as a spark. By means of one of these stratagems he gets possession of some of his grandfather's jewelry, and by throwing the suspicion of the theft upon his grandfather's mistress he causes her to be cast off by the old man. Follywit, however, has never found out the identity of his grandfather's mistress; and later chancing to meet the woman, is taken in by her pretense of modesty and virginity, artfully played by the courtesan with the help of her mother, and marries her out of hand.

His last device is to present himself and his friends, disguised as a group of actors, at his grandfather's house when a dinner is being given there. In his guise as the leader of the troup Follywit easily persuades the old man to lend him a gold chain, a jewel, and a watch, to be used as properties for the play he is to present for the entertainment of the guests. While he is giving the prologue, the other rogues are to slip out and make off with the spoil. They are caught, however, by a constable who brings them into the assembled gathering. Follywit, like many a trickster in similar emergencies, rises masterfully to the occasion, pretends that this is all part of the play, has the constable himself bound and gagged, and then goes off with his friends and the booty, leaving the domestic audience gazing in misdirected delight at the apoplectic efforts of the constable to make himself understood. Hastily throwing off their disguises, Follywit and his companions come back to the house where the trickery has at length been made clear to the old gentleman, and they hear the story of how Sir Bounteous was cozened by a band of actors. While he is commiserating with the old man and marveling that there are "such creatures," the watch Follywit has stolen strikes the hour in his pocket. His grandfather reaches into Follywit's pocket, draws forth watch, chain, and jewel, and Follywit and company stand revealed as the culprits. He can now apply to himself the generalization which he himself has unctuously pronounced earlier in the play: ". . . craft recoils in the end, like an overcharged musket, and maims the very hand that puts fire to't" (III, iii, 11-13). The young rake is confounded; but to show his grandfather that he has been intending to settle down, informs him that he has taken to himself a wife, "both a gentlewoman and a virgin" (V, ii, 273). He thereupon points to the lady, who has been attending the feast. The old man feels that the laugh vouchsafed him by this turn of the wheel is ample satisfaction for the losses he has sustained. When Follywit learns that he has married his grandfather's discarded mistress (who, indeed, had been cast off precisely as a result of one of his own tricks), he says: "Tricks are repaid, I see"; but he sticks to his contract with good grace, especially since his grandfather, having had the last laugh, is willing to give him a thousand pounds as a wedding present.

The recoil of Follywit's final trick upon its inventor is thus seen to be due to an excess of confidence and impudence in coming back with the booty in his pocket to the scene of his roguery and speaking to the one he had just deluded. At the bottom of this impudence lay a desire for exploiting a piece of deception to its utmost possibilities. It is to be noted, however, that these further possibilities lie, not along the line of more booty, but along the line of greater enjoyment of the trick for the trick's own sake. He has done this sort of thing before. When he robbed his grandfather the first time with the help of a double set of disguises, he and his accomplices could have made off with the plunder as soon as they had got their hands on it. It would then be known that the visiting "lord" and his retinue were identical with the robbers. But Follywit insisted on carrying the trick through to completion even though he recognized that it would be more risky. Shifting out of his disguise as a robber back into his disguise as Lord Owemuch, he had himself and his henchmen tied up so as to look as if they too had been robbed.

We now arrive at the most ticklish point, to rob, and take our ease, to be thieves, and lie by't: look to't, lads, it concerns every man's gullet; I'll not have the jest spoiled, that's certain, though it hazard a windpipe. I'll either go like a lord as I came, or be hanged like a thief as I am; and that's my resolution (II, v, 82-88).

The added touch, therefore, was "for wit's sake" (to use Cocledemoy's phrase), rather than prompted by a desire for more gain. So too in the last trick it is for wit's sake that he comes back to be told the story of how his grandfather was cozened and to be properly sympathetic. "A vengence of this foolery!" is the curse muttered by one of the accomplices when they are caught. It is this added foolery for the fun of it which makes the gentlemen rogues of comedy, like Follywit, different from the rogues of real life who would scamper from the scene of the crime as soon as they had got their hands on the booty. They would not stay in the vicinity or come back to follow through on a jest at the risk of hanging. They certainly would not come back with the plunder still in their pockets.

There is the other element of the "biter bit" by one of his own victims. Though Follywit does not know it, the woman he marries is the one he had driven out of his grandfather's favor by the second trick he played. This nip, therefore, is given to Follywit by one in such peculiar relations to his other victim, that his grandfather can afford to take special satisfaction from the turn of events. The grandfather ends the play with the following aphorism:

> Who lives by cunning, mark it, his fate's cast;
> When he has gull'd all, then is himself the last.

Another archdeceiver who "lives by cunning" and in the end is himself brought down by his excessive indulgence in trickery is Jonson's Volpone.[6] After he and Mosca, the parasite, have successfully fooled everybody in the first courtroom scene,

---

[6] Herford and Simpson, *Ben Jonson*, Vol. V.

Mosca feels that they will not be able to better that feat, and there is a touch of caution in his glorying:

> Here, we must rest; this is our master-peece:
> We cannot thinke, to goe beyond this (V, ii, 13-14).

Volpone thereupon begins to bring things to a conclusion. After spreading abroad the news of his "death" in order to bring his gulls flocking to his house, he provides for himself a choice vantage point from which to observe and relish the final delicious spectacle of the opening of his victims' eyes to the awful reality of their true situation and status. Yet Volpone is not satisfied with the "rare meal of laughter" furnished him by this entertainment. In order to intensify the distress of his dupes and in order to squeeze the utmost enjoyment out of their discomfiture, he has Mosca don elegant clothing in order to bring home to them what they have lost, and he himself sallies forth from his house in disguise with the purpose of torturing each of his victims in turn by pretending to have heard that he has come into Volpone's money.

Now, his victims would in all likelihood have nursed their losses and their chagrin in silence lest, as Mosca had warned them, they reveal their own complicity in Volpone's villainy; but the final turn that Volpone attempts to give to the screw snaps the head off it. For the torturing of Voltore by the parading of Mosca in magnificent garments and by the jibes of Volpone in his disguise is what finally breaks Voltore's self-control, obliterates his sense of self-preservation, and drives him in frenzy to reveal the plot against Celia and Bonario. Furthermore, in leaving his house in disguise after giving out that he was dead and in conveying the impression that Mosca was his heir, Volpone gives Mosca the opportunity of getting possession of his keys and setting up the "fox trap." In order to thwart the treachery of Mosca, Volpone has to uncover himself in court, show himself to be healthy as well as alive, and take his punishment. Volpone knows that it was by following *à outrance* his bent for trickery that he has brought ruin on himself:

> To make a snare, for mine owne necke! and run
> My head into it, wilfully! with laughter!
> When I had newly scap't, was free, and cleare!
> Out of mere wantonnesse! ô, the dull deuill
> Was in this braine of mine, when I deuis'd it;
>
> .   .   .   .   .
>
> . . . . These are my fine conceipts!
> I must be merry, with a mischiefe to me!
> What a vile wretch was I, that could not beare
> My fortune soberly? I must ha' my crotchets!
> And my *conundrums!* . . . (V, xi, 1-17).

Brief reference may be made to Marston's *Jack Drum's Entertainment,*[7] in which Brabant senior, who fancies himself a wit and practical jokester, brings a Frenchman, Monsieur John, to his home and introduces him to his wife under the pretense that the place is a house of call and she a harlot. The "wicked Jest" is turned "on his owne head," which is crowned with the horns so beloved of Elizabethan audiences.

We may now turn to some instances of intriguers' being undermined by counterdevices. These instances range from illustrations of a single successful countertrick to an example of an extended and intricate intrigue made up of an integrated series of moves and countermoves. A deft manipulator and puller of strings who tries to make one puppet too many dance to his tune is Rinaldo of Chapman's *All Fools.*[8] His successful abetting of Valerio in intriguing against the domestic peace of the jealous husband, Cornelio, rouses the victim to a counter-trick which in the end proves the undoing of Rinaldo's and Valerio's intrigue against the father, Gostanzo. When Cornelio discovers that the pair of young fellows have been deliberately

---

[7] In Wood, *Plays of John Marston,* Vol. III.
[8] In Parrott, *Plays of Chapman: Comedies.*

and deceitfully playing upon his jealousy to enjoy the complications that would arise, he sets about plotting his revenge, declaring that he will have "gull for gull" (IV, i, 359-77). He tells Rinaldo that his friend Valerio has been arrested for debt and is being held by officers at a certain tavern. He suggests that Rinaldo should bring Valerio's father, Gostanzo, to that tavern that he may redeem his son from the hands of the law. Frightened by this news, Rinaldo does just what Cornelio wants him to do; but when he and the father arrive at the tavern, they find Valerio not in custody but in his cups. Not only that, but he is dicing in the company of women—he who had been careful all along to nurse his father's delusion that he was too bashful even to look upon the face of a woman. And when one of these women turns out to be the wife whose relationship to Valerio has by means of Rinaldo's artful sleight-of-hand been kept from Gostanzo all through the play, the whole web of deception woven around the father bursts asunder. Cornelio can well feel he has put through a satisfying revenge. "Jam sumus ergo pares," he gloats. And in joining the ranks of the dupes, Rinaldo gives point and justification to the title of the play.

The title of the anonymous *Wily Beguiled* also gives a clear hint as to what the plot of the play is. Churms, a sly pettifogger, pretends to further the suit of the loutish but wealthy farmer's son, Peter Plod-all, for the hand of Lelia, and for this purpose is given ready access to the girl by her father, who is in favor of this match. The lover of the girl, a scholar who is driven away by the father, is also deceived by the lawyer, who tells him he will use his opportunities for seeing the girl to keep her in mind of her lover. Churms, of course, is bent on winning Lelia and her wealth for himself. His undoing had its source in the accidental overhearing by Lelia's recently returned brother, Fortunatus, of a gloating soliloquy of Robin, Churms' assistant, in which he reveals his and his employer's intentions and some of the means they are using to encompass their purpose. Fortunatus begins a counterplot in order that the scholar, who is his friend, may wed his sister. He informs the audience of his intentions:

> This is the trap which for him I haue laid,
> Thus craft by cunning once shal be betraid.[9]

His counterplot consists simply in having instructions brought to his sister that she is to pretend to favor Churms, ask him to assist in her flight from home and from the proposed match with the farmer's son, and lead him into an ambush prepared by her father and lover. Churms falls into the trap, is mocked by the girl and beaten by her brother. Thus easily is the supposedly wily one beguiled. Fortunatus then persuades his father, who was given a scare by the flight of Lelia with Churms, to agree to allow her to marry the scholar. In this play, therefore, we have the deceitful designs of an intriguer frustrated by counterplotting. The counterplot consists in a simple trick by which the chief deceiver is taken in.

Counterplots are also to be seen in *The Merry Wives of Windsor*, and there we find the situation of a would-be duper duped. Having convinced himself that he has spied entertainment in Mistress Ford's eye, Falstaff sets about an intrigue to translate her "out of honesty into English." It is her husband's money he is after even more than her favors. "I will use her as a key of the cuckoldy rogue's coffer" (II, ii, 285-86). Not content with one affair, he also makes overtures to Mistress Page, attempting to keep secret from each of them that he is soliciting the other. "I will be cheaters to them both, and they shall be exchequers to me. They shall be my East and West Indies, and I will trade to them both" (I, iii, 77-80). Upon receiving the letters he sends them, the indignation of the ladies knows no bounds; and when they learn from each other that this merchant of venery has wafted an argosy of temptation to them

---

[9] W. W. Greg, *Wily Beguiled*, xii; 1497-98.

both, they lay their heads together and plan to sink him and his projects.

The counterplotting of the wives and the results achieved are something in which they can take pleasure and pride. In the buck basket, in his hastily donned woman's gown and scarf which save him from being recognized but not from receiving a beating, and in his guise as Herne the Hunter, with the huge horns on his head, we see the reiterated exhibition of a would-be guller gulled.[10] It is the counterintrigue of his intended victims which brings about his discomfiture. With a crescendo in comic effect and an increase in the punishment visited upon Falstaff he falls three several times into a trap laid for him by the same persons using the same means. He has ample reason for feeling that he has lost some of his dexterity: "Have I laid my brain in the sun, and dried it, that it wants matter to prevent so gross o'erreaching as this?" (V, v, 143-45).

This chapter will close with an examination of the frustrating of a villainous intriguer by counterintrigue. In Mendoza, the villain of Marston's *The Malcontent*,[11] has been recognized a descendant in comedy of Lorenzo of *The Spanish Tragedy* and a Machiavellian self-seeking politician.[12] Malevole, as an instance of the malcontent type, has been analyzed along with others of the type by Professor Stoll.[13] Professor Oscar James Campbell has discussed the function of this character as a satiric commentator.[14] The present examination of Mendoza and Malevole centers only on their functions as agents of deception, and in Mendoza's case, as also the victim of it.

---

[10] See Thorndike, *English Comedy*, p. 128.

[11] In Wood, *Plays of John Marston*, Vol. I.

[12] Una Ellis-Fermor, *The Jacobean Drama*, second edition, p. 92. London: Methuen and Company, 1947.

[13] Elmer Edgar Stoll, "Shakespeare, Marston, and the Malcontent Type." *Modern Philology* 3:281-303, January 1906.

[14] Campbell, *Shakespeare's Satire*, pp. 142-49.

This play has no subplot to speak of. Sufficient variety is achieved, however, by the constantly shifting focus of attention from Mendoza's intriguing to Malevole's. Several minor characters who contribute little to the movement of the play serve, nevertheless, as walking illustrations of the corrupt and depraved conditions of the court of Genoa and as stimuli to the flow of misanthropic and virulent comment by the malcontent.

With the help of Mendoza's machinations and the backing of the powerful Duchy of Florence, Pietro has banished Duke Altofronto and has himself assumed control in Genoa. But disguised as a malcontent hanger-on of the court, Altofronto comes back to do what he can to regain his dukedom. Besides exploiting his guise as a malcontent to comment in unsavory language upon the passing scene, Altofronto, who now goes by the name of Malevole, uses his allowed familiarity with the new duke to inform the usurper that his minion, Mendoza, is carrying on an intrigue with his wife, Aurelia. Mendoza, however, takes advantage of a misunderstanding between him and the duchess, who has just transferred her favor to a rival of Mendoza's, and adroitly shifts suspicion from himself by exposing this new adultery to the duke. Being now more firmly than ever in the good graces of the duke, Mendoza effects a reconciliation with the duchess and plots with her the murder of her husband. Accordingly he employs the malcontent, Malvole-Altofronto, to murder Duke Pietro and to give out the false report that Pietro has committed suicide. Pretending to fall in with Mendoza's plan, Malevole informs Duke Pietro of it and persuades him to disguise himself as a hermit and corroborate the malcontent's report about the "suicide" of Duke Pietro.

Mendoza now assumes full power, banishes Pietro's duchess, and turns his attention to trying to persuade the imprisoned Maria, wife of the original duke, Altofronto, to marry him. In these negotiations he uses the disguised Malevole-Altofronto himself and the disguised Pietro as go-betweens. Since these

two, however, know of his hand in the supposed murder of
Pietro, he seeks to eliminate them by engaging each of them to
poison the other. The intended victims of this murderous double-
dealing expose the plan to each other. At this juncture, hearing
Pietro express sorrow for having usurped the duchy, Malevole
reveals himself as the deposed Altofronto. The two then plan to
bring the counterintrigue against Mendoza to a head. This they
do in one or two moves, with the result that Mendoza is banished
and Altofronto reassumes the dukedom.

This play presents us with a closely woven plot of intrigue
and counterintrigue. The villain makes use of feigned friendship
and treachery to betray or attempt to betray almost every character in the play: Pietro, Altofronto, the wives of each of them,
and the other lover of the adulterous duchess. But he is at a
decided disadvantage when he begins to use as an instrument
of his villainies the very person who, in disguise, has set himself to overthrow him and regain his rightful place in the sun.
Malevole-Altofronto in his turn uses disguise and feigns friendship not only with Mendoza but with the main victims of
Mendoza's deceptions. Only toward the end does Altofronto
uncover himself to Pietro and join him in a sincere alliance.

It is to be especially noted that the initiating agent throughout most of the play is Mendoza. Except for Altofronto's first
move in coming back to the court in disguise and his putting
into Pietro's ear the bee of suspicion about his wife and Mendoza, it is Mendoza who keeps making the moves. Each of
these is counterchecked by Altofronto, who rather makes use
of Mendoza's own advances to thwart him than initiates any
steps of his own. Thus he takes advantage of Mendoza's cuckolding of the usurper to stir suspicion against him; he works
Mendoza's employment of him to murder Duke Pietro to convince the duke of Mendoza's villainy and to bring him back in
the guise of a hermit; he turns Mendoza's diabolical attempt to
have Malevole-Altofronto and the "hermit" kill each other

into an opening for revealing himself to Pietro as Altofronto and for having him join forces with him; he merely presents to Mendoza's treacherousness the means of deceiving himself as to the poisonous qualities of the box by means of which Mendoza thought he had finally disposed of Malevole; finally, the masked dance commanded by Mendoza as the scene for his winning by hook or by crook the hand of Maria, the imprisoned wife of Altofronto, is exploited by Altofronto as an opportunity for closing in with his fellow conspirators upon the villain. His disguise gives Altofronto the advantage of waiting for his adversary to make a move before making a countermove, whereas Mendoza does not even suspect he has an enemy at such close quarters. Notwithstanding all this, Mendoza is pictured as a consummate Machiavellian. He is, therefore, a most interesting example of a villainous duper duped by counterintrigue.

In this chapter two main methods have been illustrated by which deception serves to bring about its own frustration. In the first place, the deceiver himself may be the direct cause of his own undoing. This, in turn, may happen in a number of ways: the intriguer's own device may recoil upon him by his trying to be too clever, or by his having too much confidence in himself, or by his overreaching himself and indulging in just too much trickery for his own good. The second principal way in which an initiated deception brings about its own frustration is by provoking a reaction in the shape of a successful counterintrigue. Either manner of having a deception thwarted results in the duper-duped situation. *Wily Beguiled; The Merry Wives of Windsor; All Fools; A Mad World, My Masters; Michaelmas Term; Volpone;* and *The Malcontent,* besides being examples of how deception can be employed to provide exciting force, complications, and general forward movement to a comic plot, also serve to show how one or other of the various ways in which deception is frustrated may bring a play to its denouement and conclusion.

CHAPTER VI

The Means
of Deception

At the beginning of an intrigue or a hoax an agent of deception might be asked by his accomplices or his employer to "devise the means" by which their ends might be achieved. And the trickster might well answer, as one of them indeed does, in some such terms as these: "Let me alone; I have a trick, a conceit, a thing, a device . . ." In this chapter are gathered for inspection and classification the tricks and devices which serve as the means and instruments of deception in Elizabethan comedy. The classification does not attempt to be any more rigid than the material will suffer it to be. Some instances might conceivably fit also into other pigeonholes than those into which they are here placed. It goes without saying that some of the episodes mentioned in this chapter have already been looked at in this study from other points of view. Here the focus is on the individual devices, pretenses, and stratagems rather than on the over-all plots, projects, and intrigues in which they are the wheels and cogs. The purpose of this phase of the study is to show the variety of artifices devised by tricksters and at the same time to indicate the patterns into which they fall.

One of the most obvious means by which characters in comedy are misled is the deceptive use of words. The victims may be deceived by lies or by ambiguities or by flattery or by being fed with false hopes. Many examples of these occur in the comedies under consideration.

The regularity with which lies are used to develop the plot in Elizabethan drama provokes one author to remark that "without the convention of the lie most of the action in Elizabethan plays would come to a halt."[1] At the end of *Gammer Gurton's Needle* the bailiff asks Diccon, "Hast thou not made a lie or two, to set these two by the eares?" (V, ii, 222). It is precisely by a judicious sprinkling of lies that the merry knave starts the action going, provides the complications, and sows the mischief that fills the play. In Chapman's *All Fools* Rinaldo lies to old Gostanzo in asserting that the girl they have just seen is the wife of Rinaldo's brother (I, i, 183). It is this lie that puts the plot into motion, and most of Rinaldo's dodges throughout the play are required to keep Gostanzo from finding out that the girl is really the wife of his own son. A lie which directly serves to untie one strand of the plot in *Monsieur D'Olive* (1604), by Chapman, is the one told Marcellina by Vandome to the effect that her husband is playing fast and loose with a lady of the court. This smokes her out of her self-imposed immurement into the light of day to look for her husband (V, i, 86, 245-47). The reconciliation between husband and wife is thus quite expeditiously brought about.

Ambiguous use of speech as a means of deception is frequent in Elizabethan comedy. Thorndike says of Rosalind in *As You Like It* (c. 1599) that in exploiting her disguise she speaks the simple truth and deceives her father, her lover, and Phebe.[2] Several instances of her resorting to ambiguity could be cited, but one example should be sufficient. In her disguise as a boy she says to the smitten Phebe, "I will marry you if

---

[1] Mary Crapo Hyde, *Playwriting for Elizabethans—1600-1605*, p. 153. (Columbia University Studies in English and Comparative Literature, No. 167.) New York: Columbia University Press, 1949.

[2] Thorndike, *English Comedy*, p. 114.

ever I marry woman, and I'll be married to-morrow" (V, ii, 122-23). Her statement is undoubtedly true enough, but her disguise endows it with an ambiguous coloring and she deludes the girl into indulging in fairer hopes than her real prospects warrant. And when the bright morrow dawns, Rosalind, still in disguise, boxes the unwitting girl into a marriage with the mute, inglorious Silvius:

> *Ros.* You say you'll marry me, if I be willing?
> *Phe.* That will I, should I die the hour after.
> *Ros.* But if you do refuse to marry me,
> You'll give yourself to this most faithful shepherd?
> *Phe.* So is the bargain (V, iv, 11-15).

A similar use of ambiguity is made by Mistress Low-water in Middleton's *No Wit, No Help Like a Woman's* when, disguised as a gallant and a wooer, she is challenged by Lady Golden-fleece, whom she is wooing:

> *L. Gold.* . . . . I'll put you to't, sir;
> Will you swear here you never yet knew woman?
> *Mis. Low.* Never, as man e'er knew her, by this light, widow!
>
> .   .   .   .   .
>
> Nay, since you love to bring a man on's knees,
> I take into the same oath thus much more,
> That you are the first widow, or maid, or wife,
> That ever I in suit of love did court,
> Or honestly did woo: how say you to that, widow? (II, iii, 152-60).

Another deception by the use of words which, because of the situation, do not carry their face value, occurs in Middleton's *A Trick To Catch the Old One*. After having secretly married Walkadine Hoard, the courtesan, who has been posing as a rich widow, is urged by the other old usurer, Lucre, to put away all idea of marrying Hoard and to keep herself free to marry his (Lucre's) nephew, Witgood. She makes an equivocal promise, and Lucre, not knowing she has just been married, is thus de-

luded into signing over to Witgood the property he had got from
him by usury.

> *Luc.* In the mean season,
> Will you protest, before these gentlemen,
> To keep yourself as you're now at this present?
> *Court.* I do protest, before these gentlemen,
> I will be as clear then as I am now (IV, i, 85-89).

As we have seen in preceding chapters, characters are sometimes hoodwinked with the help of flattery. By well-directed
compliments and feigned dependence on Gostanzo's assumed
ability to manage people's lives, Rinaldo in Chapman's *All
Fools* gulls the old man into gulling himself. Likewise by an
outrageous application of the trowel Dulcimel in Marston's
Parasitaster overlays her father's self-constructed image of himself as a man of wisdom and builds him up for her own purposes and his ultimate confusion. In this same play the disguised
duke, Hercules, uses flattery to draw selected victims into exhibitions of their several fatuities. A comment from an earlier
play is in place here:

> Ah sira, to see the dissimulation of a craftie counterfit knaue,
> That by flatterie can brynge to pas the thynge he would haue
>   (ll. 1255-56).[3]

In Elizabethan plays one occasionally comes across the expression "to bear in hand," which means to deceive by a course
of false pretenses or, more specifically in some cases, to delude
a person by holding out to him false hopes. This holding out
of false hopes is frequently resorted to as a means of deception.
Thus Falstaff, in his role of would-be gallant, is led on by the
merry wives to whom he has sent soliciting letters. They feed

---

[3] C. F. Tucker Brooke, editor, *Common Conditions.* (Elizabethan Club Reprints,
No. 1.) New Haven: Yale University Press; London: Oxford University Press,
1915.

him with false hopes of being successful with them by sending
messages through Mistress Quickly and appointing him a time
of meeting.[4] In order to have a constant source of ready money
to sponge on, Sir Toby Belch keeps the simple Sir Andrew Aguecheek near him by priming him with ridiculous hopes of one
day winning the hand of Sir Toby's niece, Olivia. "Send for
money, knight. If thou hast her not i' the end, call me Cut."[5]
Quintiliano in Chapman's *May Day* has the same objective in
promising the rich young gull, Innocentio, to make him his
lieutenant in an entirely imaginary company of militia (I, i,
365). Much swindling in real life, ancient as well as modern, is
based on the universal human failing of being deluded by false
hopes of getting rich quickly. The whole alchemy swindle in
Jonson's *The Alchemist,* the extravagant "projections" in his
The Devil Is an Ass, and the ensnaring of the repulsive old
harpies in *Volpone* are all traps into which the victims are
drawn by the lure of false hopes of getting rich in a hurry.
Volpone knows whereof he speaks:

> I haue no wife, no parent, child, allie,
> To giue my substance to; but whom I make,
> Must be my heire: and this makes men obserue me.
> This drawes new clients, daily, to my house,
> Women, and men, of euery sexe, and age,
> That bring me presents, send me plate, coyne, iewels,
> With hope that when I die, (which they expect
> Each greedy minute) it shall then returne,
> Ten-fold vpon them; . . .
>
> .   .   .   .
>
> All which I suffer, playing with their hopes,
> And am content to coyne 'hem into profit,
> And looke vpon their kindnesse, and take more,
> And looke on that; still bearing them in hand,

---

[4] *The Merry Wives of Windsor,* II, i, 96-100; III, iii, 205-08; IV, iv, 12-15.
[5] *Twelfth Night,* II, iii, 202-03.

Letting the cherry knock against their lips,
And, draw it, by their mouths, and back againe . . .
    (I, i, 73-90).

The telephone, which is such a frequent prop in modern
plays, was not available to the Elizabethans; but they could use
letters, and they could use them as instruments of deception.
The riddles in the forged letter written by Maria in *Twelfth
Night* are so artfully couched that Malvolio, given his propen-
sities, cannot but construe them the way he does and conclude
that greatness is being thrust upon him. The spectacle of his
decoding of these "mad Herogliphickes" to his own undoing is
one of the great scenes in comic drama (II, v). In Chapman's
Monsieur D'Olive we come across something quite similar (IV,
ii, 181-260). Commenting on this scene, Professor Parrott sees
"an amusing bit of plagiarism" in the situation wherein two
courtiers forge a letter to lure D'Olive into making a foolish
exhibition of himself before the lady he has been led to believe
in love with him. Professor Parrott, however, calls attention to
the different ways in which this trick is emphasized in the two
plays. Chapman elaborates that part of the incident which
Shakespeare leaves untouched—namely, the actual preparation
of the bait, the penning of the letter—and refrains from enlarg-
ing on elements developed with such memorable skill by Shakespeare.[6] In *The Widow*, mostly by Middleton, a forged letter is
used by a wife to deceive her husband. Philippa pretends to
receive a soliciting letter from a lover. This she has written
herself, and she shows it to her husband both to allay suspicion
of any looseness on her part and because she knows he will be
foolish enough to bring it forthwith to her lover and demand an
explanation. In this way the lover will know that the lady herself has written the letter and is thereby informing him that she

---

[6] Parrott, *Plays of Chapman: Comedies*, p. 779, note.

is willing to receive his attentions (I, i, 108 ff.; I, ii, 184 ff.). A similar use of a forged letter by Dulcimel to gull her father is found in Marston's *Parasitaster* (III, i). A forged document, not a letter, is employed by the rogue Canby in *The Blind Beggar of Bednal Green* (by Chettle, Day, and perhaps Haughton) to deceive young Strowd. Canby pretends to assist the gull in saving his father from the gallows by giving him a reprieve he says he has obtained from the Duke of Gloucester, but which he has himself counterfeited (Act II, lines 1229 and 1260).[7]

A much-used means of deception in comedy is simulating an emotion or an attitude or a relationship toward another which is at variance with the true state of affairs. Pretended friendship and assistance is one kind of simulation frequently resorted to. All through *Roister Doister* the braggart is comically abused by Merrygreek under the pretense of helping him with the widow, Custance; but this abuse really comes to a head in the farcical battle where Merrygreek repeatedly strikes poor Ralph, while making a great show of belaboring the enemy (IV, viii, 28-32). This is but a primitive form of the deception whereby one individual works under the cloak of friendship to injure another, as when a person takes advantage of a commission to further another's suit to a lady's hand and woos her for himself. This we see being done by Parson Shorthose in the subplot of *Grim the Collier of Croydon* (1600)[8] and by Proteus in *The Two Gentlemen of Verona*. Given access in the latter play to Silvia by her father that he may ween her thoughts away from her banished lover, Valentine, and direct them toward the foolish Thurio, Proteus tries to make love to the girl on his own account. But

---

[7] For another example of a forged letter used to deceive see Middleton's *The Family of Love*, V, iii, 323-39. For uses of spurious wills see *The London Prodigal*, I, i, 213-29; II, i, 152-64.

[8] In Hazlitt, *Collection of Old English Plays*, Vol. VIII. *Grim the Collier of Croydon* was first produced in 1600 and the author was probably William Haughton. See Chambers, *The Elizabethan Stage*, Vol. IV, p. 16.

he is shortly given to understand just where he stands with her: "Thou subtle, perjur'd, false, disloyal man!" (IV, ii, 95). Similarly, in the anonymous *Wily Beguiled* Churms, allowed by her father to visit a girl in order to persuade her to marry a suitor she despises, woos her for himself. We see double-dealing at work in the *Supposes* of Gascoigne, where the parasite professes to further the old lawyer's suit to Polynesta, while at the same time letting another suitor, Erostrato, believe that he is working in his behalf. Necessarily, he keeps each ignorant of his connections with the other. The purpose of this deception is, of course, to have two sources of free meals (I, iii, 29 ff.). In similar fashion Mistress Quickly (who thinks she knows Anne Page's mind) profits by not letting her right hand know what her left hand does. She encourages two of Anne's suitors and an emissary of a third to cross her palm, leading each of them along in the belief that she will speak favorably for him alone.[9] A variation on this sort of duplicity is the agreement made by the witty pages, Dromio and Riscio, in Lyly's *Mother Bombie* to cooperate with their respective masters in their projects of marrying off their foolish offspring. Instead of helping their masters, the two pages (in company with another pair of the same stripe) spend the rest of the play contriving means and ways of embarrassing them, yet all the time keeping up the pretense of collaboration.

Sometimes pretended anger is used by a character to gain his ends. The husbands of the two angry women of Abington plan and go through with a trumped-up quarrel in order to bring their wives to a reconciliation with each other. This deception brings the solution to all the complications which have arisen from the falling out between the two wives.[10] In order not to let

---

[9] *The Merry Wives of Windsor*, I, iv, 33-36, 121-29, 142-78.
[10] Henry Porter, *The Two Angry Women of Abington* (c. 1598), scenes 12 and 14. In Gayley and Thaler, *Representative English Comedies*, Vol. I.

the love between Ferdinand and Miranda advance too quickly and "lest too light winning make the prize light," Prospero, in *The Tempest* (*c.* 1611), pretends to believe that Ferdinand is not what he claims to be and, feigning anger against him, puts him to hard labor (I, ii, 451-64). After the trial scene in *The Merchant of Venice* Portia, still in her disguise as a doctor of laws, specifies as the only reward she will accept from Bassanio for the vanquishing of Shylock the ring which she herself has given him on their wedding day, and she goes off in a feigned huff when he demurs (IV, i, 427-48). He is moved to send the ring after her, and thus the situation is set up for the mock chiding of the final hundred lines of the play. Subtle in Jonson's *The Alchemist* pretends to be mightily incensed by the refusal of the truculent Ananias to supply more money until he and his Puritan brethren have received some return on their previous investments in Subtle's experiments. He even makes a show of being much annoyed that the brethren have sent to negotiate with him one with so unsanctified a name as Ananias. This rough treatment, he reasons, will be more effective than blandishments in bringing to heel the recalcitrant dupes.

> This will fetch 'hem
> And make 'hem hast towards their gulling more.
> A man must deale like a rough nurse, and fright
> Those, that are froward, to an appetite (II, v, 87-90).

Pretended love is another means of deception. In Lyly's *Endymion* (1588) the hero simulates love for Tellus, at least for a short while, in order to hide his love for Cynthia (II, i), and Tellus pretends to be in love with Corsites with the purpose, it seems, of preserving the slight liberty she enjoys in the prison presided over by that personage (IV, i). The king in Dekker's *Old Fortunatus* asks his daughter to make a show of returning Andelocia's love for her so that she may entice him to reveal the secret source of his great wealth (III, i and ii). The philandering gallant, Laxton, in *The Roaring Girl* (by Middleton and Dekker) encourages Mistress Gallipot to think him in love with her, but he plays this game only so long as she can supply him with funds filched from her husband's coffers (II, i, 88-94). In the other plot of the same play Sebastian feigns an infatuation with Moll Cutpurse with the intention of gaining his father's consent to his marriage with his beloved Mary Fitzallard. This consent the father is constrained to give in order to avoid, as he thinks, the greater of two evils. In Chapman's *Monsieur D'Olive* Vandome pretends to be in love with Eurione and asks his brother-in-law, St. Anne, to go to the lady in his behalf. This he does only to draw St. Anne out of his self-enforced retirement and get him to look on Eurione in the hope he will fall in love with the lady, who already loves St. Anne.

> 'Tis true I did dissemble love t'Eurione
> To make you happy in her dear affection
> Who more dotes on you than you can on her (IV, i, 68-70).

Merely for the sport of breaking down the resistance of Gondarino to the allurements of women the sprightly Oriana, in Beaumont's (and Fletcher's?) *The Woman-Hater* (1606), pretends to be in love with him and woos the man with all the arts and subtleties at her command (III, i). He manages to bear up stalwartly under the attack. *Wit at Several Weapons* (*c.* 1609), by Fletcher and others, shows several characters pretending to be in love with people for whom they have no affection. That he might have an opportunity of being near his beloved without letting her uncle suspect his attitude and also without permitting the niece herself to know at the outset his true feelings toward her, Cunningham allows the niece's duenna to think that he has been smitten by her more mature charms. The younger lady, in her turn, counterfeits a passion for a servingman, so that she may see the reaction of Cunningham, whom she feels to be really in love with her (I, i; II, ii).

Though ignorance is neither an emotion nor an attitude, the feigning of it sometimes sets up a relationship between two characters; and this form of deception is placed here for want of a more logical category. The lively Lodovico, in Chapman's *May Day*, is informed that his old uncle has disguised himself as a chimney sweep in order to pass unnoticed on his way to an assignation with another man's wife. Accordingly he notifies a couple of the old man's friends of the escapade in progress, and all three hurry to intercept him. Not letting him know that they think him anything else but a chimney sweep, they badger him merrily and unmercifully with general remarks about the lechery of old men and with more particular and pungent employment of his own name (III, i). In Middleton's *The Family of Love* Maria knows that the man wooing her from beneath her balcony is not her lover, Gerardine, as he claims to be, because Gerardine is with her on the balcony at the moment; but she pretends not to see through the attempted imposture in order to flout the disguised gallant and finally to send him packing with a gust of derision (III, ii, 30-99). In the same author's *A Mad World, My Masters* the courtesan, Gullman, feigning ignorance that Harebrain is eavesdropping, makes believe she is talking to Mistress Harebrain and giving her chaste and devout advice, whereas the wife is really in another room enjoying a meeting with her lover. The husband thinks he is being quite clever in checking up on his wife by listening in on this "conversation," but at the very moment he is being thoroughly abused (III, ii, 184-240). The trick to open the eyes of Benedick and Beatrice to their underlying mutual love is helped by a pretense of ignorance on the part of the "honest slanderers" in *Much Ado about Nothing* that their dupes are listening to their remarks about them (II, iii; III, i). There is another example of deceiving an eavesdropper by pretended ignorance of his presence in Haughton's *Englishmen for My Money* (IV, iii; lines 1935-65). In *The Scornful Lady*, by Fletcher and Beaumont, the heroine pretends not to see through the disguise of her lover and tortures him with a show of willingness to forget him. Twice in *The*

Coxcomb, by the same authors, Maria does not reveal the fact that she recognizes her husband under his disguises, has him beaten on one occasion, and on another gives voice to loving sentiments about him which she by no means feels (II, i; IV, i).

Characters sometimes simulate physical or mental ailments in order to attain their ends. Bellafront's counterfeit madness in the last scene of *The Honest Whore, Part I* (1604) is what arouses the pity of the duke, who then forces Matheo, the one who first corrupted her, to agree to marry her. By feigning to be at death's door, Harvey, one of the young lovers in Haughton's *Englishmen for My Money,* induces Pisaro, the usurer, who anticipates getting his hands on the young man's property, to consent to Harvey's marriage to his daughter and to forgive him his earlier debts. At the instigation of the clever Merecraft Jonson's Fitzdottrel, in *The Devil Is an Ass,* pretends to be bewitched that he may have the deed he had recently signed invalidated. Merecraft assures him that it will require no great cleverness to carry off this deception:

> It is the easiest thing Sir, to be done.
> As plaine, as fizzling: roule but wi' your eyes,
> And foame at th' mouth. A little castle-soape
> Will do't, to rub your lips: And then a nutshell,
> With toe, and touch-wood in it to spit fire.
> Did you ne're read, Sir, little *Darrels* tricks,
> With the boy o' *Burton,* and the 7. in *Lancashire,*
> *Sommers* at *Nottingham?* All these do teach it.
> And wee'll giue out, Sir, that your wife ha's bewitched you:
> .   .   .   .
> And ga' you potions, by which meanes you were
> Not *Compos mentis,* when you made your *feoffment* (V, iii, 1-12).

Volpone's "cunning purchase" of his wealth is built, of course, on his primary pretense of being sick unto death. The wife of Greenshield in *Northward Ho!,* by Dekker and Webster, pretends to be a somnambulist in order to avert the suspicions of

her husband when she wanders around the house at night and
visits her husband's friend and guest in his room.

Since deceivers are usually unable to present bona-fide credentials and endorsements, they are often under the necessity
of manufacturing the means of recommending themselves to
prospective victims and securing their confidence. These false
qualifications may take the shape of pretensions to extraordinary knowledge, pretensions to virtue and respectability, or
misrepresentations of financial status.

It is unnecessary here to do more than remind the reader of
the tricks of those rogues who impress their dupes and delude
them by exhibitions of mock conjuring and other fabricated
manifestations of supernatural and otherwise extraordinary
knowledge. Such are the prophesies and hocus-pocus of Trappola *(The Bugbears)*, Cacurgus *(Misogonus)*, and George Pieboard and his accomplice, the captain *(The Puritan)*. Then
there are Diccon's mystifying and terrifying of Hodge in *Gammer Gurton's Needle* with his intimations of knowledge communicated by the devil. And no one can forget the archsciolist
of them all, Jonson's Subtle, whose polysyllabic disquisitions
throughout *The Alchemist* on the virtues of the "stone" and on
the processes perfective thereof compose the stock in trade
which dazzles the dupes led to him by Face. In Day's *Law Tricks*
(*c.* 1607) pretensions to skill in the black art are employed for
other purposes. By seeming to bring back to life his "dead"
aunt Polymetes uses mock conjuring to force a confession from
the wicked pair of would-be murderers who had attempted to
poison her (V, ii; ll. 2208-31).

In assumed virtue and respectability is to be found another
means of deception. The *meretrix* in Gascoigne's *The Glass of
Government* (1575), with the help of the sly parasite, Eccho,
ensnares the young and unexperienced Philosarchus by feigning
to be "very demure and modest" (II, vi). When her "aunt"
pretends to object to the indecorum of a young woman speaking

with a man on the street, he is allowed to follow them home. The chorus after the second act makes clear to the spectators the intention of these fowlers:

> These parasites, and bawdes have quickly caught,
> The careless byrds, who see not their deceyptes.

Employing a similar subterfuge, another courtesan in Middleton's *A Mad World, My Masters* sets out to compass a more respectable alliance. Pretending to be a virgin, and a bashful one at that, Gullman hooks and nets a husband who has himself been deceiving others all through the play (IV, v). The courtesan in one of the plots of *Northward Ho!*, by Dekker and Webster, sets herself up in a house and poses as a respectable and well-to-do lady, having some member of her trade pose as her reverend father, and a couple of hangers-on as her servants. In the course of this deception she induces each of three gulls to believe she is in love with him and wheedles money separately out of each of them. There is no call here to touch upon the hypocrisy of Dame Purecraft and Zeal-of-the-land Busy *(Bartholomew Fair)*, because neither the pietism of the one nor the casuistical trumpeting of the other deceives anyone. Nor need we give examples of such pretensions as are paraded by braggart soldiers, would-be gallants, and other types of those who would seem what they are not, because these delusions deceive only those who suffer from them. Those gulls, on the other hand, whose self-deception is played upon by shrewder people than themselves are with more propriety bracketed with their peers in the chapter on the dupes.

In Elizabethan comedies victims are sometimes deluded by imposters who misrepresent their financial status. By posing as a rich knight with lands and a castle the penniless Sir Petronel Flash in *Eastward Ho!* induces Gertrude, the gullible daughter of Touchstone, to marry him and give him control of her property. A long and successful imposture is the rich-widow game played by the courtesan in *A Trick To Catch the Old One* by Middleton. Exploiting this device under the able direction of Witgood, she deceives practically every other character in the comedy, notably the two old money grabbers. The same trick with the same successful results is to be seen in Lording Barry's *Ram-Alley*. We may also mention the foisting of Sir Walter Whorebound's castoff mistress, in Middleton's *A Chaste Maid in Cheapside* (*c.* 1611), upon the Yellowhammer family as a Welch heiress and her marriage, under these false pretensions, to the addlepated Tim. Middleton seems to have liked disposing of this type of character in some such fashion.[11]

A character in a play may not only pretend to have other qualifications or attitudes than he actually has but may also pretend to be someone else than he really is. This deception, being a falsification of identity, is an ampler form of imposture than misrepresentation of personal attribute or qualification. The most common form of doing this in Elizabethan comedy is to assume a disguise. On the other hand, a character may impersonate another character without the help of disguise when neither the imposter nor the one he is impersonating is known to those he is imposing on. This seems to be the case in Gascoigne's *Supposes*, where a credulous old stranger is frightened into willingness to impersonate a young man's father and to assure a fraudulent security to a bond. There is no indication that the old man changes his appearance in any respect in order to carry out his part in the deception (II, ii; IV, v). Again, a

---

[11] The deceptive marriage was of frequent occurrence in Restoration comedy and in his treatment of the subject, Gellert S. Alleman divides such marriages into two types: "the 'tricked marriage'—so called because it involves an error as to the identity, fortune, or quality of the person married—and the 'mock marriage'—a ceremony invalid, on the stage at least, because performed by a pretended clergyman" (Gellert S. Alleman, *Matrimonial Law and the Materials of Restoration Comedy*, p. 34. Wallingford: The Author, 1942. See also pp. 60-79 of the same book.) For the purposes of the present work it was more convenient to arrange such deceptive marriages in other groupings.

character, without pretending to be someone else who actually exists, can invent an entirely new identity. This last form of deception can be either by way of disguise or without one according to whether or not the impostor is known to those he is to deceive. Thus, Master Ford in *The Merry Wives of Windsor* visits Falstaff under the name and the person of a character not heard of before (Brook), but he does so in disguise because, presumably, Falstaff knows what Ford looks like. Another imposture met with in Elizabethan comedy and in its sources is the device of substitution, sometimes called the "bed trick." This too may be considered as a falsification of identity.

Disguise need not always be adopted with purposes of deception. It may be resorted to primarily as a means of concealment and of self-protection. This is sometimes the motive, initially at any rate, back of the assumption of boy's garb by girls in romantic comedies. Witness Julia's reason in *The Two Gentlemen of Verona:*

> *Luc.* But in what habit will you go along?
> *Jul.* Not like a woman, for I would prevent
> The loose encounters of lascivious men.
> Gentle Lucetta, fit me with such weeds
> As may beseem some well-reputed page (II. vii, 39-43).

But when the objective is deception of other characters, disguise is an apt means, at least on the stage, to this end. It was seen in great frequency on the Elizabethan stage and its dramatic uses have been thoroughly treated by Victor Oscar Freeburg.[12] For the purposes of the present chapter it will be sufficient to indicate the classification in which Freeburg arranges the numerous instances of disguise he has found. First, however, it will be convenient to recall a definition and some necessary distinctions which are set down with admirable precision by Free-

---

[12] Freeburg, *Disguise Plots.*

burg. Dramatic disguise he defines as "a change of personal appearance which leads to mistaken identity."[13] By means of a double test—namely, change and confusion—we can discern the difference between disguise and various similar devices. Thus, the trick of substitution in a dark chamber is not disguise, nor is the twin motive of *The Comedy of Errors* based on disguise. Though confusion arises in each case, it is not due to any change of costume and facial appearance. Conversely, change of appearance may not always lead to mistaken identity. Deception results from Volpone's efforts at looking like a dying man, but his dupes mistake his condition, not his identity. Nor is one inclined to make a false judgment about the identity of a person one perceives to be wearing a mask or a fantastic costume. One would rather suspend decision until some sign of identification should be detected.

As a basis for the division of his material Freeburg uses the disguise situation as such and arrives at a classification of disguises consisting of five categories. In one class are placed all cases of girls disguised as boys, no matter what the motive prompting the girls to assume the disguise. All women disguised as boys or men he calls female pages. Boys or men disguised as women he treats in a chapter entitled, "The Boy Bride," even though not all boys in girl's clothing get as far as a wedding ceremony. All spy situations where disguise is employed make up a third group. Examples of the lover in disguise comprise a fourth. Plays in which a single character, usually a rogue, impersonates many parts with lightning changes of costume are discussed in a chapter entitled "The Rogue in Multi-Disguise." Only a few examples of each type of disguise need here be mentioned. Of female pages there are Julia, Rosalind, Viola, and Portia, in *The Two Gentlemen of Verona, As You Like It, Twelfth Night,* and *The Merchant of Venice,* respectively;

---

[13] *Ibid.,* p. 2.

Martia in *The Widow* and Mistress Low-water in *No Wit, No Help Like a Woman's*, both by Middleton. We find boys or men disguised as women in *George a Greene* (by Robert Greene?),[14] *A Mad World, My Masters* (Middleton), *Law Tricks* (Day), and *Epicoene* (Jonson). Multidisguise is employed in *The Blind Beggar of Bednal Green* (Chettle and Day), *The Blind Beggar of Alexandria* (Chapman), *The Dutch Courtesan* (Marston), and Middleton's *The Family of Love* and *Michaelmas Term*.[15] The lover in disguise is seen in the *Supposes* (Gascoigne) and the later adaptations of this play, *The Taming of a Shrew* and *The Taming of the Shrew;* also in Dekker's *The Shoemakers' Holiday* (1599) and Jonson's *The Devil Is an Ass.* Plays in which the disguised-spy situation is found have been discussed or mentioned in the third chapter and it would be superfluous to name them again here.

The pretended yielding to the solicitations of a would-be seducer and the substitution of another woman in the place of the solicited one is a deception made familiar enough by Shakespeare's use of it in *All's Well That Ends Well* (*c.* 1602) and *Measure for Measure*.[16] The unknown author of *Grim the Collier of Croydon* employs this device of substitution, but he complicates it to a degree far beyond anything Shakespeare would attempt to achieve. Honoria is in love with young Musgrave; her father wishes her to marry Lacy, earl of Kent; she has just been cured from dumbness by a devil who is spending a sabbatical

---

[14] F. W. Clarke and W. W. Greg, editors, *The Comedy of George a Green—1599* (Malone Society Reprints. London: Malone Society, 1911). The date of first production is *c.* 1590.

[15] See William J. Lawrence's essay on the complex-disguise play in his *Pre-Restoration Stage Studies*, pp. 277-98.

[16] Pretended yielding to solicitation uncombined with the trick of substitution is done by Franceschina in Chapman's *May Day*, II, i, 383-85; in *The Merry Wives of Windsor*, II, i, 96-100; and in *The Blind Beggar of Bednal Green*, I, 385-402, by Ellanor, who agrees to meet the cardinal but goes away, instead, with Gloucester.

year on earth masquerading as a human doctor; and he, in his disguise, has put in a claim for the girl's hand. Her father goes about settling things in his own involute way. He persuades Marian, Honoria's cousin, that her cooperation will both help Honoria marry her beloved, Musgrave, and get a rich husband for herself. Marian's cooperation consists in allowing herself to be married to the doctor, who will be told the marriage must take place in the dark in order to deceive the bride, Honoria, who has refused to consider him as a suitor, and who will herself, he is told, be under the impression she is marrying her beloved. Honoria and Marian are also deceived as to the identity of the man Honoria is really marrying. This is not Musgrave, but Lacy, the earl whom the father has favored all along. Honoria is told her marriage must take place in the dark because they must deceive the doctor, who thinks he is marrying her, whereas it is Marian he is wedding. This all goes through as planned by the father, and thus this conniving old gentleman deludes his daughter, his niece, and the doctor (not to speak of young Musgrave, who is left completely out of things), each of whom thinks he or she is helping deceive someone else, and two of whom are mistaken as to the identity of their respective spouses.[17]

In Fletcher's *Monsieur Thomas* (*c.* 1615) there is an incipient substitution of a blackamoor for Thomas' mischievous mistress (V, i). There appears to be an instance of a use of the "bed trick" in *Blurt Master Constable* (V, ii, 116-45); but Bullen, who includes this play in his edition of Middleton's works, though it is probably by Dekker,[18] believes that a lack

---

[17] Other cases of substitution are in the anonymous *Fair Em the Miller's Daughter* (in Brooke, *Shakespeare Apocrypha*) and in Thomas Heywood's *The Wise Woman of Hogsdon*. The dates are respectively *c.* 1590 and 1604.

[18] See Harbage, *Annals of English Drama*, p. 68. Chambers (*The Elizabethan Stage*, Vol. III, p. 439) lists *Blurt Master Constable* among Middleton's works. The date is *c.* 1601.

of clarity in the play has caused the second scene of the fifth act to be misunderstood.[19]

A second trick of substitution, though rather grimmer than what is usually indicated by the term in Elizabethan comedy, is to be found in *Measure for Measure*. The duke, disguised as a friar, in order to thwart Angelo, who has ordered Isabella's brother to be beheaded, persuades the provost of the prison to anticipate the execution of another condemned prisoner by a few hours and send his head to Angelo instead of Claudio's. The timely death of a third prisoner relieves them of the necessity of hastening anybody's execution, and they use the detached head of the dead prisoner to satisfy Angelo's demand for proof of Claudio's dispatch (IV, iii, 73-84).

An age-old variation of the substitution trick is the *Amphitruo* situation. In Plautus' version the god Jupiter assumes the shape and the appearance of a definite individual named Amphitryon, and takes his place in his wife's welcoming embraces, while Amphitryon is still on his way home from a military expedition. Jupiter is assisted in carrying through this deception by Mercury, who takes on the appearance of Amphitryon's slave, Sosia. Such a disguise, of course, achieves a completeness of transformation impossible to mere mortal impostors, for the deceivers not only imitate the outward shape of Amphitryon and Sosia but know their inmost thoughts and use this knowledge to their own advantage and to the discomfiture of the deluded mortals.[20] The second act of Heywood's *The Silver Age*, not a comedy but a dramatization of classical legend, presents this situation, and the earlier and anonymous *The Birth of*

---

[19] Bullen, *Works of Thomas Middleton*, Vol. I, pp. xxi-iii.

[20] There are many adaptations of the *Amphitruo* plot in other literatures and some in other periods of English drama than the Elizabethan. See Karl von Reinhardstöttner, *Plautus: Spätere Bearbeitungen Plautinischer Lustspiele*, pp. 115-229 (Leipzig: W. Friedrich, 1886) and W. B. Sedgwick, "The History of a Latin Comedy," *Review of English Studies* 3:346-49, July 1927.

Hercules (*c.* 1604) is a very readable adaptation of the Plautine *Amphitruo.*[21]

False reports of their own death are sometimes given out by characters who then assume a disguise in order to spy on relatives or friends and test their fidelity. Several uses of this device are discussed by Freeburg in his chapter on the spy-in-disguise plot.[22] This combination of falsified report of death and disguise is found in *Michaelmas Term, Volpone,* Chapman's *The Widow's Tears,* Day's *Law Tricks,* Fletcher's *The Scornful Lady,* and the anonymous *The London Prodigal.* The combination of a pretended death and resurrection of the "corpse" is in *The Puritan* and in *Westward Ho!* The use of a sleeping potion to induce a simulated death is to be seen in *The Honest Whore, Part I* and in *The Puritan.* In neither of these cases does the one who is put to sleep know beforehand of the plan to do so. He is accordingly among the victims of the deception. In this way the situation differs from the use of the sleeping potion in *Romeo and Juliet.*[23] One remembers also the ruse devised by the friar of the reported death of Hero in *Much Ado about Nothing.*

To facilitate presentation and to underscore similarities, the foregoing illustrative instances of the different means and instruments of deception were organized in groups which ranged from the use of language and the use of such instruments as fraudulent documents up through various simulated attitudes,

---

[21] In R. Warwick Bond, editor, *The Birth of Hercules* (Malone Society Reprints. London: Malone Society, 1911). Other cases of gods or devils taking human shape in Elizabethan comedy occur in *Grim the Collier of Croydon* and in Jonson's *Cynthia's Revels* (*c.* 1601) and *The Devil Is an Ass.*

[22] Freeburg, *Disguise Plots,* pp. 144-47.

[23] Other plays, both tragedies and comedies, in which sleeping potions are used are mentioned by Forsythe, *The Relations of Shirley's Plays to the Elizabethan Drama,* p. 74. For comment on the use in the *commedia dell' arte* of the sleeping potion, the devices of disguise, concealment, and substitution, and several other kinds of tricks mentioned above, see K. M. Lea, *Italian Popular Comedy,* Vol. I, pp. 174, 182, 184-85; Vol. II, pp. 409-10 (London: Oxford University Press, 1934).

qualifications, and conditions to, finally, such falsifications of identity as impersonation, disguise, and substitution. This arrangement resulted in something of a design which showed the varying degrees of fullness of participation with which the deceiver could enter into his deception, or more exactly, could identify himself with the means of deception he was employing. The mere number and diversity of these instances, which are by no means exhaustive, point to the pervasiveness of deception in the action of Elizabethan comedies, and at the same time serve as a partial index to the taste of the Elizabethan audience for trickery in the plays they attended.

The Audience Appeal
of Deception

J ust what was it in the theatrical employment of deception that Elizabethan theatergoers found so interesting and so funny? More explicitly, what dramatic values and what comic effects, achieved with the help of deception as an element of technique, appealed to Elizabethan audiences? In the answering of this question much of the data already presented will be scanned from a new point of view.

The most obvious as well as the most prevalent use of deception in Elizabethan comedy was its organic employment in plot structure. Such arrangements as a dupe being used as an unwitting instrument in the deceiving of another, the situation of a dupe assisting in his own duping, and the situation of a pair of dupes being manipulated by a trickster as reciprocal instruments of each other's confusion are not static arrangements at all but dynamic relationships which constitute, in part at least, the mechanism of the plays in which they find themselves. In the frustration of trickery, too, by the excessive use of it or by the mistakes of the intriguer or by the recoil of his own device upon the inventor there is perceptible an articulated framework of exciting force, complication, and resolution. In *Michaelmas Term*, for instance, the reversal of the main plot is brought about by the excessive resort to trickery by Quomodo, the interlocked phases of whose swindling of Easy out of his property had constituted the forward movement of the plot. Then again, the interacting forces of deception may be a means of artistically connecting the subplot to the main plot of a play. Thus, the tricksters in the main plot of Chapman's *All Fools* are repaid in their own coin by the victim of their conniving incursion into the subplot. This plot, therefore, is connected with the main story first of all by the trick played upon Cornelio by the young Rinaldo and Valerio. Next, in the turning of Cornelio upon his victimizers the eyes of the chief dupe of the main plot (Gostanzo) are opened to his own gulling. Thus it is by the finesse of Cornelio that the denouement of the main plot is brought about.

Perhaps the most masterful employment on the Elizabethan stage of trickery as the very framework and fabric of a comedy is Jonson's *The Alchemist*. As in *Volpone*, a number of intrigues are set successively in motion, but here more than in *Volpone* it is essential that the various dupes be prevented from discovering one another's connection with the rogues. Much of the interest and suspense, therefore, is aroused by the exhibition of the parties who are involved in the separate intrigues following each other in an accelerating rate onto the one unchanging scene of action. As the pace increases, the anticipation of collisions is repeatedly sharpened and then pleasurably frustrated by Face's demonstrations of quick thinking in emergency. But the feeling continues to grow that, with each new averting of a snarling of the lines on which their puppets are strung, still greater ingenuity must be exerted by the rogues to prevent complete and final catastrophe. Then in the fourth act, when the disguised Surly's counterintrigue begins, the audience knows that the pace cannot keep up for long. Even this danger injected by Surly is nullified by Face's exploiting of the stupid Kastrill's quarreling humor and of the truculent Ananias' zealous antagonism to Spanish slops. Thus two dupes are manipulated into helping their chief duper outface the very one who is trying to open their eyes, and thus components of a pair of hitherto carefully separated intrigues are in the emergency combined by the trickster to set up a buffer against a threatening counterintrigue. Finally, the rogues themselves fall out, and in the dizzying whirl of the last few scenes the audience asks itself which of the two rogues will come out on top. To this there can be but one answer, for Face all along has shown himself more canny and shifty than Subtle in dodging counterchecks.

This brief indication of the use of deception as a structural element in *The Alchemist* may fittingly be closed with a quotation from a brilliant analysis to which the preceding paragraph is not a little indebted.

> As a piece of almost geometrical form, this play appears to be without a companion in the drama with which I am acquainted. The flawless art with which the action is maintained through the steadily increasing tempo of the last two acts and the exquisite proportioning of that acceleration, where the slightest misjudgement would have ruined the subtly articulated balance of movements, must be an unfailing source of aesthetic delight.[1]

One ingredient of this aesthetic delight, which was aroused in Elizabethan audiences not only by *The Alchemist* but also in varying degrees by the plays immediately to be mentioned, was an increasingly sophisticated pleasure of seeing dramatic conflict work itself out in terms of deception. This pleasure was catered to by a long development extending from the simple sequences of tricks which provided such elementary complications as were to be seen in *Roister Doister* and *Gammer Gurton's*

---

[1] Ellis-Fermor, *The Jacobean Drama*, pp. 46-47. For a discussion of the intrigue plot and Elizabethan experiments in plotting see also Madeleine Doran, *Endeavors of Art: A Study of Form in Elizabethan Drama*, pp. 152-56, 295-340 (Madison: The University of Wisconsin Press, 1954). Professor Doran's admirable book was published too recently to be of service in the writing of the present work.

Needle (*c.* 1553 for both of them), through the growing complexity of imitations of classical and Italian models like *The Bugbears* (*c.* 1564), *Supposes* (1566), *Mother Bombie* (*c.* 1589), *The Taming of the Shrew* (*c.* 1594), and *Wily Beguiled* (*c.* 1602), to the artfully interwoven intrigue of *All Fools* (*c.* 1604), *The Malcontent* (1604), *A Trick To Catch the Old One* (*c.* 1605), *Ram-Alley* (1608), and the massively architectonic masterpieces, *Volpone* (*c.* 1606) and *The Alchemist* (1610). In the later stages, at least, of this development there was much intellectual stimulation for the audience in keeping up with the thrust and parry of intrigue and counterintrigue. Hamlet's remark to his mother, "O, 'tis most sweet/ When in one line two crafts directly meet" (III, iv, 209-10), voiced a sentiment even more applicable to comedy than to tragedy; and it expressed, no doubt, the Elizabethan reaction to the spectacle of "wits at war with wits."

With the emergence of romantic comedy and its perfecting in the hands of Shakespeare, love interest took its place as an important element in the audience appeal of Elizabethan comedies. Nevertheless those audiences, it must be noted, never lost their taste for plays founded on trickery and intrigue. They certainly saw many of them, as can be gathered from the examples of the classical imitations, realistic comedy of London life, humor comedy, and satirical comedy analyzed in the foregoing chapters.

What is not so readily appreciated is the fact that even in romantic comedies the machinery of movement is effectively lubricated by the use of deception. One would, no doubt, expect to find trickery in the subplot of *Twelfth Night*, the most Jonsonian of Shakespeare's comedies, but it should not be overlooked that the romantic main plot also is founded on Viola's deceiving of both Orsino and Olivia as to her sex and that it is this mild deception which involves her, not entirely to her liking, in the fooleries of the subplot. It is Proteus' duplicity that initiates the difficulties of Valentine in *The Two Gentlemen of Verona*. It is with the help of Portia's deceiving of everybody in the courtroom as to her identity that Antonio's difficulties are resolved and the minor comic possibilities of *The Merchant of Venice* are entangled. Rosalind's merry mystifications and ambiguities under the cloak of her disguise deceive father, lover, and the shepherdess Phebe, and furnish *As You Like It* with such light intrigue as is required to slide it into its multimarriaged ending. In *Much Ado about Nothing* there are the lying and calumniating of Don John and the counterplotting by the friar in the pretense of Hero's death and the "substitute" bride for the repentant Claudio. And in the same play we find the merry trick played successively on Benedick and Beatrice by their "honest slanderers." Again, commentators have pointed to the amount of lying and trickery resorted to by Helena of *All's Well That Ends Well*.[2] It is true that in this play the heroine's devices have not so amiable an air about them as surrounds much of the trickery in the Shakespearean comedies preceding *All's Well That Ends Well*; but it must not be forgotten that in those plays, as well as in this one, Shakespeare supplied his audience with the tricks and intrigue it took pleasure in. In Dekker's romantic comedy *The Shoemakers' Holiday* young Rowland Lacy finds it no shame "To clothe his cunning with the Gentle Craft" so that by means of his disguise as a shoemaker he may possess the "happie presence" of his Rose. And his final plan to carry her off and marry her at the Savoy chapel is successful only because the pursuit of his uncle and Rose's father is directed to the wrong church by a trick played on them by Simon Eyre's merry journeyman, Firk.

In addition to giving pleasure to Elizabethan theatergoers by its organic uses in plot structure, deception could be relied upon to appeal to the audience as an exercise in intellectual

---

[2] See, for instance, Chambers, *Shakespeare: A Survey*, pp. 206-07.

wit. Virtuosity in trickery was deemed interesting for its own sake. This interest generally was brought to focus on the chief deceiver of the comedy. There was much to fascinate the audience in the cleverness and dexterity of such tricksters as Trappola, Cocledemoy, Smallshanks, Face, Merecraft, Mosca, Lemot, Lodovico, and Rinaldo. The very names given to Brainworm, Savorwit, Witgood, Wittypate, Truewit, and others of that ilk show by what aspect of their character their creators sought to appeal most to the audience. The spectators would note with keen appreciation and appraisal of comparative merits the exercise of the special talents of these characters: how they managed and manipulated the other characters, even their own confederates; with what canniness they selected the precise weakness of prospective victims; with what deft handling they prepared them for a fall; how they exploited each new opportunity presented by new arrivals or chance occurrences. What must have delighted the audience as much as anything else was to behold a trickster caught in an embarrassing contretemps and to surmise with eager anticipation by "what trick, what device, what starting hole," he would extricate himself or hide from open and apparent shame. Intensified suspense would be the natural dramatic effect of such moments.

Then there was the joyous exuberance flowing out from these tricksters. Some of them took such a bumptious and lively pleasure in their own cleverness, even apart from whatever ulterior motives they had in exercising it, that they often elaborated upon their tricks far beyond necessity, ornamenting them with interlacing weavings and windings that could serve no purpose but to give full and uninhibited play to their ingenuity.

The buoyant gaiety of these fellows was of considerable service also in producing another comic effect; namely, the heightening of the spirit of mirth and laughter. To see the truth of this statement one has but to cast an eye back on a few characters: on Merrygreek, who would not give up the sport he got out of playing hoaxes on Roister Doister if he had to live on bread and cheese; on Diccon, whose pranks led to such confusion and turmoil in Gammer Gurton's village; on the sprightly mischievousness of Lyly's pages in *Mother Bombie* and *Midas* (*c.* 1589); on Chapman's trio of merry and energetic gullers, Lemot, Lodovico, and Rinaldo; on the irrepressible Cocledemoy and the breezy Smallshanks; on Jonson's Brainworm and True-wit; on Shakespeare's Maria.

The exhilaration of such characters often communicated itself to confederates and abettors, and we see the latter entering into the game with equally high spirits. These confederates often voice their appreciation of the cleverness of the chief trickster or show palpitating eagerness for the sport they see in prospect. Sir Toby is all ears when Maria promises to gull Monsieur Malvolio into a nayword: "Possess us, possess us."[3] And when she has merely indicated how she will go about it, he quivers like a hound on a hot scent: "Excellent! I smell a device" (II, iii, 176). His admiration for her wit, when he sees the effects of its workings upon Malvolio, is in the same strain and needs no further illustration. So too the gentleman in *The Puritan,* who, though strictly speaking no confederate of George Pieboard, does help him dodge the officers who have apprehended him for debt and expresses his enthusiastic appreciation of the trick by which George eludes the officers: "By my troth, an excellent deuice" (III, iv, 87). The only sentence Justice Clement passes on Brainworm when he hears of his day's mischief is to command Brainworm to pledge him in a cup of sack. In the opinion of the merry officer Brainworm has done nothing which does not deserve to be pardoned "for the wit o' the offence."[4] A phrase used by Face's master, Lovewit, on the latter's unexpected arrival, expresses a laudatory attitude often

---

[3] *Twelfth Night,* II, iii, 149.
[4] *Every Man in His Humor,* V, iii.

shown in Elizabethan comedies to the clever trickery of the comic intriguers:

> What deuice should he bring forth now!
> I loue a teeming wit, as I loue my nourishment.[5]

Volpone's enjoyment of Mosca's cleverness will be commented on later in this same chapter.[6]

The reader will further appreciate what mirth and laughter were excited in audiences by the comic employment of deception if he will recall certain hilarious scenes: the tricking of Beatrice and Benedick in *Much Ado about Nothing*, the gulling of Malvolio and the trumped-up duel between Viola-Cesario and Sir Andrew Aguecheek in *Twelfth Night;* the adaptation of this last trick in the playing off of La Foole and Daw against each other in *Epicoene;* the great scene of bluff and double bluff in *All Fools,* in which Gostanzo, who believes himself a crafty manager of other people's business, contributes handsomely to his own gulling; the party at the Blue Anchor Tavern in *Eastward Ho!* at which the usurer Security, who is duped into helping his own wife desert him, pledges with unconscious but with reverberating irony all those who "are going eastward to night towardes Cockolds Haven." Finally, it is not so much the moonlight or the music that sets the dominant tone of the last scene in *The Merchant of Venice* as the merry teasing of Bassanio and Gratiano by their wives over the matter of the rings. This pleasant torturing of their husbands is made possible by the game of deception begun at the trial and here continued by the ladies until they have reduced the men almost to a state of frenzy. It is the spirit of gaiety that rides high at the end of this play, higher even than the romantic mood engendered by the poetry and the music of the last scene. Yet the deliberate trick-

---

[5] *The Alchemist*, V, i, 15-16.
[6] *Infra*, pp. 150-51.

ery of disguises and the consequent mistaken identity are what this gaiety is built upon.

In addition to being made to concur in the heightening of the spirit of fun and merriment, deception was also obliquely used by Elizabethan dramatists to prevent the atmosphere from thickening and a tragic tone from building up in scenes and episodes in which other elements would have combined to produce such an effect. Here again a glance may be given to the *The Merchant of Venice*. It might be thought that the romantic poetry and lighthearted tricks of the final scene were introduced by the author principally in order to ease the tensions and dissipate the tragic atmosphere of the trial scene. It may well be asked, however, whether anything like a really tragic atmosphere was allowed to develop in that previous scene. We have no reason to doubt that the audience was expected to know who the young lawyer and clerk from Padua were. From the moment of Portia's entrance the audience knew the secret kept from all the characters on the stage except the girls. There would be some suspense about how and when Portia would thwart Shylock, but there would be no real doubt on the part of the audience that thwart him she would. Furthermore, even in moments when a modern audience would not be looking for comedy, Shakespeare exploited the comic possibilities of the disguise situation and the deception of the husbands as to the identity of the lawyer and clerk. Just before Antonio bares his breast for the knife, Bassanio and Gratiano protest that they would sacrifice their wives along with everything else dear to them to save Antonio from Shylock's hatred. And immediately comes Portia's dry remark to Bassanio that his wife would give him little thanks for his protestation if she were to hear it—a sentiment echoed by Nerissa. What could an Elizabethan audience do but enjoy this comically ironic situation and laugh when the irony was made explicit by such innuendoes? How, then, could a really tragic atmosphere have a chance to develop?

In this connection *Volpone* comes to mind. It is common experience to find scholars speaking of an element in this play which "trenches on the tragic,"[7] of the serious tone of this play,[8] or of the impression of unlimited possibilities of evil conveyed by the characters.[9] It is possible, however, to overemphasize the tragic or semitragic elements of the play.[10] Indeed, it is hard to see how anything approaching a tragic atmosphere could develop in a work so full of laughter. Yet this laughter is the expression of the pleasure, pervasive and eruptive, taken by Volpone and Mosca in their own cunning. The whole play, of course, is built around deception; and though this deception is a means whereby Volpone secures his victims' money and property and attempts to satisfy his lust, it is his love, nevertheless, of trickery and deception for its own sake that seems to be even more operative than greed or lechery as a motive force. He glories more, he says, in the cunning purchase of his wealth than in its glad possession, since he gains in no common way. Though, too, he is prostrated by the miscarriage of his attempt to bring Celia to his embraces, he is most appreciative of Mosca's ingenuity in extricating him from the consequences of this frustrated attempt. This appreciation is directed, not only toward the release from danger, but to the cleverness itself by which he was saved. In fact, he says he enjoyed the spectacle of his henchman's courtroom maneuvers more than if he himself had succeeded with Celia. "The pleasure of all womankind's not like it" (V, ii, 11). At the beginning of the play, too,

---

[7] Morris, *Studies in Jonson's Comedy*, p. 70.

[8] Schelling, *Elizabethan Drama*, Vol. I, p. 534.

[9] Herford and Simpson, *Ben Jonson*, Vol. II, p. 55.

[10] See Parrott and Ball, *Short View of Elizabethan Drama*, p. 139; Ralph Nash, "The Comic Intent of *Volpone*," *Studies in Philology* 44:26-40, January 1947. Louis Kronenberger finds it difficult to decide whether the play is essentially a comedy or not. See his *The Thread of Laughter: Chapters on English Stage Comedy from Jonson to Maugham*, pp. 28-29 (New York: Alfred A. Knopf, 1952).

Mosca's plying of the dupes makes it difficult for Volpone to contain his "flux of laughter," and the villain must leap out of his bed when Corbaccio has left.

> O, I shall burst;
> Let out my sides, let out my sides—
>
> .   .   .   .   .
>
> O, but thy working, and thy placing it!
> I cannot hold; good rascall, let me kisse thee:
> I neuer knew thee, in so rare a humour (I, iv, 132-38).

So, too, after the disturbing excitement of his first appearance in court he feels the need of some merriment, but he thinks that some device of "rare ingenious knauery" which would possess him with a violent laughter would lift up his spirits again. Therefore he and Mosca set the stage for what they expect will be the final act in the gulling of their dupes. And as Volpone chooses for himself a vantage point from which to view the bouleversement of Voltore, Corbaccio, and Corvino, and tells Mosca to play the artificer and "torture them rarely," any group of spectators will share his gleeful anticipation and will enjoy the same "rare meal of laughter" as they together with him watch his victims squirm and writhe at the revelation of how they have been foxed.

Volpone and Mosca, however, are by no means just jolly knaves with an itch for mischief and a merely incidental interest in other people's money. They are truly malicious. Their villainy, nevertheless, is counteracted, as far as any depressing effect upon the audience is concerned, by their cleverness and by their exuberant enjoyment of their own cleverness. What helps to keep the atmosphere from thickening and the audience from being repelled is the laughter that billows through the play in gusty waves. It is a laughter communicated from Volpone and Mosca to the audience and arising, at least partially, from the interflowing intellectual delight taken by both deceivers and audience in the artful practice of trickery.

It is in this entertainment value of deception as a dramatic and comic element that we may find an approach to a problem which has exercised scholars for many years. It was stated in the discussion in a previous chapter of *Measure for Measure* that a much more functional use was made of the disguised-duke device and its attendant deceptions than had been achieved in other contemporary plays using the same device or similar ones.[11] There is, to be sure, an abundance of deception in *Measure for Measure*, but the question may be asked: How necessary, artistically speaking, was all this trickery? The duke himself calls his devices a physic "that's bitter to sweet end," but the sweet end could have been achieved without all the bitterness of Isabella's grief over her brother's supposed death, without the feigned threatening of the two women, Isabella and Mariana, by the returned duke, and without the suspicion cast upon the "friar," under whose directions they had done all they had done.

Evaluations and explanations of the doubling and redoubling indulged in by the "duke of dark corners" are numerous and diversified. Professor Van Doren feels that the duke mixes matters wantonly and is tortuously slow in putting things to rights.[12] E. K. Chambers looks for the reason of this "superfluous mystification," as he calls it, in the intent of the author, and divines a "satirical intention of Shakespeare towards theories about the moral government of the universe which, for the time being, at least, he does not share." He sees in the duke's part a symbol of the working of Providence, but the treatment is, he says, ironical, and he finds in this play a nascent pessimism which has "advanced to the point of finding ineffectiveness and not deliberate ill will in the ordering of things."[13] Professor

---

[11] *Supra*, pp. 63-64.
[12] Mark Van Doren, *Shakespeare*, p. 218. London: George Allen and Unwin, 1941.
[13] Chambers, *Shakespeare: A Survey*, pp. 215-16.

O. J. Campbell, seeing in this play Shakespeare's second contribution, with original developments, to the new type of "comicall satyre" which Ben Jonson had invented, argues that the duke's manipulation of events is not wanton, but is a means of exposing and humiliating the foolish and evil characters.[14] This theory puts the play in a definite dramatic convention and explains its structure and the function of the duke by reference to that framework. The question may still be asked, however, whether even to lay bare the "ugly scars in Angelo's nature" this excessive exhibition of finesse on the part of the duke, especially in the last scenes, was required. It could have been done as effectively by downright accusation and exposure.

Another explanation, which perhaps is less profound, is here suggested. In the light of the foregoing discussion of the entertainment value of deception it would seem that Shakespeare in the last scenes of *Measure for Measure* was simply catering to the taste of his audience for exhibitions of trickery and artifice in the sort of character who manipulated the strings. The Elizabethans cried out for tricks, devices, and mystifications, and the playwright who knew his clientele as well as did any of his fellow craftsmen was supplying them withal. The yielding to this taste by playwrights often resulted in faulty structure and excrescences, but these excrescences were sometimes highly dramatic in themselves. So too here, at the end of the play, we have an effective scene in which all the threads are gathered together and subjected tantalizingly to even further entanglements before being unknotted and smoothed out. In this process each successive revelation—unhooding, exposure of villainy, and the "resurrection" of Claudio—is withheld till the right moment, so that emotions of humiliation and deep repentance

---

[14] Campbell, *Shakespeare's Satire*, p. 133. For another explanation of the duke's delays based on an examination of the play in the light of contemporary dramatic genres see Murray Krieger, "*Measure for Measure* and Elizabethan Comedy," *PMLA* 66:775-84, September 1951.

are followed by the cry of Isabella's joy and the quickening in the eye of Angelo. There were surprises enough for the *dramatis personae;* but the audience, having knowledge of the underlying deception, had been looking for these all along. This does not mean that the spectators did not enjoy these moments or that the dramatic impact was less. Their pleasure consisted in the anticipation of revelations which they knew were bound to come and also in the very real suspense of wondering just how those revelations were to be made. And when those moments were delayed by the author as long as possible and then sprung at the most effective juncture, the ebullient disclosure was none the less pleasurable because it was anticipated.

It is possible, therefore, to demur at the observation that Shakespeare "might after the dark shadows of the preceding intrigue, have ended *Measure for Measure* as a tragedy, had he so chosen, but he determined that it should close in the spirit of comedy."[15] Dark shadows may have been hanging over the characters of the play, but the spectators could not have been enveloped in those shadows nor could they have been affected by them as they would have been if they were witnessing an ordinary Shakespearean tragedy. They knew almost from the beginning that a protective and guiding figure was lurking benevolently in such shadows as there were, who could dispel them in a moment and who at any rate would in the end see that no disastrous consequences would eventuate. When the audience is aware of such an element all through the play, there is no possibility of sustaining authentic tragic atmosphere.[16]

---

[15] William Witherle Lawrence, *Shakespeare's Problem Comedies*, pp. 117-18. New York: The Macmillan Company, 1931.

[16] Support for this position is found in a brief passage in an article read after the above was written: "It should be noted that the Duke's continuous and assuring presence, demanded by his function as intriguer, does prevent the romantic element from involving too dangerous a situation; we see here how a Jonsonian device helps maintain the play as comedy" (Krieger, *"Measure*

Perhaps it is only by adverting to the existence of the Elizabethan interest and pleasure in the dramatic presentation of
deception that we can approach an explanation of the excessive
exhibition of duplicity by Cleanthes, the intriguer of Chapman's
The Blind Beggar of Alexandria. The chief motive behind most
of his disguises, lies, perjuries, and other knaveries is personal
gain or the satisfaction of his lust; and to the extent that these
deceptions aid him in accomplishing these objectives they may
be considered as having functional uses in the plot. But in that
episode in which he marries two women under two distinct disguises, keeping each wife ignorant that he has another, and
alternately cuckolds himself by seducing wife A in the disguise
in which he is known to wife B and wife B in the disguise in
which he is known to wife A—in that episode it cannot be
merely to satisfy his lust that he doubles and redoubles these
turnings, because he thereby adds no length to the tether of his
roaming passions. All this postulates in him a fund of decep-
tiveness which derives its best satisfaction from the contemplation of its own involutions:

> Oh, this is old excellent!
> Now who can desire better sport?
> This night my other wife must lie alone,
> And next night this wife must do the like.
> Now will I woo the other as the Count,
> Which if she grant, and they do break their troth,
> I'll make myself a cuckold 'twixt them both (v, 139-45).

The mere presentation of such an episode on the Elizabethan
stage is an indication of what the audience could absorb. And

---

for Measure and Elizabethan Comedy," *PMLA* 66:783, September 1951).
A remark by Professor Alfred Harbage about Shakespeare's comic method is
relevant here: "As a rule, in . . . fables destined to end well, the episodes
are treated in a tone befitting the facts as they appear to the audience rather
than as they appear to the characters in the play . . ." (Alfred Harbage,
As They Liked It, p. 135. New York: The Macmillan Company, 1947).

the fact that the spectators could absorb it is itself something of an explanation of why Chapman could offer it to them. This excessive and perverted ingenuity was no doubt interesting to them as an exhibition of virtuosity in trickery.

Another source of audience appeal in the dramatic use of deception on the Elizabethan comic stage was its effectiveness in stimulating an ironic and satiric temper in the spectators. Irony and satire are not, of course, one and the same thing, nor are the terms here used synonymously. Satire, for one thing, can be injected into a literary work without the help of irony, and conversely not all irony need be satirical. A character, for instance, may be placed in an ironical situation and have coruscating verbal ironies playing around his unsuspecting head without being ridiculed by the author or derisively laughed at by the audience. Such is the case with King Oedipus in Sophocles' play of that name. So too the ruefully ironic remarks made about their own predicament by some of Shakespeare's disguised heroines in boys' clothing would not arouse satirical reactions in any audience. Yet irony can be a most effective instrument in the hands of a satirist.

For proof of the existence of a taste for satire among Elizabethan theatergoers the reader must be referred to other works.[17] In these works will also be found fuller illustration both of the general pervasiveness of satire in Elizabethan comedies and of its concentration in the more specialized form of drama known as "comicall satyre." It will be sufficient here to remind the reader of the various tribes of dupes who were paraded on the Elizabethan stage for the delectation of the audience. An undoubted element in this enjoyment would be the pleasure of

---

[17] Schelling, *Elizabethan Drama*, Vol. I, pp. 473-91; Baskervill, *English Elements in Jonson's Early Comedy*, pp. 144-213; Herford and Simpson, *Ben Jonson*, Vol. I, pp. 376-99; Henry W. Wells, *Elizabethan and Jacobean Playwrights*, pp. 189-211 (New York: Columbia University Press, 1939); and the whole of Campbell's *Comicall Satyre*.

recognizing and seeing duped not only types indigenous to contemporary London, such as Puritans, fops, usurers, and foreigners, but also types associated with the life and stage of
many ages and countries, such as dotards, braggarts, and those
with foolish pretensions of all sorts.

Often enough the laughter aroused by the antics and the
embarrassments of such types must have been of the derisive
nature which would indicate a response proper to satire. There
were, of course, a number of ways in which characters could
be made to look ridiculous and their follies made to draw satiric
laughter from the audience. In some cases (as it was with
Stephen and Matthew in *Every Man in His Humor*) they were
merely put into juxtaposition to more normal exemplars of
social traits and behavior, and the resultant contrast was immediately perceptible and laughter-provoking. Sometimes satiric commentators like Malevole *(The Malcontent)*, Hercules
(Parasitaster), and Macilente *(Everyman Out of His Humor)*
by their continuous animadversion made very clear to the audience the desired attitude to be directed to the follies and vices
displayed. Again, the innate emptiness of certain gulls (such
as Slender in *The Merry Wives of Windsor* and Fungoso in
Everyman Out of His Humor) would float to the surface in a
bubbling display of inanity without any active stirring of the
waters by either commentators or tricksters.

Very frequently, however, it was by deliberately contrived
situations, deftly planted booby traps, mischievous intriguing,
that eccentric characters were displayed, "humors" emphasized,
and follies and vices exposed. The initiating and guiding hand
in this particular manner of exhibiting and exposing follies,
humors, and vices would usually be that of the deceiver of the
play. It was by this aspect of their character and this typical activity that such individuals as Lemot, Rinaldo, Maria,
Dulcimel of *Parasitaster*, Brainworm, Mosca, and Face were
used as the agents of their authors' satirical intentions. So too

characters like Macilente and the duke of *Measure for Meas*
in addition to exercising their functions as satiric comment
would sometimes employ trickery to play upon their v
and draw them into situations rich in satiric effects. In
adaptability as an instrument of satire, therefore, lay one o
the sources of audience appeal in the use of deception.

In a number of places throughout this study attention has
already been called both to ironic implications of situations
based on deception and to verbal highlighting of such ironies.
Some of the scenes already mentioned will be here briefly re-
called and a few other examples will be adduced. Since, however, the concept of irony has justly been complained of as
taking as many shapes as the Old Man of the Sea *(Proteusartig)*,
it would be well, before proceeding to the examples, to indicate
clearly the sense in which irony is used here.

Scholars differentiate several species of irony, the foremost
among them being rhetorical, Socratean, and dramatic.[18] Our
concern is with dramatic irony, and this may be described as
"a device whereby incongruity is introduced into the very structure of a play, by having the spectators aware of elements in
the situation of which one or more of the characters involved
are ignorant."[19] Its essential features, therefore, are these: (1) a
discrepancy or incongruity between appearance and reality or
between expectation and event; (2) ignorance of the discrepancy
on the part of at least one of the characters; (3) awareness of
the discrepancy by the spectators.[20] All of these features may
be found not only in tragic situations but in comic situations as

[18] G. G. Sedgewick, *Of Irony, Especially in Drama*, second edition, pp. 3-27
(Toronto: University of Toronto, 1948) ; Alan Reynolds Thompson, *The Dry
Mock: A Study of Irony in Drama*, pp. 5-12 (Berkeley and Los Angeles:
University of California Press, 1948).

[19] Joseph T. Shipley, editor, Dictionary of World Literature, article "Irony." New
York: The Philosophical Library, 1943.

[20] See Thompson, *The Dry Mock*, p. 10; Sedgewick, *Of Irony*, pp. 48-49.

well and may be productive of comic effects, in which case we have comic irony. Now, discrepancies and incongruities are everywhere; but what we normally call irony is a striking discrepancy, one which is artfully arranged to draw attention to itself, or which, though occurring by chance, likewise compels our notice.[21]

One of the most effective means of making the irony of a situation manifest itself is the use of verbal irony; that is, ambiguous language which can be used either innocently by the character ignorant of the true nature of his predicament or with knowledge and intention by a character who, together with the audience, is aware of the reality as well as of the appearances of the situation.[22]

The specific objective of this part of our study is to illustrate the precise relationship existing between irony and deception. As has been noted, an essential feature of irony is the ignorance on the part of at least one character of the real state of affairs. Now, this ignorance may be the result of any one of a number of causes. It may result from an accidental arrangement of circumstances, such as happens in a situation based merely on mistaken identity, in which nobody tries actively to deceive anyone else. This is the genesis of the ignorance upon which most of the farcical complications in *The Comedy of Errors* are founded. Secondly, the ignorance may be induced by the self-deception of the victim himself. Finally, the ignorance may be directly caused by the active and positive tricking of one character by another. Deception, therefore, is one of the means by which irony may be introduced into a play, and in this use of

---

[21] See Thompson, *ibid.*

[22] Of the first kind there are famous instances in Sophocles' *Oedipus Tyrannus* and of the second kind examples are to be found in the speeches of Clytemnestra as she welcomes home her husband in Aeschylus' *Agamemnon*. See J. A. K. Thomson, *Irony: An Historical Introduction*, pp. 56-68 (London: George Allen and Unwin, 1926); Sedgewick, *Of Irony*, pp. 62-68.

deception in effecting irony and stimulating an ironic response in the spectators lies one of its sources of audience appeal.

This calls for illustration. In a sense all situations in which some characters are deceived by others or act as unwitting instruments in the deception of others, or in which characters cooperate in their own duping, are at least latently ironical because they are situations in which a character acts in ignorance of his true condition whereas the real state of affairs is understood by the audience. (If of course the audience is not informed of the deception, there is no irony.) But only situations in which the discrepancy "leaps to the eye" will be cited.

There is the "biter bit" situation in Middleton's *A Mad World, My Masters* in which Follywit, who has been gulling his grandfather all through the play, takes to wife a woman who deludes him into thinking her a virgin but who is his grandfather's castoff mistress. The pleasure of the audience at this juncture would be greatly enhanced by such bits of verbal irony as the following ecstatic remarks by Follywit:

> Those bashful maiden humours take me prisoner. . . . Give me a woman as she was made at first; simple of herself, without sophistication, like this wench: I cannot abide them when they have tricks, set speeches, and artful entertainments (IV, v, 55-63).[23]

He is at the very moment being effectually tied hand and foot by just such tricks and artful entertainments.

Irony is to be detected in the whole movement of Middleton's *A Trick To Catch the Old One*, in which two covetous old rivals, Hoard and Lucre, are seen sedulously busy in their efforts to trick each other and young Witgood—efforts which are directed by Witgood to their undoing.[24] Each of them prides himself on

---

[23] Further examples of verbal irony in this play may be found in I, ii, 30-45; I, ii, 155-66; III, ii, 252; V, i, 51-54.

[24] For a discussion of this play from another aspect see *supra*, pp. 87-89.

making use of Witgood and the "widow" as a means of distressing the other and increasing his own wealth, while Witgood and the "widow" (who is his penniless mistress) are actually using the greed and mutual animosity of the old men as an instrument in victimizing both of them. Therefore, though the last line in the play is not ironical, since Hoard, who speaks it, has at last had his eyes opened, it ruefully sums up the ironical burden of the whole play: "Who seem most crafty prove ofttimes most fools."

In addition to this pervasive irony in *A Trick To Catch the Old One* there are incidental bits of verbal irony which serve both to emphasize the irony of the situation and to remind the audience of the core of deception around which it is built. In that scene where Lucre first learns of his nephew's reputed hopes of marrying a rich widow, he thinks he is cleverly pumping a servant of the lady's and drawing out of him a secret which his nephew does not wish revealed. Lucre does not know, however, that this "servant" is really Witgood's tool (the host), sent expressly to feed the uncle this information without letting him realize how anxious they are to have him get it. Lucre's assumption of superior adroitness at the very moment he is being drawn by the "servant" toward a trap is emphasized by such lines as his complacent asides: "A good, blunt honesty"; "A simple country fellow—I'll work't out of him" (II, i, 30 and 62-63).

When the "widow" is approached by the other victim, Hoard, with a proposal of marriage, she favors him with a timid and apprehensive sigh: "The world is so deceitful!" (III, i, 211). She is assured that there is no deceit in this wooer; and the irony of the situation lies in the fact that, though he thinks he is deceiving her as to how full of guile he is, she is entirely aware of his intentions, whereas he does not know that she who gives utterance to such womanly apprehension is even now ensnaring him in a mesh that will hold him for life.

The best bit of comic irony in the play, and perhaps in all of Middleton, occurs in the scene where Hoard in self-congratulating anticipation of a rich match comes to a tavern to meet the "widow" who has promised to run off with him and marry him. Upon inquiring if a gentlewoman has put in an appearance, he is informed by a merry waiter that none has come in yet but a "Dutch widow." This is a new phrase to the old fellow; and being in high spirits over outwitting as he be-lieves, his enemy and Witgood, he asks what a Dutch widow might be. "That's an English drab, sir," replies the drawer, and the prospective bridegroom is tickled with this new bit of learn-ing. "I shall remember a Dutch widow the longest day of my life," he tells his friend with a laugh (III, iii, 20), and one can readily imagine the roar of laughter that must have come from the Elizabethan audience at that remark. Hoard would certainly have occasion to remember that phrase. His statement is loaded with a delayed-action fuse which will detonate only when he discovers that he himself has married an English drab and a penniless one at that. In that illuminating moment the phrase of the merry drawer pops before his mind's eye like a death's head on a spring and he hops around in a fury of frustration, howl-ing: "A Dutch widow! a Dutch widow! a Dutch widow!" (V, ii, 108).

Irony is also to be seen in the situation of those whose self-deception provides the occasion or the opening for the active wiles of deceivers. Such, for example, are Gostanzo of Chap-man's *All Fools*, Gonzago of Marston's *Parasitaster*, and Mal-volio. At the root of Gostanzo's plight are his conception of himself as a clever man of the world who knows both how to bring up his own son and how to manage other people's affairs, and his contempt for his neighbor, Marc Antonio, because of the latter's apparent lack of such excellencies.[25] The clash be-

---

[25] See *supra*, pp. 76-78.

tween this view of himself and reality is frequently lit up by
such verbal ironies as the following vaunt made in the presence
of Marc Antonio:

> As you have usd him [Marc Antonio's son], therefore, so you
>   have him.
> Durst my son thus turn rebel to his duty,
>
> .   .   .   .   .
>
> Durst my son serve me thus?[26]

And the audience knows, of course, that his son jolly well does
dare to serve him thus. The son is not quite the "tame and
thrifty" fellow his father believes him to be. No more is needed
here than reference to the discussion of Marston's *Parasitaster*
in a previous chapter, in which the irony of Gonzago's self-
deception and hoodwinking by his daughter have been adum-
brated.[27] As for Malvolio, it will be sufficient merely to advert
to the ringing overtones of irony in "Some are born great, some
achieve greatness, and some have greatness thrust upon them."
Though these are not his own words originally, Malvolio applies
them to himself with a readiness and an assurance entirely fore-
seen and counted upon by Maria. Here is self-deception being
worked upon by a clever deceiver with devastating effect.

Shakespeare draws much comic irony out of disguise situations. As a single example there may be mentioned the running
and ironical game of cat-and-mouse played at odd moments
throughout *Measure for Measure* by the disguised duke with the
loose-tongued Lucio, who finally takes upon himself to unhood
the "friar" and in that moment discovers which of the two of
them is the mouse. For further illustration of irony and disguise
situations in Shakespeare the reader is referred to Victor Oscar
Freeburg's monograph.[28]

---

[26] *All Fools*, II, i, 5-10.
[27] *Supra*, pp. 78-81.
[28] Freeburg, *Disguise Plots*, pp. 76-78.

For an example of irony arising out of a disguise situation in Ben Jonson's work we may turn to *The Devil Is an Ass.* The minor devil, Pug, who has been granted a day upon earth to work mischief and who has been masquerading as a servant in the household of Fitzdottrel, the chief gull of the play, offers to extricate Fitzdottrel from a bad situation. In practically the only moment in the play when Fitzdottrel is not being gulled by someone, he rejects the proffered help with scornful unbelief.

> You most infernall counterfeit wretch! Avaunt!
> Do you thinke to gull me with your Aesops Fables?
>
> .   .   .   .
>
>   Like a lying raskall
> Told me he was the *Diuel* (V, v, 29-34).

As an illustration of Chapman's use of irony in disguise situations, the following may be quoted from his *May Day:*

> Twenty to one she is some honest man's wife of the parish, that steals abroad for a trimming, while he sits secure at home, little knowing, God knows, what hangs over his head, the poor cuckold esteeming her the most virtuous wife in the world. And should one tell him he had seen her dressed like a page, following a knave thus, I'll lay my life he would not believe it (IV, iv, 17-23).

These half-amused, half-somber reflections of Quintiliano, who does not know that the disguised page he perceives to be a woman is his own wife, are more pertinently applicable to him and to his wife than he realizes.

Dupes are often made to give utterance to smug appreciations of themselves and their cleverness at the very moment they are being hoodwinked or just before they are to discover they have been ensnared. *"Fallere fallentem non est fraus,"*[29] is

---

[29] An apt translation of this phrase is furnished by the title of a lost play of Henry Chettle's, *'Tis No Deceit To Deceive the Deceiver.* See Harbage's *Annals of English Drama* under date of 1598.

Throat's comment in *Ram-Alley* about his own cleverness at the
moment he is actually being outwitted by the one he thinks he
is deceiving.[30] And not long before his eyes are opened he exults
with the anticipation of the affluence he believes his chicanery
has won him:

> I now in pompe will ride, for 'tis most fit,
> He should haue state that riseth by his wit (III, i, 1513-14).[31]

Finally, there is Bassiolo's complacency when he is being
adroitly used, in Chapman's *The Gentleman Usher*, as a mere
instrument by Margaret and her lover:

> For he that cannot turn and wind a woman
> Like silk about his finger is no man (III, ii, 372-73).

These examples should suffice to illustrate the relationship
between deception and irony. Deception is one of the means by
which irony may be introduced into a play, and it is this added
value, this ironic bloom upon a comic situation, that constitutes
one of the sources of audience appeal in the use of deception.
Irony, however, is not only an effect of deception; it reciprocally
serves to emphasize the functional significance of deception by
sharpening the audience's awareness of both the discrepancies
in the situation and of the victim's ignorance of them. The
result, of course, will be a heightening in the audience of the
sense of the ridiculous. For further indication of the possible
effect of comic irony upon the Elizabethan audience a description of the effect of comic irony upon an ancient Roman audience may be pressed into service:

> The effects of this comic irony range all the way from what
> Aristotle terms educated insolence (πεπαιδευμένη ὕβρις) to
> genial and sympathetic fellow-feeling, according as the victim

---

30 Hazlitt, *Collection of Old English Plays*, Vol. X, p. 302.
31 *Ibid.*, p. 335 (end of Act III).

of the delusion is a villain, a braggart, a buffoon, or a harmless innocent. The foreknowledge which the audience has of
what the players are unconsciously stumbling into provides
both the "sense of superiority," which Plato found to be an
effect of comedy, and the enjoyment of the incongruous which
moderns have often considered its chief ingredient.[32]

We can with perfect justice apply to the sort of writing
which has been analyzed in the foregoing pages the tribute half
grudgingly accorded the metaphysical poets by Dr. Johnson,
that to write in this manner, it was at least necessary to think.
And conversely, it might with equal justice be said of the audience for which this sort of thing was written that to enjoy it, it
was at least necessary to be mentally alert. Chapman and
Middleton and Jonson and Shakespeare and the other Elizabethans who made definite efforts to achieve comic irony must
have expected their audience to be on the *qui vive* and they
must have found that they were, or they would not have continued writing in this way.

---

[32] Tenney Frank, *Life and Literature in the Roman Republic*, p. 111. (Sather
Classical Lectures, Vol. VII.) Berkeley: University of California Press, 1930.

CHAPTER VIII

Conclusion

This study took its rise from the desire to discover whether the tricks and stratagems, the presence of which in Elizabethan comedy any reader will at least occasionally notice, were in large part no more than episodic and disconnected jokes or booby traps, and had no more functional use than to provide merely incidental entertainment. "Deception," the concept and term used to bring to focus the subject to be studied, is, it is true, rather abstract; but the subject was found susceptible of concrete treatment in a series of converging approaches. The agents of deception, their characteristics and their ways of operating; the several types of victims and their contribution to the action; the checks and reversals to trains of deception; the multiplicity and variety of the tricks themselves; the reasons for the appeal to the Elizabethan audiences in all this contriving and its estimated effects upon those audiences—all of these facets of the subject, when submitted to scrutiny, not only revealed the ubiquity of deception in Elizabethan comedies but also furnished enough evidence to warrant the conclusion that deception was put in those comedies to a number of definitely structural and functional uses. In order to arrive at a summary of those functions and to see what the upshot of the whole investigation is, it will be profitable to cast a reflective eye over the more significant observations made in the course of the work.

167

Analysis of the objectives and methods of the agents of deception in Elizabethan comedy showed that those characters were by no means as stereotyped or conventionalized as were the deceivers of other times and stages, such as the classical tricky slave and the medieval Vice. Yet all the members of the different categories of deceivers here discussed employed deception to gain their ends; and if guile and deceitfulness did not constitute the most salient trait of each and every one of them, it was mainly by deception, nevertheless, that they maneuvered their way through the plays, manipulated the other characters, and contributed materially to the dramatic movement of the plot. Thus the starting of a train of deception by an arch-deceiver, the momentary embarrassments, checks, and obstacles he ran into, the countermovements his activities stimulated, the successful outcome or the final frustration he met with, supplied not only much of the story material but the forward movement from situation to situation, the exciting incident, the complication, and often enough the denouement of many an Elizabethan comedy. The deceiver, too, was often operative in grouping other characters and getting them on and off stage, in displaying and exposing them and in inducing changes in them. Functioning in these ways, the agents of deception manifested, despite individual variations, certain archetypal resemblances in character traits and in behavior.

So too, in turning to the victims: no observer could fail to note what variety of feather fluttered through that comic aviary of Elizabethan gulls, woodcocks, and dotterels; and discrimination was carefully made in these pages between the several kinds of ways in which they were deceived. Nevertheless, it became apparent that the characteristic manner in which most dupes definitely furthered the dramatic movement of plays was their active cooperation, in varying degrees, in their own duping. In the course of this cooperation they betrayed the fact that they were not all equally foolish. The discovery of this divergence brought to the fore an interesting problem. The question arose whether any correspondence was observable in Elizabethan comedy between the degree of intelligence shown by the one deceived and the facility with which he was actually deluded. Was less ingenuity displayed by a deceiver in gulling a ninny than in outfoxing a cunning opponent? An examination of the plays provided a definite no as answer to this question, and the significance of the answer seemed to be that what determined the degree of difficulty experienced by a deceiver and the amount of trickery exhibited by him was the Elizabethan author's desire to satisfy both the exigencies of his plot and the interest of contemporary audiences in trickery for its own sake. Hence it may be inferred that in this aspect, at least, of such situations the Elizabethan comic dramatist did not attempt a realistic approach to the conditions of a corresponding situation in real life.

Just as unifying elements, in other aspects of this study, were found in the midst of variety, so too in the cataloguing of the diversified profusion of dodges and devices employed by tricksters the outlines of a pattern emerged, and the result was a design which revealed the different degrees of fullness with which a deceiver could identify himself with the means of deception he was using. The mere number and diversity of the devices catalogued also added to the growing impression of what an astonishing amount of the action of Elizabethan comedies, even of romantic comedies, moved through situations of deceiving and being deceived.

When an attempt was made to determine wherein lay the appeal to Elizabethan audiences in all this deceiving and being deceived, the answer seemed to be that what attracted the Elizabethans were certain dramatic values and comic effects which were inherent in deception as a dramatic element or achieved by means of its help. One of these values was the attractiveness of deception as machinery of intrigue. As the Elizabethan age progressed, this value was injected by writers into their comedies in intensifying complexity in order to cater to the increasingly sophisticated interest on the part of the audience in seeing dramatic conflict work itself out in deception.

One does not have to subscribe without reservation to Brunetière's conflict theory of drama to admit that conflict does play a large part in dramatic representation. Now, it should be apparent from this study that one of the most prevalent means by which conflicting forces get under way and move through complications into climax and resolution in Elizabethan comedy is trickery. Boy wants to marry girl; rogue tries to get his hands on someone else's property; mischief-maker sets out to stir up hilarious trouble; exhibitors and exposers seek to draw their victims into prolonged display of their follies or betrayal of their vices; enviers move malevolently toward their designs— and all meet with obstacles, of one kind or another, to their will and intention. And the most common manner and means in Elizabethan comedy of moving toward objectives and circumventing obstacles are indirection, trickery, deception. The obstacles themselves are often the product of deception on the part of adversaries, and the adversaries are beaten by being outwitted, and they are outwitted by a more effective employment of deception than they themselves are able to bring to bear. Consequently, if conflict be essential to drama, or at any rate an important element in it, then deception, as far as Elizabethan comedy is concerned, is conflict's most pervasive and most dynamic manner and medium of operation.

Deception also appealed to the audience as an exercise in intellectual wit, an exhibition of virtuosity in trickery interesting for its own sake. This interest was brought to focus on the chief deceivers, whose special talents seemed to fascinate not only the audience but the playwrights, who sometimes highlighted such characters beyond the demands of their original function of manipulating the intrigue. Trickery furthermore appealed to the audience in that it served to heighten the spirit of mirth and laughter in a play and at times to lighten the atmosphere of comedies which might otherwise tend toward a tragic mood.

Another source of audience appeal in the dramatic use of deception was its effectiveness in stimulating an ironic and satiric temper. This reaction, elicited chiefly by witnessing from the superior station of informed spectators the predicaments of the victims of deception, was an emotional and intellectual satisfaction by no means peculiar to Elizabethan audiences. Certainly, the audiences that witnessed the productions of Plautus (if not Terence) must have extracted great pleasure and perhaps some profit from ironical situations based upon deception. The same kind of pleasure must have been felt by the respective audiences at a typical performance of the *commedia dell' arte* and at a showing of any one of a number of Molière's comedies, as well as by the patrons of English comedy down through the Restoration.

Consideration of this appeal of deception to audiences of the past naturally stimulates curiosity as to whether audiences of today are as attracted toward this sort of thing as were those earlier audiences. One way of finding out the answer to this question would be to examine the comedies that are being written for them and have been written for them in the past twenty or thirty years. Is trickery, for instance, employed nowadays as an element of plot structure? Is there such a thing in comedy anymore as "gull for gull, and wits at war with wits"? What has been put into modern plays in the nature of comic irony and to what extent is comic irony introduced by means of deception? Are modern audiences ever granted the spectacle of unwary but supremely confident dupes following each other in sapient sequence into the jaws of traps laid for them by their natural enemies, the clever and the witty, to ancient ancestors of whom past audiences have with genial perversity given their sympathy and their plaudits?

To answer these questions would, of course, require a study by itself. This can now be said, at any rate, that if there be any interest in the dramatic uses of deception in modern comedy, it certainly cannot compare with the interest in it shown by the Elizabethans. They liked it and looked for it, and it was given to them in abundance. In its abundance it served as the very stuff of incident, episode, and story, as machinery and framework of dramatic action, and as instrument in the display of character and in the production of such dramatic values as gaiety, satire, irony, and the sparkle of intellectual virtuosity.

A. Dramatic Texts[1]

Abrams, William Amos, editor. *The Merry Devil of Edmonton—1608, And a Reprint of The Life and Death of the Merry Devil of Edmonton, by T. B., 1631.* Durham: The Duke University Press, 1942.

Amyot, Thomas, and others, editors. *A Supplement to Dodsley's Old Plays.* 4 vols. London: Shakespeare Society, 1853.

Barry, Lording. *Ram-Alley or Merrie-Trickes—A Comedy by Lording Barry,* edited by Claude E. Jones. (Materials for the Study of the Old English Drama, Vol. XXIII.) Louvain: Uystpruyst, 1952.

Beaumont, Francis, and Fletcher, John. *The Works of Francis Beaumont and John Fletcher,* edited by Arnold Glover and A. R. Waller. 10 vols. Cambridge: Cambridge University Press, 1905-1912.

Bond, R. Warwick, editor. *The Birth of Hercules.* (Malone Society Reprints.) London: Malone Society, 1911.

———, editor. *Early Plays from the Italian.* London: Oxford University Press, 1911.

Brooke, C. F. Tucker, editor. *Common Conditions.* (Elizabethan Club Reprints, No. 1.) New Haven: Yale University Press; London: Oxford University Press, 1915.

———, editor. *The Shakespeare Apocrypha.* London: Oxford University Press, 1908.

Chapman, George. *The Plays and Poems of George Chapman: The Comedies,* edited by Thomas Marc Parrott. London: George Routledge and Sons; New York: E. P. Dutton and Company, 1914.

---

[1] Anonymous plays and collections of plays by miscellaneous authors are listed under names of editors or compilers.

173

174 Deception in Elizabethan Comedy

Chettle, Henry; Day, John; and (?) Haughton, William. *The Blind Beggar of Bednall Green*, edited by W. Bang. (Materialien zur Kunde des älteren englischen Dramas, Vol. I.) Louvain: Uystpruyst, 1902.

Clarke, F. W., and Greg, W. W., editors. *The Comedy of George a Green—1599*. (Malone Society Reprints.) London: Malone Society, 1911.

Day, John. *Law Tricks—1608*, edited by John Crow and W. W. Greg. (Malone Society Reprints.) London: Malone Society, 1950.

Dekker, Thomas. *The Dramatic Works of Thomas Dekker*, edited by Fredson Bowers. Vol. I. Cambridge: Cambridge University Press, 1953. (Only the first volume of this edition has been published thus far. It is anticipated that the edition will contain four volumes when completed.)

Farmer, John S., editor. *Five Anonymous Plays*, Fourth Series. London: Early English Drama Society, 1908.

Field, Nathan. *The Plays of Nathan Field*, edited by William Peery. Austin: The University of Texas Press, 1950.

Gascoigne, George. *The Complete Works of George Gascoigne*, edited by John W. Cunliffe. 2 vols. Cambridge: Cambridge University Press, 1907-1910.

Gayley, Charles Mills, and Thaler, Alwin, editors. *Representative English Comedies*. 4 vols. New York: The Macmillan Company, 1903-1936.

Greg, W. W., editor. *The Weakest Goeth to the Wall—1600*. (Malone Society Reprints.) London: Malone Society, 1913.

———, editor. *Wily Beguiled—1606*. (Malone Society Reprints.) London: Malone Society, 1913.

———, editor. *The Wit of a Woman—1604*. (Malone Society Reprints.) London: Malone Society, 1913.

Haughton, William. *William Haughton's Englishmen for My Money or A Woman Will Have Her Will*, edited by Albert Croll Baugh. Philadelphia: no publ., 1917.

Hazlitt, W. Carew, editor. *A Select Collection of Old English Plays Originally Published by Robert Dodsley in the Year 1744*, fourth edition. 15 vols. London: Reeves and Turner, 1874-1876.

Heywood, Thomas. *The Dramatic Works of Thomas Heywood.* 6 vols. London: John Pearson, 1874.

Horne, Herbert P., and others, editors. *Nero and Other Plays.* (The Mermaid Series.) London: T. Fisher Unwin; New York: Charles Scribner's Sons, n.d.

Jonson, Ben. *Ben Jonson,* edited by C. H. Herford, Percy Simpson, and Evelyn Simpson. 11 vols. London: Oxford University Press, 1925-1952.

Leishman, J. B., editor. *The Three Parnassus Plays.* London: Ivor Nicholson and Watson, 1949.

Lyly, John. *The Complete Works of John Lyly,* edited by R. Warwick Bond. 3 vols. London: Oxford University Press, 1902.

Manly, John Matthews, editor. *Specimens of the Pre-Shakespearean Drama.* 2 vols. Boston: Ginn and Company, 1897.

Marston, John. *The Plays of John Marston,* edited by H. Harvey Wood. 3 vols. Edinburgh and London: Oliver and Boyd, 1934-1939.

Middleton, Thomas. *The Works of Thomas Middleton,* edited by A. H. Bullen. 8 vols. London: J. C. Nimmo, 1885-1886.

Plautus, Titus Maccius. *T. Macci Plavti Comoediae,* edited by W. M. Lindsay. 2 vols. London: Oxford University Press, 1904-1905.

Shakespeare, William. *The Complete Works of Shakespeare,* edited by George Lyman Kittredge. Boston: Ginn and Company, 1936.

Sharpham, Edward. *The Fleire,* edited by Hunold Nibbe. (Materialien zur Kunde des älteren englischen Dramas, Vol. XXXVI.) Louvain: Uystpruyst, 1912.

Simpson, Percy, editor. *Fidele and Fortunio—The Two Italian Gentlemen.* (Malone Society Reprints.) London: Malone Society, 1910.

Skelton, John. *Magnyfycence, a Moral Play by John Skelton,* edited by Robert Lee Ramsay. (Early English Text Society, Extra Series, No. 98.) London: Kegan Paul, Trench, Trubner and Company, 1906.

Spencer, Hazelton, editor. *Elizabethan Plays.* Boston: D. C. Heath and Company, 1933.

Terence, Publius. *P. Terenti Afri Comoediae,* edited by Robert Kauer and Wallace M. Lindsay. London: Oxford University Press, 1926.

Webster, John. *The Dramatic Works of John Webster,* edited by William Hazlitt. 4 vols. London: John Russell Smith, 1857.

Wood, A. C., editor. *The Cobler's Prophecy—1594.* (Malone Society Reprints.) London: Malone Society, 1914.

B. Historical and Critical Works

Alleman, Gellert S. *Matrimonial Law and the Materials of Restoration Comedy.* Wallingford: The Author, 1942.

Aydelotte, Frank. *Elizabethan Rogues and Vagabonds.* (Oxford Historical and Literary Studies, Vol. I.) London: Oxford University Press, 1913.

Balch, Marson S. *The Dramatic Legacy of Thomas Middleton.* Unpublished dissertation, Harvard University, 1931.

Baldwin, Thomas Whitfield. *Shakespeare's Five-Act Structure: Shakespeare's Early Plays on the Background of Renaissance Theories of Five-Act Structure from 1470.* Urbana: The University of Illinois Press, 1947.

Baskervill, Charles Read. *English Elements in Jonson's Early Comedy.* (Bulletin of the University of Texas, No. 178; Humanistic Series, No. 12; Studies in English, No. 1.) Austin: The University of Texas, 1911.

Brooke, C. F. Tucker. *The Tudor Drama: A History of English National Drama to the Retirement of Shakespeare.* Boston: Houghton Mifflin Company, 1911.

Campbell, Oscar James. *Comicall Satyre and Shakespeare's Troilus and Cressida.* San Marino: Henry E. Huntington Library and Art Gallery, 1938.

——— *Shakespeare's Satire.* London and New York: Oxford University Press, 1943.

Chambers, E. K. *The Elizabethan Stage.* 4 vols. London: Oxford University Press, 1923.

——— *Shakespeare: A Survey.* London: Sidgwick and Jackson, 1925.

Chandler, Frank Wadleigh. *The Literature of Roguery.* 2 vols. Boston: Houghton Mifflin Company, 1907.

Charlton, H. B. *Shakespearean Comedy.* New York: The Macmillan Company, 1938.

Christian, Mildred Gayler. *Non-Dramatic Sources for the Rogues in Middleton's Plays.* Chicago: University of Chicago Libraries, 1936.

Creizenach, Wilhelm. *English Drama in the Age of Shakespeare,* translated by Cécile Hugon. London: Sidgwick and Jackson, 1916.

Cushman, L. W. *The Devil and the Vice in the English Dramatic Literature before Shakespeare.* (Studien zur englischen Philologie, Hft. VI.) Halle: Max Niemeyer, 1900.

Dilley, M. Evelyn. *The Parasite: A Study in Dramatic Development.* Unpublished dissertation, University of Chicago, 1924.

Doran, Madeleine. *Endeavors of Art: A Study of Form in Elizabethan Drama.* Madison: The University of Wisconsin Press, 1954.

Draper, John W. "Mistaken Identity in Shakespeare's Comedies." *Revue anglo-américaine* 11:289-97, avril 1934.

Duckworth, George E. *The Nature of Roman Comedy: A Study in Popular Entertainment.* Princeton: Princeton University Press, 1952.

Dunkel, Wilbur Dwight. "The Authorship of *The Puritan.*" *PMLA* 45:804-08, September 1930.

———— *The Dramatic Technique of Thomas Middleton in His Comedies of London Life.* Chicago: University of Chicago Libraries, 1925.

Ellis-Fermor, Una. *The Jacobean Drama,* second edition. London: Methuen and Company, 1947.

Evans, Viola Mitchell. *Self-Deception in the Plays of Six Comic Dramatists.* Unpublished dissertation, University of California, 1935.

Forsythe, Robert Stanley. *The Relations of Shirley's Plays to the Elizabethan Drama.* (Columbia University Studies in English and Comparative Literature, No. 48.) New York: Columbia University Press, 1914.

Frank, Tenney. *Life and Literature in the Roman Republic.* (Sather Classical Lectures, Vol. VII.) Berkeley: University of California Press, 1930.

Freeburg, Victor Oscar. *Disguise Plots in Elizabethan Drama: A Study in Stage Tradition.* (Columbia University Studies in English and Comparative Literature, No. 51.) New York: Columbia University Press, 1915.

Gordon, George. *Shakespearean Comedy and Other Studies.* London: Oxford University Press, 1944.

Harbage, Alfred. *Annals of English Drama—975-1700.* Philadelphia: University of Pennsylvania Press, 1940.

Harbage, Alfred. *As They Liked It.* New York: The Macmillan Company, 1947.

———— *Shakespeare's Audience.* New York: Columbia University Press, 1941.

Herrick, Marvin T. *Comic Theory in the Sixteenth Century.* Urbana: The University of Illinois Press, 1950.

Heseler, Maria. *Studien zur Figur des Gratioso bei Lope de Vega und Vorgängern.* Hildesheim: Franz Borgemeyer, 1933.

Hough, J. N. "The Understanding of Intrigue: A Study in Plautine Chronology." *American Journal of Philology* 60:422-35, 1939.

Howell, James. *The Rogue in English Comedy to 1642.* Unpublished dissertation, University of North Carolina, 1941.

———— *The Rogue in Non-Dramatic English Literature to Robert Greene.* Unpublished thesis, University of North Carolina, 1931.

Hyde, Mary Crapo. *Playwriting for Elizabethans—1600-1605.* (Columbia University Studies in English and Comparative Literature, No. 167.) New York: Columbia University Press, 1949.

Jenkins, Antoinette S. *The Jealous Husband in the Plays of Chapman, B. Jonson, Heywood, and Shakespeare.* Unpublished thesis, University of North Carolina, 1928.

Judges, A. V., editor. *The Elizabethan Underworld.* London: George Routledge and Sons, 1930.

Kreider, Paul V. *Elizabethan Comic Character Conventions as Revealed in the Comedies of George Chapman.* (University of Michigan Publications in Language and Literature, Vol. XVII.) Ann Arbor: The University of Michigan Press, 1935.

Krieger, Murray. "*Measure for Measure* and Elizabethan Comedy." *PMLA* 66:775-84, September 1951.

Kronenberger, Louis. *The Thread of Laughter: Chapters on English Stage Comedy from Jonson to Maugham.* New York: Alfred A. Knopf, 1952.

Lawrence, William J. *Pre-Restoration Stage Studies.* Cambridge: Harvard University Press, 1927.

Lawrence, William Witherle. *Shakespeare's Problem Comedies.* New York: The Macmillan Company, 1931.

Lea, K. M. *Italian Popular Comedy.* 2 vols. London: Oxford University Press, 1934.

Legrand, Philippe E. *The New Greek Comedy*, translated by James Loeb. London: William Heinemann, 1917.

McCloskey, John C. "The Plot Device of False Report." *Shakespeare Association Bulletin* 21:147-58, 1946.

Michaut, Gustave Marie. *Histoire de la comédie romaine: Plaute.* 2 vols. Paris: E. de Boccard, 1920.

Milligan, Burton Alviere. *Rogue Types and Roguery in Tudor and Stuart Literature.* Unpublished dissertation, Northwestern University, 1939.

Morris, Elizabeth Woodbridge. *Studies in Jonson's Comedy.* (Yale Studies in English, No. 5.) Boston: Lamson, Wolffe, and Company, 1898.

Mueschke, Paul, and Fleisher, Jeanette. "Jonsonian Elements in the Comic Underplot of *Twelfth Night.*" *PMLA* 48:722-40, September 1933.

Nash, Ralph. "The Comic Intent of *Volpone.*" *Studies in Philology* 44:26-40, January 1947.

Parrott, Thomas Marc. *Shakespearean Comedy.* New York: Oxford University Press, 1949.

———— and Ball, Robert Hamilton. *A Short View of Elizabethan Drama.* New York: Charles Scribner's Sons, 1943.

Raphael, Maxwell I. *The Lover's Helper: Studies in the Development of a Literary Type.* Unpublished dissertation, Harvard University, 1937.

Reinhardstöttner, Karl von. *Plautus: Spätere Bearbeitungen Plautinischer Lustspiele.* Leipzig: W. Friedrich, 1886.

Schell, Jack Steward. *The Gull as a Type Character in the Plays of G. Chapman, B. Jonson, and Shakespeare.* Unpublished thesis, University of Southern California, 1933.

Schelling, Felix E. *Elizabethan Drama—1558-1642.* 2 vols. Boston: Houghton Mifflin Company, 1908.

Schild, Erich. *Die dramaturgische Rolle der Sklaven bei Plautus und Terenz.* Basel: Hirzen, 1917.

Sedgewick, G. G. *Of Irony, Especially in Drama,* second edition. Toronto: University of Toronto, 1948.

Sedgwick, W. B. "The History of a Latin Comedy." *Review of English Studies* 3:346-49, July 1927.

Shipley, Joseph T., editor. Dictionary of World Literature. New York: The Philosophical Library, 1943.

Snuggs, Henry L. "The Comic Humours: A New Interpretation." *PMLA* 62:114-22, March 1947.

Sprague, Arthur Colby. *Shakespeare and the Audience: A Study in the Technique of Exposition*. Cambridge: Harvard University Press, 1935.

Stoll, Elmer Edgar. "Shakespeare, Marston, and the Malcontent Type." *Modern Philology* 3:281-303, January 1906.

Stonex, Arthur Bivens. "The Usurer in Elizabethan Drama." *PMLA* 31:190-210, 1916.

Thompson, Alan Reynolds. *The Dry Mock: A Study of Irony in Drama*. Berkeley and Los Angeles: University of California Press, 1948.

Thomson, J. A. K. *Irony: An Historical Introduction*. London: George Allen and Unwin, 1926.

Thorndike, Ashley H. *English Comedy*. New York: The Macmillan Company, 1929.

Van Doren, Mark. *Shakespeare*. London: George Allen and Unwin, 1941.

Vandiver, E. P., Jr. "The Elizabethan Dramatic Parasite." *Studies in Philology* 32:411-27, July 1935.

Ward, A. W. *A History of English Dramatic Literature to the Death of Queen Anne*. 3 vols. London: Macmillan and Company, 1899.

Wells, Henry W. *Elizabethan and Jacobean Playwrights*. New York: Columbia University Press, 1939.

Wieand, Helen E. *Deception in Plautus: A Study in the Technique of Roman Comedy*. Boston: Richard G. Badger, 1920.

Withington, Robert W. " 'Vice' and 'Parasite': A Note on the Evolution of the Elizabethan Villain." *PMLA* 49:743-51, September 1934.

INDEX

Accomplices
  as distinguished from tools, 72
  as victims of deception, 71-72, 76
  deceivers' use of, 72-73, 75-76
  of agents of deception, 147
Adaptations of Italian plays, 23, 26, 28
Admiration for agents of deception,
   147-48
Adolescens in Roman comedy, 25, 28,
   29, 37, 92
Adultery in Elizabethan drama and
   Italian stories, 91 *note*
Aemilia, 32-33
Aeschylus, 159 *note*
Affected fools, 93, 94
Agamemnon, 159 *note*
Agents of deception, 8-41, 42-70, 105-18,
   167
  accomplices of, 147
  admiration for, 147-48
  as agents of authors' satirical intentions, 157-58
  as victims of deception, 105-18
  characteristics of, 46, 67-70, 146-47
  cleverness of, 51-52, 54, 58, 67, 68,
   146
  daughters as, 78, 85
  dramatic action and, 9, 13-14, 33-36
  dupes played off against each other
   by, 84-89, 142-43
  duping of, 105-18
  emergencies cleverly met by, 35-36,
   55, 68, 142, 146
  enjoyment of own trickery by, 150-51,
   155
  enviers as, 42, 64-65
  excess of confidence of, 109

  excessive indulgence in trickery by,
   105-12
  exhibitors of folly as, 12, 12 *note*, 16-
   23, 37, 80-81, 157-58
  exposers of wickedness as, 42, 58-64,
   157
  exuberance of, 146
  fathers as, 60-62
  frustration of, 27, 53, 55, 105-18
  gaiety of, 146-49
  husbands as, 59-60, 81-84
  ingenuity of, 54, 67
  lack of resourcefulness of, 27
  less stereotyped than Latin tricky
   slave or medieval Vice, 65-66
  lovers as, 37-41
  lovers' helpers as, 23-38
  manipulation of other characters by,
   17, 20, 22, 69, 157-58, 168
  mischief-makers as, 9-15
  motives of, 9, 16, 17-18, 19, 22-23, 28-
   29, 41, 43, 58-59, 61, 64-65, 66, 150-
   51, 155
  names indicative of characteristics of,
   146
  objectives of, 8, 9, 23, 58-59, 66-67,
   68-69
  principles underlying discussion of, 9
  protectors as, 42, 58-64
  purpose of treatment of, 5
  resourcefulness of, 35-36, 55, 67, 68,
   142, 146
  revengers as, 42, 64
  rogues as, 42-59, 142-43
  self-reliance of, 28, 54, 67
  self-reliant lovers as, 37-41
  tactical behavior of, 67

testers as, 42, 58-64
unifying and diversifying principles
  of discussion of, 9
use of accomplices by, 72-73, 75-76
use of tools by, 72, 74
volubility of, 25-26, 131
women as, 78-79, 82, 114-15, 145
See also Anthony; Aurelius *(Taming
  of a Shrew)*; Bellemont; Biondello; Brainworm; Canby;
  Cleanthes *(Blind Beggar of
  Alexandria)*; Cocledemoy; Courte-
  san *(Northward Ho!)*; Diccon;
  Don John; Duke Vincentio; Dul-
  cimel; Dulippo; Face; Father
  (Captain); Father of Flowerdale
  (London Prodigal); Follywit; For-
  tunatus; Franceschina *(Dutch
  Courtesan)*; Friscobaldo; George
  Pieboard; Gerardine; Glister;
  Gullman; Harebrain; Hercules;
  Justiniano; Lemot; Lodovico; Lu-
  centio; Macilente; Malevole-
  Altofronto; Maria *(Twelfth
  Night)*; Mendoza; Merecraft;
  Merrygreek; Mistress Low-water;
  Mosca; Oriana; Pages *(Mother
  Bombie)*; Peter Fabel; Quomodo;
  Rinaldo; Savorwit; Sebastian
  Wengrave; Shortyard; Sir Petronel
  Flash; Smallshanks; Subtle;
  Truewit; Volpone; Wellbred;
  Witgood; Wittypate
Alchemist, 26, 52, 94, 95, 123, 148 *note*
  deception as structural element in,
    142-43
  dupes played off against each other
    in, 142-43
  pretended anger in, 127
  volubility of Subtle in, 131
Alessandro, 32
All Fools, 2 *note*, 32, 68, 90, 95-96, 100,
    118, 120, 122, 142, 144, 148
  counterintrigue in, 112-13
  dupe's cooperation in own duping in,
    76-78
Alleman, Gellert S., 133 *note*

All's Well That Ends Well, 136, 145
Altofronto. *See* Malevole-Altofronto
Ambiguity as means of deception, 120-
    22, 145
Amedeus, 24, 25, 26, 90
Amica, 25
Ampedo, 1
Amphitruo situation, 138-39
Ananias, 94, 127, 142
Andelocia, 1-2, 127
Angelo, 32-34
Annals of English Drama—1558-1642, 5,
    5 *note*, 137 *note*, 164 *note*
Anthony, 30-31
Antonio *(Coxcomb)*, 91
Antonio *(Merchant of Venice)*, 145, 149
Archetypal deceiver of Elizabethan
    comedy, 67-70
Arlequino, 34
As You Like It, 120-21, 135, 145
Asinaria, 38
Astrologer, impersonation of, 28
Astrological hocus-pocus, 26
Atmosphere, influence of deception on
    of *Measure for Measure*, 154
    of *Merchant of Venice*, 148-49
    of *Volpone*, 150-51
Audience appeal of deception, 1, 6-7,
    141-66, 169-72
  See also Sources of audience appeal
    in dramatic uses of deception
Aurelio, 32-33
Aurelius *(Taming of a Shrew)*, 38
Aydellotte, Frank, 42 *note*, 43 *note*,
    44 *note*, 50 *note*, 94 *note*

Bacchides, 12 *note*, 76 *note*
Baldwin, Thomas Whitfield, 12 *note*
Ball, Robert Hamilton, 84 *note*
Barry, Lording, 56
Bartholomew Fair, 64, 132
Baskervill, Charles Read, 16 *note*,
    93 *note*, 156 *note*
Bassiolo, 96, 165
Beatrice, 129, 143, 145
Beaumont, Francis, 4, 59, 100
"Bed trick," 134, 137

Bellemont, 84
Benedick, 98, 129, 145, 148
Bianca, 29-30
Bibliography, 173-80
Biondello, 24, 25
Birth of Hercules, 138-39
"Biter bit" situation, 110, 160
Blind Beggar of Alexandria, 22, 136, 155
Blind Beggar of Bednal Green, 43-44, 69, 94, 97, 125, 136
Blurt Master Constable, 137
Bogus settlement of quarrels, 52-53
Bonario, 111
Bond, R. Warwick, 24 *note*
Booby traps, 157
"Boy Bride," 135
Boys
   disguised as women, 135
   girls disguised as, 134, 135
Brabant senior, 112
Braggarts, 10, 11, 157
Brainworm, 22, 23, 36-37, 147, 157
Brandino, 82-83, 91
Brother of William Smallshanks, 72-73
Brunetière's conflict theory of drama, 170
Buffone, 21-22
Bugbears, 23-26, 68, 90, 101, 131, 144
Bullen, A. H., 50 *note*, 137-38

Cacurgus, 9, 28-29, 131
Campbell, Oscar James, vii, 16 *note*, 20 *note*, 115, 153, 156 *note*
Canby, 43-44, 69, 97, 125
Captain, 62
Captivi, 12 *note*, 35 *note*
Celia, 26, 111, 150
Chambers, E. K., 18 *note*, 28 *note*, 53 *note*, 56 *note*, 59 *note*, 93 *note*, 105 *note*, 125, 137 *note*, 152
Chandler, Frank Wadleigh, 42 *note*, 43 *note*
Chapman, George, 2 *note*, 15, 18, 22, 32, 33, 34, 59, 76, 81, 92, 93, 96, 112, 120, 122, 123, 124, 128, 164
   intriguers in comedies of, 18 *note*
   irony in disguise situations in comedies of, 164
   structural use of agents of deception in comedies of, 16, 33-34
   technique of comic structure in comedies of, 34
Characteristics of agents of deception, 46, 67-70, 146-47
Chaste Maid in Cheapside, 133
Chettle, Henry, 125, 164 *note*
Christian, Mildred Gayler, 42 *note*
Churms, 93, 96, 113-14, 126
Claudio *(Measure for Measure)*, 138, 153
Claudio *(Much Ado about Nothing)*, 65, 98, 145
Cleanthes *(Blind Beggar of Alexandria)*, 22, 155
Cleanthes *(Supposes)*, 26
Clever servants, 24-25, 26-27, 28, 30, 32-34, 34-36, 36-37, 40
   See also Latin tricky slaves
Cleverness of agents of deception, 22, 46, 51-52, 54, 58, 67, 68, 146
   attitude toward, 147-48
Clytemnestra, 159 *note*
Cocledemoy, 9, 44-46, 68, 97, 110, 147
Comedy
   Elizabethan, 2-5, 65-66, 67, 156, 168
   Greek New, 11
   humor, 5, 16, 37, 144
   of intrigue, 3-4
   realistic, 5, 144
   restoration, 171
   Roman, 11 *note*, 25, 28, 38, 90
   romantic, 5
   satiric, 5, 156-58
   See also Structural use of deception
Comedy of Errors, 4, 135, 159
Comic effects of deception, 115, 141, 145-51, 169, 172
Comic interest and deception, 34, 50
Comic irony and deception, 82, 158, 163-65, 171
   See also Irony
Comic possibilities of disguise situation, exploitation of, 149, 163-64

Comic structure, Chapman's technique of, 34

"Comicall satyre," 153, 156

Commedia dell' arte, 90, 171

Commodity swindle, 47-50, 50 *note*

Common Conditions, 122 *note*

Conceited fools as victims of deception, 96

Confidence men, 48, 51

Confidence of deceivers, excess of, 109

Confidence of dupes, means of securing, 25, 77-78

Conflict and deception, 143-44, 170

Confusion, dupes as reciprocal instruments of others', 84-89

Conjurer, impersonation of, 24, 54

Construction of plot and deception. *See* Structural use of deception

Conycatchers, 44 *note,* 94

Cooke, Jo., 93 *note*

Cooperation of dupes
in own duping, 49, 56-58, 71-89
necessary for dramatic action, 103-04

Cornelio, 90, 112-13

Corporal *(Puritan),* 74-75

Counterfeit law officers, 47

Counterintrigue
and intrigue, 52, 112-18, 143, 144
frustration of deception by, 53, 112-18

Courtesan *(Northward Ho!),* 132

Courtesans, 25

Coxcomb, 59, 91, 130

Cozeners, 43, 44

Creizenach, Wilhelm, 94 *note*

Cuckolding, 81

Cunnion, Theodore J., S.J., vii

Curculio, 12 *note*

Cushman, L. W., 14 *note*

Cynthia's Revels, 139 *note*

Dame Chat, 12-13, 97

Dapper, 49 *note,* 94, 95

Daughters as agents of deception, 78, 85

Day, John, 125, 131

Deceivers. *See* Agents of deception

Deception
appeal of to Elizabethan audiences, 1, 6-7, 141-66, 169-72
as exercise in intellectual wit, 145-46, 170
as ingredient in Elizabethan comedy, 168
as machinery of intrigue, 21, 141-45, 168, 169
as virtuosity in trickery, 145-46, 155-56, 170
atmosphere and, 148-51
audience appeal of, 1, 6-7, 141-66, 169-72
comic effects of, 115, 141, 145-51, 169, 172
comic interest and, 34, 50
comic irony and, 82, 158, 163-65, 171
conflict and, 143-44, 170
deceivers' enjoyment of, 150-51, 155
dramatic action and, 3, 13-14, 15, 35, 50-51, 64, 69-70, 140, 141-45, 167-68
dramatic values of, 6-7, 141, 143-44, 169, 172
employed for its own sake, 9, 145-46, 155-56, 170
entertainment values of, 6-7, 145-56
frustration of, 6, 27, 53, 55, 62, 105-18
fun and, 9-15, 44, 146-51
hilarious scenes built on, 148
in modern comedy, 172
indulging in too much for deceivers' own good, 105-12
intellectual delight in, 151
interest of Elizabethan audiences in, 1, 6-7, 103, 140, 143, 144, 153, 155-56, 172
irony and, 50, 61, 76, 81-82, 83, 158-68, 171
lovers' unassisted use of, 37-41
meaning of, 3
mischief and, 9-15
motives for, 9, 16, 17-18, 19, 22-23, 28-29, 41, 43, 58-59, 61, 64-65, 66, 150-51, 155
organic employment of, 32-33, 141-45
recoil of upon itself, 59, 105-12, 118

revenge as motive for, 19, 64

romantic comedy and, 144-45

satire and, 69, 157-58

self-deception and, 77-81, 162-63

spirit of gaiety and, 148-49

susceptibility to, 5-6, 95-103

suspense and, 50, 146

ubiquity of in Elizabethan comedy, 167

See also Agents of deception; Dramatic action; Functional use of deception; Means of deception; Structural use of deception

Deceptive use of words as means of deception, 119-22

Dekker, Thomas, 1, 39, 60, 61, 84, 136, 137

Delirio, 20-22

Devices, 1, 2, 6, 31, 45, 54, 61, 67, 81, 119, 136-39, 153

See also Means of deception

Devil Is an Ass, 4, 26, 52, 101, 123, 130, 136, 164

Diccon, 9, 12-14, 15, 68, 84-85, 97, 120, 131, 147

Dilley, M. Evelyn, 11 *note*

Disguise

as means of deception, 6 *note*, 19, 29, 31, 37, 39, 45, 47, 59-64, 82, 106, 108, 111, 134-36, 155

as means of exposing wickedness, 62-64

definition of, 135

irony and, 163-64

Shakespeare's exploitation of comic possibilities of, 149

spy situations and, 59-64, 135-36

Disguised dukes, 62-64, 116, 152

Disguised fathers, 60-61

Disguised husbands, 60

Disguised kings, 62

Disguised lovers, 136

Disguised rogues, 45, 46, 47, 135

Disguised spies, 135-36

Diversifying principle of discussion of deceivers, 9

Doctor Caius, 85, 92

Doctor Rat, 13

Dodges and devices. *See* Devices; Means of deception

Domestic fool, 28

Don John, 64-65

Doran, Madeleine, 143 *note*

Double-dealing, 16, 17, 22, 63, 96, 126

Drama, Brunetière's conflict theory of, 170

Dramatic action

contribution to by agents of deception, 9, 13-14, 33-36

contribution to by victims of deception, 71-89, 103-04, 141, 168

deception and, 3, 13-14, 15, 35, 50-51, 64, 69-70, 140, 141-45, 167-68

directed and controlled by trickery, 15

See also Structural use of deception

Dramatic conflict, development of from simple sequences of tricks to complex intrigues, 143-44

Dramatic irony, 158

See also Irony

Dramatic use of deception

interest of Elizabethan audiences in, 1, 6-7, 143, 144, 153, 155-56, 172

taste of Elizabethan audiences for, 103, 140

Dramatic values of deception, 6-7, 141, 143-44, 169, 172

See also Functional use of deception

Draper, John W., 4

Duckworth, George E., 14 *note*

Duke Altofronto. *See* Malevole-Altofronto

Duke Vincentio, 9, 63-64, 69, 152, 158

Dukes in disguise, 62-64, 116, 152

Dulcimel, 41, 62, 68, 78-79, 82, 122, 125, 157

Dulippo, 26-27

Dunkel, Wilbur Dwight, 42 *note*, 53 *note*, 107 *note*

Duper duped. *See* Frustration of deception

Dupers. *See* Agents of deception

Dupes. *See* Victims of deception

Dutch Courtesan, 44-46, 65, 94, 136

Eastward Ho! 81-82, 91, 94, 96, 132, 148

Easy, 47-51, 94, 98, 102, 142

Eavesdroppers, 129

"Education drama," 28

Elizabethan audiences, appeal of deception to. *See* Sources of audience appeal in dramatic uses of deception

Elizabethan comedy
agents of deception in less stereotyped than Latin tricky slave or medieval Vice, 65-66
archetypal deceiver of, 67-70
deception as ingredient in, 168
satire in, 156
types of, 5, 144
ubiquity of deception in, 167

Elizabethan drama, adultery in, 91 *note*

Elizabethan dramatists, aims of, 103

Elizabethan gulls. *See* Gulls

Elizabethan London, types indigenous to, 157

Ellis-Fermor, Una, 115 *note*, 143 *note*

Emergencies, cleverness of deceivers in meeting, 35-36, 55, 68, 142, 146

Endymion, 127

Englishmen for My Money, 30-31, 33, 68, 92, 93, 94, 96, 100, 130

Entertainment values of deception, 6-7, 145-56

Enviers as agents of deception, 42, 64-65

Epicoene, 26, 86, 136, 148

Epidicus, 38

Erostrato, 26-27, 126

Evans, Viola Mitchell, 4

Every Man in His Humor, 22, 36-37, 40, 90, 94, 95, 147 *note*, 157

Everyman Out of His Humor, 8, 19-23, 157

Ewen, C. L'Estrange, 56 *note*

Exhibition of folly by means of deception, 12, 12 *note*, 16-23, 37, 69, 80-81, 157-58

Exposers of wickedness as agents of deception, 42, 58-64, 157

Exuberance of agents of deception, 146

Face, 49 *note*, 52, 131, 142, 147, 157
more canny and shifty than Subtle, 143

Fair Em the Miller's Daughter, 137 *note*

Fair Maid of the Exchange, 93

Fallax servus, 38
See also Latin tricky slaves

False counsel as means of deception, 10

False hopes, raising of as means of deception, 122-24

False pretences, 47

False report of death as means of deception, 106, 139
See also Pretended death and resurrection as means of deception

Falsification of financial status as means of deception, 56, 132-33

Falsification of identity as means of deception, 133-39
See also Disguise; Impersonation as means of deception

Falstaff *(Henry IV)*, 95

Falstaff *(Merry Wives of Windsor)*, 85, 91, 95, 122-23, 134

Family of Love, 39, 125 *note*, 129

Fastidious Brisk, 20-22, 94

Father *(Captain)*, 62

Father *(Grim the Collier of Croydon)*, 136

Father *(Misogonus)*, 28

Father *(Supposes)*, 26, 27, 30

Father *(Taming of the Shrew)*, 30, 72

Father of Flowerdale *(London Prodigal)*, 60-61, 73

Father of girl *(London Prodigal)*, 63, 73

Father of Sebastian Wengrave, 39, 96-97, 128

Father of William Smallshanks, 72-73, 91

Fathers
as agents of deception, 60-62
as victims of deception, 14-15, 24, 28, 30-31, 34, 39, 77-81, 89-90, 94
in disguise, 60-61

Fathers *(Bugbears)*, 24, 90

Female pages, 135

Field, Nathan, 41 *note*

Fitzdottrel, 52, 101, 130, 164

Flattery as means of deception, 77-78, 79-81, 122

Fletcher, John, 59, 62, 82, 100, 137

Florilla, 18, 94

Flügel, Edward, 10

Folly, exhibition of, 12, 12 *note*, 16-23, 37, 69, 80-81, 157-58

Follywit, 41, 53, 100, 107-10, 160

Fool
affected, 93, 94
conceited, 96
domestic, 28

Foolish pretensions, 157

Fops, 7, 20, 157

Foreigners as victims of deception, 30-31, 85, 92, 94, 157

Forged documents as means of deception, 44

Forged evidence as means of deception, 39

Formosus, 23-24

Forsythe, Robert S., 90 *note*, 139 *note*

Fortunatus, 113-14

"Fox trap," 111

Framework of plays. *See* Structural use of deception

Franceschina *(Dutch Courtesan)*, 65

Franceschina *(May Day)*, 33

Frank, Tenney, 166 *note*

Freeburg, Victor Oscar, 6 *note*, 46, 59, 61, 62, 134-35, 139, 163

Friscobaldo, 61

Frustration of deception, 6, 27, 53, 55, 62
by counterintrigue, 112-18
by recoil of trickery upon itself, 105-12

Fun and deception, 9-15, 44, 146-51

Functional use of deception
in displaying intellectual wit and virtuosity in trickery, 9, 145-46, 153-55
in exhibiting and exposing folly, 16-22, 37, 69, 80-81, 157-58
in heightening spirit of mirth, 9-16, 146-54

in influencing atmosphere, 149-54

in stimulating ironic and satiric temper, 156-66

See also Comic effects of deception; Dramatic values of deception; Structural use of deception

Gaiety, 172
of agents of deception, 146-49
See also Mirth and laughter

Gammer Gurton, 12, 13, 97

Gammer Gurton's Needle, 4, 12-14, 68, 84-85, 95, 120, 131, 143-44

Gascoigne, George, 26, 131

Gayley, Charles Mills, 10 *note*

Gentleman Usher, 96, 165

Gentlemen rogues, 53-58, 73

George a Greene, 136

George Pieboard, 53-55, 73-75, 101, 131, 147

Gerardine, 39-40, 41, 129

Gertrude, 132

Girls disguised as boys, 134, 135

Glass of Government, 131

Glister, 39-40, 85-86, 96, 99

Go-between, 23 *note*
See also Lovers' helpers

Gonzago, 78-81, 90, 162, 163

Gostanzo, 77-78, 90, 95-96, 100, 112-13, 121, 122, 148, 162

Gracioso, 41

Grazzini, Antonfrancesco, 23

Greek New Comedy, 11

Greene, Robert, 136

Greene's Tu Quoque, 93

Greenshield, 84, 130

Grim the Collier of Croydon, 125, 136, 139 *note*

Gripe, 94, 96, 100

Gudgeon, 85-86, 92

Guilpin, Everard, 78

Gulled gallants, 86, 92, 96

Guller gulled, 115
See also Frustration of deception

Gullers. *See* Agents of deception

Gullibility, 104
of dupes, 68, 83

Gullman, 129, 132
Gulls, 16, 33, 37, 44 *note*, 78, 93-94,
    105, 157
    See also Victims of deception

Harbage, Alfred, vii, 5, 155 *note*,
    164 *note*
Harebrain, 83, 91, 100, 129
Haughton, William, 30, 125, 125 *note*
Hazlitt, William, 61
Helena, 145
Helpers, lovers', 23-38, 40, 68, 76-78
Henry IV, 95
Hercules, 80, 122, 157
Herford, C. H., 2 *note*, 52 *note*,
    150 *note*, 156 *note*
Heseler, Maria, 41 *note*
Heywood, Thomas, 137 *note*, 138
Hoard, 75, 76, 88, 96, 99, 101, 121,
    160-62
Hoaxes, 2, 25, 35, 84, 119
Hodge, 13, 95, 97, 131
Honest Whore, Part I, 139
Honest Whore, Part II, 61-62
Howell, James, 42 *note*
Humor comedy, 5, 16, 37, 144
Humor types, 16, 37
Humorous Day's Mirth, 15, 68, 91, 94,
    95
Humors, 16, 20, 37, 157
Husbands
    as agents of deception, 59-60, 81-84
    as victims of deception, 81-84, 90-91,
        94, 148
    in disguise, 60
    spying, 59, 60
Hyde, Mary Crapo, 120 *note*

Ignorant characters as victims of de-
    ception, 98
Impersonation as means of deception,
    24, 28, 47, 54, 133-34
    See also Disguise
Incongruous, enjoyment of, 166
Ingenuity of agents of deception, 54, 67
    See also Cleverness of agents of
        deception

Innocentio, 94, 95, 123
Instruments of deception. *See* Means of
    deception
Intellectual delight in trickery, 151
Intellectual virtuosity, 172
Intellectual wit, deception as exercise
    in, 145-46, 170
Intelligence, levels of among victims of
    deception, 95-103, 169
Intrigue, 33, 38, 40, 44, 51, 68, 87, 119
    and counterintrigue, 52, 112-18, 143,
        144
    comedy of, 3-4
    deception as machinery of, 21, 141-45,
        168, 169
    love, 40, 41
    mischievous, 2, 9, 157
    varied application of the term, 3
    villainous, 1, 64-65, 115-18
    See also Deception; Structural use of
        deception
Intriguers, 7, 34, 51, 68, 69
    frustration of villainous, 115-18
    in Chapman's comedies, 18 *note*
    rogue, 42, 53
    See also Agents of deception; Clever
        servants; Rogues
Investigation
    limitations of, 8
    material for, 5
    method followed in, 7
    unifying and diversifying principles
        of discussion of deceivers in, 9
Irony, 172
    comic, 82, 158, 163-65, 171
    concept of, 158
    deception and, 50, 61, 76, 81-82, 83,
        158-68, 171
    distinction between satire and, 156
    dramatic, 158
    essential features of, 158-59
    in "biter bit" situation, 160
    in disguise situations, 163-64
    latent, 160
    of situation, 160-64
    pervasive, 80-82, 161
    rhetorical, 158

self-deception and, 162-63
Socratean, 158
species of, 158
verbal, 159, 160, 160 *note*, 161
Italian plays, adaptations of, 23, 26, 28
Italian stories, adultery in, 91 *note*

Jack Drum's Entertainment, 86, 112
Jenkins, Antoinette S., 91 *note*
Jones, Claude E., 56 *note*
Jonson, Ben, 4, 19-20, 22, 23, 36, 52, 81,
    82, 86, 93, 101, 110, 123, 127
  disguise situations in comedies of,
    164
  enjoyment of trickery in comedies of,
    37, 147-48, 150-51
  exhibition of folly in comedies of,
    19-22, 37
  satire in comedies of, 23, 153
  structural use of deception by,
    142-43
Judge, John F., vii
Justice Clement, 147
Justice Overdo, 64
Justiniano, 60

Kastrill, 142
Kenna, Catherine, vii
King Oedipus, 156
Kings in disguise, 62
Kitely, 37, 90
Knowell, 36, 90
Kreider, Paul, 18 *note*, 33
Krieger, Murray, 153 *note*, 154 *note*
Kronenberger, Louis, 150 *note*

La Besha, 91, 94, 95
Lady Goldenfleece, 121
Latent irony, 160
Latin tricky slaves, 13, 14 *note*, 23, 25,
    27, 28, 34, 36, 38, 65, 66
  See also Clever servants
Laughter and mirth, 146-51, 171
Law Tricks, 131, 136, 137
Lawrence, William J., 6 *note*, 136 *note*
Lawrence, William Witherle, 154 *note*
Lawyer *(Supposes)*, 91

Lawyers as victims of deception, 56-58,
    72-73, 93, 96
Laxton, 92, 127
Lea, K. M., 139 *note*
Le Moyne College, vii
Legrand, Philippe E., 12 *note*, 14 *note*
Lemot, 9, 15-18, 22, 23, 68, 147, 157
Leno as victim of trickery in Plautus,
    92
Letters as means of deception, 18, 82,
    96, 124-25
Lies as means of deception, 13, 45-46,
    57, 77, 119-20, 145, 155
Limitations of investigation, 8
Lipsalve, 85-86, 92
Lodovico, 32-34, 69, 129, 147
London Prodigal, 60-61, 73, 91-92,
    125 *note*, 139
Lorenzo, 33, 91, 94, 115
Louts as victims of deception, 95
Love intrigue, 40, 41
Lovers
  in disguise, 136
  relationship between helpers and, 23,
    27, 29-30, 40, 41
  ridiculous as victims of deception, 85,
    91, 94
  self-reliant, 37-41
  unassisted use of deception by, 37-41
Lovers' helpers, 23-38, 40, 68, 76-78
Lucentio, 29-30
Lucre, 75, 87-88, 96, 101, 121-22, 160-61
Lyly, John, 14, 59, 127, 147

Machine à fraude, 69
Machinery of intrigue, deception as, 21,
    141-45, 168, 169
  See also Structural use of deception
Machinery of plot, swindling as, 48,
    50-51, 52-53, 142-44
Macilente, 8, 16, 19-23, 157, 158
Macpeak, Thomas J., vii
Mad World, My Masters, 40, 41, 53, 83-
    84, 91, 100, 118, 129, 132, 136, 160
  irony in, 83
  recoil of trickery upon trickster in,
    107-10

Magician, impersonation of, 28

Malcontent, 62, 115-18, 144, 157

Malcontent type, 115-16

Malevole-Altofronto, 115-18, 157

Malheureux, 65

Malvolio, 4, 94, 95, 99, 100, 124, 147, 148, 162, 163
    main victim of deception in *Twelfth Night*, 18-19

Manipulation of characters by agents of deception, 17, 20, 22, 69, 157-58, 168

Manly, John Matthews, 10 *note*, 12 *note*

Maria *(Family of Love)*, 39, 129

Maria *(Twelfth Night)*, 16, 124, 147, 157, 163
    main agent of deception in *Twelfth Night*, 18-19, 18 *note*

Marriage situation, secret, 24-25, 34-36, 77

Marston, John, 40, 44, 62, 81, 86, 112, 115

Massinger, Philip, 59 *note*

Material for investigation, 5

May Day, 40, 69, 91, 94, 95, 123, 129, 136 *note*
    deception as structural element in, 32-34
    irony and disguise in, 164

McCloskey, John C., 6 *note*

Means of deception, 6, 119-40, 169
    ambiguous use of speech as, 120-22, 145
    deceptive use of words as, 119-22
    disguise as, 6 *note*, 19, 29, 31, 37, 39, 45, 47, 59-64, 82, 106, 108, 111, 134-36, 155
    false counsel as, 10
    false report of death as, 106, 139
    falsification of financial status as, 56, 132-33
    falsification of identity as, 133-39
    flattery as, 77-78, 79-81, 122
    forged documents as, 44
    forged evidence as, 39
    impersonation as, 24, 28, 47, 54, 133-34

letters as, 18, 82, 96, 124-25

lies as, 13, 45-46, 57, 77, 119-20, 145, 155

mock conjuring as, 131

pretended anger as, 56, 126-27

pretended death and resurrection as, 60, 131, 139

pretended diabolic possession as, 52, 53

pretended friendship as, 125-26

pretended ignorance as, 128-30

pretended knowledge as, 54, 131

pretended love as, 127-28

pretended virtue as, 83, 108, 131-32

pretended yielding to solicitation as, 136-37

raising false hopes as, 122-24

rich-heiress trick as, 56-58

rich-widow trick as, 75-76, 87-88, 132-33, 161-62

simulated ailments as, 31, 130-31

simulation as, 52, 53, 83, 108, 125-33

spurious precontract of marriage as, 88

spurious will as, 60, 73

substitution as, 136-39

Measure for Measure, 62, 63-64, 69, 136, 138, 152-54, 163
    evaluations of trickery in, 152
    functional uses of deception in, 63, 152-54
    influence of deception on atmosphere of, 154

Medieval moralities, Vice of, 11 *note*, 14, 23, 28, 65

Men disguised as women, 135

Mendoza, 115-18

Merchant of Venice, 91, 127, 135, 145
    influence of deception on atmosphere of, 148-49

Merecraft, 26, 52, 101, 130

Meretrix, 131

Merry Devil of Edmonton, 31-32, 90

Merry Wives of Windsor, 85, 90, 91, 92, 95, 118, 134, 136 *note*, 157
    frustration of deception by counter-intrigue in, 114-15

Merrygreek, 10-12, 15, 68, 125, 146-47
Method followed in investigation, 7
Michaelmas Term, 59, 94, 95, 98, 102,
    136, 139
    deception as structural element in,
      46-52, 141-42
    duper duped in, 106-07, 118
Michaut, Gustave Marie, 11 *note*,
    12 *note*, 14 *note*
Midas, 147
Middleton, Thomas, 4, 34, 39, 40, 46, 48,
    62, 75, 82, 102, 106, 133, 137
    cynicism of, 84
    dramatic art of, 50-51
    gentlemen rogues in comedies of, 53
    irony in comedies of, 81-82, 160-62
Midsummer Night's Dream, 10
Miles Gloriosus, 38
Milligan, Burton Alviere, 42 *note*,
    50 *note*
Mirth and laughter, 146-51, 171
Mischief and deception, 9-15
Mischief-makers, 9-10, 13, 14, 16, 17,
    18, 23, 84
Mischievous intriguing, 2, 9, 157
Misogonus, 28
Misogonus, 28, 131
Mistress Gallipot, 128
Mistress Low-water, 69, 121, 136
Mistress Mulligrub, 45-46
Modern comedy, deception in, 172
Molière, 171
Monsieur D'Olive, 124
Monsieur D'Olive, 120, 124, 128
Monsieur Thomas, 137
Morris, Elizabeth Woodbridge, 37 *note*,
    150 *note*
Mosca, 55 *note*, 87, 101, 110-11, 150,
    151, 157
Mostellaria, 38
Mother Bombie, 14-15, 23, 69, 90, 126,
    144, 147
Motives
    false color on, 22
    of agents of deception, 9, 16, 17-18,
      19, 22-23, 28-29, 41, 43, 58-59, 61,
      64-65, 66, 150-51, 155

    of Cacurgus, 28-29
    of Cleanthes in *Blind Beggar of*
      Alexandria, 155
    of Lemot, 17-18
    of Macilente, 22-23
    of Maria in *Twelfth Night*, 19
    of Merrygreek, 11-12
    of Tranio, 30
    of Volpone, 150-51
Much Ado about Nothing, 64-65, 98,
    129, 139, 145, 148
Mulligrub, 44-46, 94, 97
Multidisguise, rogues in, 46, 135-36

Names of tricksters, indications of
    characteristics in, 146
Nash, Ralph, 150 *note*
Nevill, 41 *note*
Nicholas, 73-74, 94, 95
Nincompoops as victims of deception,
    95, 96
No Wit, No Help Like a Woman's, 69,
    90, 92, 121, 136
    clever servant in, 34-36
Northward Ho! 84, 130, 132

Objectives of agents of deception, 8, 9,
    23, 58-59, 66-67, 68-69
Oedipus, 156
Old Fortunatus, 1, 127
Old men as victims of deception, 25,
    33, 94
Organic function of deception. *See*
    Structural use of deception
Oriana, 128
Othello, 71

Pages, female, 135
Pages *(Midas)*, 147
Pages *(Mother Bombie)*, 14-15, 23, 69,
    126, 147
Parasitaster, or The Fawn, 40, 41, 62,
    68, 90, 122, 125, 157
    dupe as instrument of own duping in,
      78-81
    irony and deception in, 80-81
Parasite, 11, 12 *note*

Parents as victims of deception, 85, 90
  See also Fathers
Parody on disguised exposer and protector, 64
Parrott, Thomas Marc, 18, 34, 84 *note,* 91 *note,* 124, 150 *note*
Pedant *(Taming of the Shrew),* 72
Perjuries, 155
Perkinson, Richard H., vii
Pervasive irony, 80-82, 161
Peter Fabel, 31-32
Peter Plod-all, 95, 113
Peter Skirmish, 74-75
Pettifoggers, 96
  See also Lawyers as victims of deception
Phoenix, 62-63
Phormio, 12 *note*
Pisaro, 30-31, 130
Plautine tricky slaves. *See* Latin tricky slaves
Plautus, Titus Maccius, 76
  comedies of, 11 *note,* 12 *note,* 24, 25, 37, 38, 40, 76, 92, 138-39, 171
  relationship between young lovers and tricky slaves in, 38
Plot, swindling as machinery of, 48, 50-51, 52-53, 142-44
  See also Structural use of deception
Poggio, 96
Polynesta, 26, 29, 126
Porter, Henry, 126 *note*
Portia, 127, 145, 147
Precontract of marriage, spurious, 88
Pre-Restoration Stage Studies, 6 *note*
Pretended ailments as means of deception, 31, 130-31
Pretended anger as means of deception, 56, 126-27
Pretended death and resurrection as means of deception, 60, 131, 139
  See also False report of death as means of deception
Pretended diabolic possession as means of deception, 52, 53
Pretended friendship as means of deception, 125-26

Pretended identity. *See* Falsification of identity as means of deception
Pretended ignorance as means of deception, 128-30
Pretended knowledge as means of deception, 54, 131
Pretended love as means of deception, 127-28
Pretended virtue as means of deception, 83, 108, 131-32
Pretended yielding to solicitation as means of deception, 136-37
Preternatural manifestations, 25-26
Principles, unifying and diversifying of discussion of deceivers, 9
Prodigal son, 28-29, 60-61
"Projects" and "projectors," 52, 119
Prospero, 127
Protectors as agents of deception, 42, 58-64
Proteus, 125-26, 144-45
Pseudolus, 38
Puck as "manipulator of mischief," 9-10
Puritan, 2 *note,* 53-55, 73-75, 95, 101, 131, 139, 147
Puritan lady, 17
Puritans as victims of deception, 7, 44-46, 54, 73-75, 94, 157
Puritans *(Puritan),* 54, 73-75, 94, 101
Purposes of agents of deception. *See* Objectives of agents of deception

Quintiliano, 33, 123, 164
Quomodo, 59, 102
  as mastermind among swindlers, 47-52
  undone by excessive indulgence in trickery, 106-07, 141-42

Ralph Roister Doister, 10, 11, 147
Ram-Alley, 69, 72-73, 76, 89, 91, 93, 96, 133, 144, 165
  cooperation of dupe in own duping in, 57-58
  gentleman rogue in, 56-58
  rich-heiress trick in, 56-58
Raphael, Maxwell I., 23 *note*

Rascality, 2

Realism, advance in, 14

Realistic comedy, 5, 144

Recoil of deception upon itself, 59, 105-12, 118

"Regular" comedies, first, 4

Reinhardstöttner, Karl von, 138 *note*

Resourcefulness of agents of deception, 35-36, 55, 67, 68, 142, 146
lack of, 27

Restoration comedy, 171

Revenge as motive for deception, 19, 64

Revengers as agents of deception, 42, 64

Rhetorical irony, 158

Rich-heiress trick as means of deception, 56-58

Rich-widow trick as means of deception, 75-76, 87-88, 132-33, 161-62

Rinaldo, 32, 40, 100, 120, 122, 147, 157
seizes upon weak point of dupe, 76-78
undermined by counterdevice, 112-13

Roaring Girl, 39, 41, 96, 127-28

Roderigo *(Othello)*, 71

"Rogue in Multi-Disguise," 135

Roguery, 2
exposing of, 62
hierarchy of, 43, 46

Rogues, 7, 44, 45, 46
as agents of deception, 42-59, 142-43
classification of, 43
dominant characteristic of, 43
gentlemen as, 53-58, 73
in disguise, 45, 47
in multidisguise, 46, 135-36

Roister Doister, 4, 10-11, 68, 125, 143

Roman comedy, 11 *note*, 25, 28, 38, 90
See also Latin tricky slaves; Plautus, Titus Maccius; Terence, comedies of

Roman tricky slaves. *See* Latin tricky slaves

Romantic comedy, 5
deception as structural element in, 144-45

Romeo and Juliet, 139

Rosalind, 145

Rosamunda, 24, 25

Rowland Lacy, 145

Rowley, William, 4, 59 *note*

Rudens, 12 *note*

Satire
deception and, 69, 157-58
distinction between irony and, 156
in Elizabethan comedies, 156
in Jonson's comedies, 23, 153
in *Measure for Measure*, 152-53
See also Satiric commentators

Satiric comedy, 5, 156-58

Satiric commentators, 8, 20, 115-16, 157, 158

Saviolina, 20-22

Savorwit, 34-36, 37

Schell, Jack Steward, 93 *note*

Schelling, Felix E., 4, 5 *note*, 150 *note*, 156 *note*

Schild, Erich, 14 *note*

Scope of inquiry, 4-5

Scornful Lady, 68, 100, 129

Sebastian Wengrave, 39, 41, 97, 105, 128

Secret marriage situation, 24-25, 34-36, 77

Security, 91, 94, 96, 148
cooperating in own duping, 81-82

Sedgewick, G. G., 158 *note*

Sedgwick, W. B., 138 *note*

Self-deception, 4, 96, 104
deception and, 77-81, 162-63
irony and, 162-63

Self-reliance
of agents of deception, 28, 54, 67
of lovers, 37-41

Servants. *See* Clever servants; Latin tricky slaves

Shakespeare, William, 4, 18, 29, 63, 64, 86, 94, 124
comedies of, 144-45, 152-54, 163
comic irony in comedies of, 163
disguise situations in comedies of, 148-49, 163
employment of device of substitution by, 136
employment of satire by, 152-53

functional uses of deception in comedies of, 152-54
use of trickery by, 152-53
See also the individual comedies
Shakespeare Apocrypha, 2 *note*, 137 *note*
Sharpers, 43, 46-53
Shift, 20-21
Shipley, Joseph T., 158 *note*
Shirley, James, 34, 139 *note*
Shoemakers' Holiday, 136, 145
Shortyard, 47-51, 99, 102, 106
suave practitioner in his own right, 51
Shrewd characters as victims of deception, 81-82, 87-89, 96-97, 110-12, 113-14
Shylock, 149
Silver Age, 138-39
Sim, 95, 98-99, 102, 106
Simpletons, 95, 96
Simulated ailments as means of deception, 31, 130-31, 160-61
Simulation as means of deception, 52, 53, 83, 108, 125-33
Sir Andrew Aguecheek, 86, 91, 94, 95, 100, 105, 123, 148
Sir Arthur Clare, 32, 90
Sir Bounteous Progress, 91, 107-08
Sir Giles Goosecap, 92
Sir Oliver Twilight, 34-35, 90
Sir Petronel Flash, 81-82, 132
Sir Toby Belch, 18 *note*, 19, 105, 147
Slave-dealing procurers as victims of · deception, 92
Slaves. *See* Latin tricky slaves
Slender, 85, 95, 157
Smallshanks, 9, 56-58, 69, 72, 89, 91, 147
Socratean irony, 158
Son, prodigal, 28-29, 60-61
Sophocles, 156, 159 *note*
Sources of audience appeal in dramatic uses of deception
attractive qualities of tricksters, 146-48
intellectual wit, 145-46

irony, 156, 158-66
machinery of movement and structure, 13-14, 33-35, 71-89, 103-04, 141-45
satire, 156-58
virtuosity in trickery, 155-56
Spanish Tragedy, 115
Spencer, Hazelton, 61 *note*
Spurious precontract of marriage as means of deception, 88
Spurious will as means of deception, 60, 73
Spy situations, disguise in, 59-64, 135-36
Spying fathers, 60-61
Spying husbands, 59, 60
Stanton, Rose Marie, vii
Stephen, 37, 94, 95, 157
Stichus, 12 *note*
Stoll, Elmer Edgar, 115
Stonex, Arthur Bivens, 92 *note*
Stratagems, 2, 54, 96, 119
Structural use of deception
contribution of dupes to, 71-89, 103-04, 141, 168
counterintrigue and, 112-18
development in, 143-44
exhibition of folly and, 12, 12 *note*, 16-23, 37, 69, 80-81, 157-58
exploitation of swindling devices as, 46-59, 142-44
exposing of wickedness and, 62-64, 157
in *Alchemist*, 142-43
in *All Fools*, 112-13
in *Bugbears*, 24-26
in *Devil Is an Ass*, 52-53
in *Dutch Courtesan*, 46
in *Englishmen for My Money*, 30-31
in *Every Man in His Humor*, 36-37
in *Everyman Out of His Humor*, 19-23
in *Gammer Gurton's Needle*, 12-14
in *Humorous Day's Mirth*, 16-18
in *Mad World, My Masters*, 107-10
in *Malcontent*, 115-18
in *May Day*, 32-34
in *Measure for Measure*, 62-63, 153-54
in *Merry Wives of Windsor*, 114-15

in *Michaelmas Term,* 46-52, 106-07, 141-42
in *Mother Bombie,* 14-15
in *No Wit, No Help Like a Woman's,* 34-36
in *Puritan,* 73-75
in *Roister Doister,* 10-12
in romantic comedies, 144-45
in *Volpone,* 87, 110-12
in *Wily Beguiled,* 113-14
lovers' helpers and, 23-37
manipulation of characters and, 17, 20, 22, 69, 157-58, 168
mischief-makers and, 9-15, 22-23, 28-29, 58-59
recoil of deception upon itself and, 59, 105-12, 118
roguery and, 42-59, 142-44
See also Dramatic action; Functional use of deception
Stupidity among dupes, 95-103
"Substitute" bride, 145
Substitution as means of deception, 136-39
Subtle, 26, 49 *note,* 52, 127, 131
less canny and shifty than Face, 143
Superiority, sense of, 166
Supposes, 26-27, 29, 30, 38, 91, 97, 126, 133, 136, 144
Susceptibility of dupes to deception, 5-6, 95-103
Suspense and deception, 50, 146
Swindlers, 43, 94
Swindling, 25-26, 46-50, 52, 53, 102-03, 106, 107
as machinery of plot, 50-51, 52-53, 142-44
based on false hopes, 123

Taming of a Shrew, 38, 136
Taming of the Shrew, 29-30, 68, 72, 97, 136, 144
Tavern host *(Trick to Catch the Old One),* 75, 76
Tempest, 127
Terence, comedies of, 12 *note,* 25, 37, 171

Testers as agents of deception, 42, 58-64
Thompson, Alan Reynolds, 158 *note,* 159 *note*
Thomson, J. A. K., 159 *note*
Thorndike, Ashley H., 10, 115 *note,* 120
Throat, 56-58, 72-73, 76, 93, 96, 99, 165
Thurio, 95, 125
Tom Strowd, 43-44, 94, 97
Tools
as distinguished from accomplices, 72
deceivers' use of, 72, 74
Tragic elements in *Volpone,* overemphasis of, 150
Tranio, 29-30, 72, 90
Trappola, 24-26, 101, 131
Traps, 1, 2, 47
Tribulation, 94
Trick to Catch the Old One, 53, 69, 93, 96, 101, 121, 133, 144
cunning dupes in, 87-89
deceiver's use of accomplices in, 75-76
irony in, 160-62
rich-widow trick in, 75-76, 87-89
Trickery. *See* Deception
Tricks. *See* Means of deception
Tricksters. *See* Agents of deception
Tricky servants. *See* Clever servants; Latin tricky slaves
Truewit, 86
Twelfth Night, 86, 87, 91, 94, 95, 105, 135, 144, 147 *note,* 148
letter trick in, 124
Malvolio as main victim in, 18-19
Maria as main deceiver in, 18-19, 18 *note*
Two Angry Women of Abington, 126 *note*
Two Gentlemen of Verona, 95, 98, 125, 134, 135, 145
Types
of deceivers, 9, 37, 42, 64, 157-58
of Elizabethan comedy, 5, 144
of victims of deception, 89-94, 156-57

Ubiquity of deception in Elizabethan comedy, 167
Udall, Nicholas, 10

Unifying principle of discussion of deceivers, 9

Unwary characters as victims of deception, 98-99

Uses of deception. *See* Comic effects of deception; Dramatic values of deception; Functional use of deception; Structural use of deception

Usurers as victims of deception, 30-31, 56-58, 87-89, 92-93, 94, 96, 157

Valentine, 98, 125, 145

Van Doren, Mark, 152

Vandiver, E. P., Jr., 11 *note*

Vega, Lope de, 41

Verbal irony, 159, 160, 160 *note*, 161

Vice of medieval moralities, 11 *note*, 14, 23, 28, 65

Vices, exposing of, 157

Victims of deception, 5-6, 7, 12, 26, 71-104, 167-69

accomplices as, 71-72, 76

agents of deception as, 105-18

as instruments of others' confusion, 84-89

conceited fools as, 96

contribution to dramatic action by, 71-89, 103-04, 141, 168

cooperation of in own duping, 49, 56-58, 71-89

cooperation of necessary for dramatic action, 103-04

fathers as, 14-15, 24, 28, 30-31, 34, 39, 77-81, 89-90, 94

foreigners as, 30-31, 85, 92, 94, 157

gullibility of, 68, 83

husbands as, 81-84, 90-91, 94, 148

ignorant characters as, 98

in Plautus' comedies, 25, 92

lawyers as, 56-58, 72-73, 93, 96

leno as, 92

levels of intelligence among, 95-103, 169

louts as, 95

nincompoops as, 95, 96

old men as, 25, 33, 94

parents as, 85, 90

played off against each other, 84-89, 142-43

problem posed by levels of intelligence among, 99-103, 169

Puritans as, 44-46, 54, 73-75, 94

ridiculous lovers as, 85, 91, 94

securing confidence of, 25, 77-78

shrewd characters as, 81-82, 87-89, 96-97, 110-12, 113-14, 160-61

slave-dealing procurers as, 92

stupidity among, 95-103

susceptibility of to deception, 5-6, 95-103

types of, 89-94, 156-57

unwary characters as, 98-99

usurers as, 30-31, 56-58, 87-89, 92-93, 94, 96, 157

witless pretenders as, 93

would-be gallants as, 93

See also Amedeus; Ananias; Bassiolo; Beatrice; Benedick; Bonario; Brabant senior; Brandino; Brother of William Smallshanks; Buffone; Celia; Churms; Claudio *(Much Ado about Nothing)*; Cleanthes *(Supposes)*; Cornelio; Corporal *(Puritan)*; Dame Chat; Dapper; Delirio; Doctor Caius; Doctor Rat; Easy; Falstaff *(Merry Wives of Windsor)*; Fastidious Brisk; Father *(Misogonus)*; Father *(Supposes)*; Father *(Taming of the Shrew)*; Father of girl *(London Prodigal)*; Father of Sebastian Wengrave; Father of William Smallshanks; Fathers *(Bugbears)*; Fitzdottrel; Florilla; Gammer Gurton; Gertrude; Gonzago; Gostanzo; Greenshield; Gripe; Gudgeon; Hoard; Hodge; Innocentio; Kastrill; Kitely; Knowell; La Besha; Lady Goldenfleece; Lawyer *(Supposes)*; Laxton; Lipsalve; Lorenzo; Lucre; Malheureux; Malvolio; Mendoza; Mistress Gallipot; Monsieur D'Olive; Mulligrub; Nicholas; Pedant *(Taming of the*

Shrew); Peter Plod-all; Peter Skirmish; Pisaro; Proteus; Puritans *(Puritan)*; Ralph Roister Doister; Roderigo *(Othello)*; Saviolina; Security; Shift; Sim; Sir Andrew Aguecheek; Sir Arthur Clare; Sir Bounteous Progress; Sir Oliver Twilight; Slender; Stephen; Tavern host *(Trick to Catch the Old One)*; Throat; Thurio; Tom Strowd; Trappola; Tribulation; Valentine; Viola-Cesario; Voltore; Weathercock; Wholesome; Wife of Delirio; Yellowhammer family
Villainous intrigue, 1, 64-65
  frustration of, 115-18
Viola-Cesario, 86, 100, 105, 144, 148
Virtuosity in trickery, 145-46, 155-56, 170
Volpone, 2, 26, 55 *note*, 87, 123, 130, 135
  motives of, 150-51
  undone by excessive resort to trickery, 110-12
Volpone, 2, 55 *note*, 101, 118, 123, 139, 142, 144
  dupes played off against each other in, 87
  enjoyment of trickery in, 150-51
  influence of deception upon atmosphere of, 150-51
  overemphasis of tragic elements in, 150
  structural use of deception in, 87, 110-12
Voltore, 101, 111, 151
Volubility of agents of deception, 25-26, 131

Ward, A. W., 10-11, 107 *note*
Weathercock, 73, 91
Webster, John, 60, 84
Wellbred, 36, 37, 40
Wells, Henry W., 156 *note*
Westward Ho! 60, 139
Wholesome, 94
Widow, 82-83, 91, 124, 136
Widow's Tears, 59, 139
Wieand, Helen E., 14 *note*
Wife of Delirio, 20-22
Wife of Mulligrub, 45-46, 94
William Smallshanks. *See* Smallshanks
Wily Beguiled, 93, 95, 96, 113-14, 118, 126, 144
Wise Woman of Hogsdon, 137 *note*
Wit at Several Weapons, 128
Wit-intriguer, 21
Witgood, 53, 69, 75-76, 101, 121-22, 133
  rich-widow trick played by, 75-76
  shrewd victims played off against each other by, 87-89, 160-61
Withington, Robert W., 11 *note*
Witless pretenders as victims of deception, 93
Wittypate, 146
Woman-Hater, 128
Woman in the Moon, 59
Women
  as agents of deception, 78-79, 82, 114-15, 145
  boys or men disguised as, 135
Would-be gallants as victims of deception, 93

Yellowhammer family, 133
Your Five Gallants, 62, 92